The Speaking Window

The Speaking Window

Tales from a Bloodied Timeline

SANDEEP DUTT, FAISAL HAYAT, AND RITIKA

OXFORD
UNIVERSITY PRESS

OXFORD
UNIVERSITY PRESS

Oxford University Press is a department of the University of Oxford.
It furthers the University's objective of excellence in research, scholarship,
and education by publishing worldwide. Oxford is a registered trade mark of
Oxford University Press in the UK and in certain other countries

Published in India by
Oxford University Press
22 Workspace, 2nd Floor, 1/22 Asaf Ali Road, New Delhi 110 002, India

ISBN-13 (hardback): 978–9–39–105073–3
ISBN-10 (hardback): 9–39–105073–5

ISBN-13 (eBook): 978–9–35–497296–6
ISBN-10 (eBook): 9–35–497296–9

ISBN-13 (oso): 978–9–35–497297–3
ISBN-10 (oso): 9–35–497297–7

DOI: 10.1093/oso/9789391050733.001.0001

Typeset in Minion Pro 10.5/14
by Newgen KnowledgeWorks Pvt. Ltd., Chennai, India

Printed and bound in India by
Replika Press Pvt. Ltd

Contents

Introduction

Survival has never been about only the heroic tales of singing Kumbaya in the moments of fear; when it is the question of life and death, everything narrows down to the instinct of staying alive. And, those who fail to adapt or change, their existence disappears as if was never there in the first place. This is where the Darwinian theory of survival of the fittest comes in.

Since the very existence of this life-sustaining planet Earth, be it the search for food or a new water resource or a place fit for shelter to sustain life, almost every living being has had to travel hundreds and thousands of miles when needed.

Like any other species, migration is not a new term to human beings. Since their origin, first it was starvation and then growth, from the stone age to the present techno-savvy era, migration has only become more and more important. Even the wars within and against the countries resulted in it. This book is about the world's biggest migration in human history, which was not a choice of those who migrated!

After a long period of struggle for independence when a nation fought for its freedom to liberate itself from the shackles of slavery, little did they know the cost to be paid would come in the form of a new pair of chains— the partition, the scars of which are remnant till date. The partition of 1947 claimed millions of lives and affected countless families which got burnt in the fire of communal violence. And this fire of abhorrence has been fanned for decades and decades to come.

Fast forward to 70 years later, a young man who was then living in Ludhiana, Punjab, India, in search of his artistic pursuits, quits his job and ends up in an Urdu class of an 87-year-old Prem Singh Bajaj, who had been teaching Urdu for the last 22 years. He sparks a fascination in his student's curious mind with his survivor story of the 1947 partition. This young fellow was Sandeep Dutt, who then decided to go on a quest to find more like-minded people across the border who were yet not blinded by the hate, and it was at that point when, through a Facebook Group

The Speaking Window. Sandeep Dutt, Faisal Hayat, and Ritika, Oxford University Press.
© Oxford University Press India 2023. DOI: 10.1093/oso/9789391050733.001.0001

'Aman-Ki-Asha,' he met a 19-year-old journalism student, Faisal Hayat from Rawalpindi, who shared the same love and interest as him and had no hate for the people on the other side. And then Sandeep found Ritika, who was working as a teacher then in the same city as him.

And just like that, Bolti Khidki—The Speaking Window was formed that started to find people on both the sides who suffered partition to take a trip to the past through their memories and discover how it was like before the fateful day of partition and how it changed their worlds upside down.

The first story that was collected for this initiative was of the same man who sparked the idea and became the inspiration behind the whole project, Mr. Prem Singh Bajaj. His experiences from both the former and the current Punjab are documented in Chapter 41 titled 'The Light Preserver'.

Initially, the trio used to post their stories on Facebook under the page name Bolti Khidki—The Speaking Window, which soon started to gather attention and admiration among the youth of both the countries. So many stories unfold the tales of lost brotherhood and warmth they used to have, and even after suffering so much, they still wish to re-live the same childhood they had once. The youngsters would relate to the experience, share their own ancestor's stories, and some even would offer help to those storytellers who needed it. Such was the story of a cloth seller, which is documented under the title 'Abandoned Virtue', Chapter 36.

Soon the group realized these stories were supposed to be heard by masses. This was made possible under the guidance of Oxford University Press and the narration of these experiences started to take the form of more serious storytelling. Another eighteen months were spent in search of more and more survivors. Over 200 people were approached and over a 100 were interviewed with the help of volunteers who joined their initiative.

During this time, Ritika had moved to Canada and now the trio had to work in three different time zones being in three different countries. Countless days and sleepless nights were spent in the search and research of the stories, and their handwork paid off in 2019 when the first draft was submitted in October and the final one is now in your hands.

Unfortunately, many of the storytellers passed away during this time period, but this book is an effort to acknowledge the facts which were collected from those survivors who suffered the atrocities of times and still could muster the courage to rise again.

This book has 47 such stories covering 52 cities, across 5 countries, with the sole aim of bringing forward the real-life experiences of the people who faced partition and still feel it should be the harmony and peace that one must seek in their respective story over the violent behaviour of mankind in desperate times for no communal or cultural difference is enough of an excuse to justify the bloodshed. When, in the end, peace is the only way, then it must be one's first choice.

Acknowledgements

Before we begin our long list of thankyous, we all would like to express our gratitude with a heartfelt THANK YOU to YOU, our readers who have picked up this book who believe in the value that this book hopes to provide you.

Some of you may feel tingling in their hearts, some may feel warmth and some cold … some would be excited to see the stories of their fore-fathers, and some may relate fractions of these stories with their ances-tors' experience. For some, this may be the first experience of a book like this, and which will fill them with a roller-coaster of feelings. And to some, it may be a curiosity voyage. So, before we embark on this journey, we would like to thank you. We may never meet, or perhaps we will but know so, we will always think of you very fondly. This one is for YOU.

To our family and friends …

Sandeep Dutt would like to thank his parents and siblings for being supportive to this project and his teachers for always believing in him. A special note to his school Principal Mrs. Leena Taparia who has been a great influence on him. To Madam Navneet Kaur and the whole team of LPU Distance Education and the NGO RudAbha for their constant support. To his friends, Himanshu Sachdeva, Anjum Khan, and Sakshi Khurana for their undying faith in him. To the universe for imparting the wisdom and providing the strength.

Ritika is indebted to her mother, Sunita Rani, and siblings for where she is today, as it wouldn't be possible without them. To Baghi, she should have treated him with more doggie-treats for being such a patient com-panion in her journey. To her friends, Ishpreet Kaur, Supreet Kaur, Alisha Mathews, and Babita Ahuja for being her cheering squad. A special thanks to both Jaspal Kaur and Karan Pratap Singh who recognized and admired the writer within her. And at the end of the day, to the Almighty! For making every fall less painful and every rise much higher!

Faisal Hayat would like to express his gratitude towards his parents who gave him the opportunity to grow and to all his friends who supported him throughout this difficult journey. A special note to thank Mian Hamid Ejaz from Lahore who helped him in meeting partition survivors for three consecutive days during his Lahore trip. To Hazqeel Haider, his senior university fellow who took care of his Narowal-trip. To Malik Faheem Jillani who took him to the village Sheikhupura to help him meet partition survivors. To his class fellow, Raja Naveed who helped him meet Mr. Riaz in Gujjar Khan. To Allah, for showing him the ways whenever he was faced with dead ends.

And it is time to mention those, to whom no amount of thank you notes would be sufficient to express authors' gratitude for the work they have put in to make this book a reality!

To the Oxford University Press that became the Genie-in-the-lamp for making this dream come true and for all the support to shape up this book.

To Sonia, who never gave up on us and always guided and supported us throughout the journey.

A special thanks to Late Mr. Prem Singh Bajaj who inspired this whole project.

A special thanks to Beena Sarwar, the editor of Aman Ki Asha, for providing a beautiful cross-border-dialogue platform between India–Pakistan. An important mention of Divya Goyal, for being the first person from the media to notice our efforts. Thank you, Divya!

Thanks to Facebook, for connecting us to many partition survivors and their relatives. Thanks to Google, for helping us in verifying a lot of facts narrated by the survivors and also in tracing their fore-mentioned locations.

To the gems who had been voluntarily helping behind the curtains in spreading the word, in traveling and arranging accommodation in their respective cities while searching partition survivors, approaching them and in a few cases, even collecting the stories on our behalf. Our heartfelt thanks to:

Aakruti Dalmia, Anika Mohla, Anwar Raza, Bhavey Nagpal, Deepak, Faizan Naqvi, Gurleen Kaur, Harleen Kaur, Jasmeet Singh, Jawahar Malhotra, Karan Taneja, Khalid Ghaznavi, Manpreet Kaur, Mujahid Eshai, Navreet Rajwan, Najjam Ul Assar, Pallav Singh, Pooja Acharya, Parveen Sethi, Preet Baweja, Raghav Gund, Rahul Rangappa, Raja Rohit

Karmani, Rajinder Rajan, Ravinandan Sharma, Ravi Singh Rajput, Simran Bansal, Simran Kaur, Surjit Anand, and Vaishali Kanojia.

Out of these, special regards to Simran Kaur for solely covering the regions of Bhopal and Calcutta and to Aakruti Dalmia for solely covering the city of Surat.

To our mentor, a loving friend, Rajat Ahuja, whose brotherly love, firm support, and belief in us empowered us to never give up on this project.

To our friend Sage Kaleke (Jaswant Singh Gill), who stayed at Sandeep's place for a month to help us complete this book in time.

And, to all those people who are directly or indirectly linked to this initiative and contributed their efforts in making it possible.

Thank you, all.

Disclaimer

The stories mentioned in the book are written based on the personal experiences of the survivors. The authors have only put into words the incidents which were narrated by the storytellers, irrespective of the authors' personal opinions related to that matter. This book doesn't aim to hurt the sentiments of any individual or group. The readers of this book are advised to use discretion while reading the stories included in it.

1

Pain of Punjab

PUNJAB RAI TALWAR
RAJA JANG - LUDHIANA

THE SPEAKING WINDOW

Not so long ago from now, in Shamchaurasi, Hoshiarpur, I felt and witnessed the same pain my family once suffered and I suffer every day and,
that too was when Shafqat took some soil from the ground and collected
it in his handkerchief. After a really long time, I met someone who shared
the same pain and brought a flood of memories of that time.

Born in a really big reputed family of landlords and owners of cattle,
in a big house, I shared my childhood with four elder brothers and a
younger sister in Raja Jang, Lahore. My father was a renowned wrestler
in our area and a farmer too. He used to ride a Kabuli horse to his fields.
My grandfather owned a sweet shop in front of our house. Every walk
of life had been lived with peace and harmony there. No one bothered
about who belonged to Islam or Hinduism. May be that was the beauty
of our place, we celebrated every festival, including the famous fair of
Baba Thamman that our neighbouring village used to organize with
great enthusiasm. I still remember that pond and the temple over there.

The Speaking Window. Sandeep Dutt, Faisal Hayat, and Ritika, Oxford University Press.
© Oxford University Press India 2023. DOI: 10.1093/oso/9789391050733.003.0001

I certainly remember Mandhi, my best friend, we used to play in the streets of Raja Jang.

The news of the partition was a bolt from the blue. As a boy of six years, it was really hard for me to understand it. I remember my mother cooking in the kitchen, when my father returned home and told us we had to leave. Our neighbours, who preached Islam, came crying and requested us not to leave and assured us to keep us safe but my father was not willing to risk the safety of the family. But, we decided to leave our grandparents with them at their request as, due to their age, they could not travel in such dangerous circumstances. So, we decided to leave them behind; thinking we would return to our home once things settled. We did not take anything with us but my mother had a savings of Rs. 250 silver coins, which she took with her. Our cattle and the horse were left in the care of a Muslim friend of my father. We reached the railway station by the evening where the Station Master, Khushi Ram, told us that the two previous trains came bathed in blood so, he would not allow the departure of the train in the absence of the army. Fortunately, the next train had the Gorkha regiment in it. The soldiers were half-naked, cladded in short pants, with their guns pointed outside the train. As there was no room in the train to accommodate as many passengers as there were, the station master Khushi Ram brought a ladder for people to climb onto the roof of the train and people travelled on the roof of the train. I remember my father untying his black turban to tie it around us to ensure we do not fall off. Because of starvation, my 2.5-year-old sister Sheela fell unconscious. Everyone took her to be dead and advised us to throw her from the train. But, when the train stopped at some place, luckily finding a pond nearby, my father took some water in his shoe, as we had no utensils to hold water to pour into my sister's mouth. And finally, her eyes opened.

The journey was full of dangers. The extremists were laced with long Tukwe (a U-shaped sharp metal, tied on a long wooden rod), on both sides of the train but could not harm us because of the presence of the army. Thus, we reached Firozpur safe and sound.

I still can recall the plane, which was throwing food packets near the railway station which we collected to eat. There, the roads were flooded with corpses. It was a horrifying scenario. With a great difficulty, we got to a two-story building of a school, where a refugee camp was set up. After a few days, my father found a deserted house and we started living there.

But then the fate disclosed another card of miseries; the floods, it was as if the nature was punishing us for all our doings and we were, too, helpless in front of it. During that calamity, my father was out for work. By the time he returned, the flow of water had grown much stronger. We ran from there. My elder brother was insisting my father to pick me up but I told him that I could run. So I did. We sought help from a truck driver to reach Moga, where we lived in a temple that was exactly opposite to its railway station. After some days, my father decided to get settled in a big city, Ludhiana. So, we got shifted there. There we stayed at the Talaab Mandir for some time and then got a house in the street opposite to the same temple. As my father was so good at running a cattle business and curing cattle diseases, we started doing the same and used to sell milk in the nearby villages on a bicycle. For six months after the partition, we remained in touch with our friends, back in our native village via letters. We soon realized that the partition was very much real and we decided to bring our grandparents. So we wrote our friends to meet us at the border so that we could receive our grandparents. When my father went to receive them on the border, my grandfather told him, 'Even you have not taken care of us so well in our entire life as much as these people did in the last six months'.

In the late 1950s, my father and my elder brother went to Lahore for a match but they went to the village instead where the whole village exclaimed, 'sadde pehalwan ji aa gye, sadde pehalwan ji aa gye! (Our wrestler has come, our wrestler has come)'. It seemed as if there was a celebration underway which lasted for whole two days and two nights as the villagers used to gather around a gas-lamp, tied to a pole for chit-chat… there were laughter and joy all around for that timeframe. The friend of my father to whom he gave his horse and cattle took my brother to his home. He opened an almirah, full of clothes and gold and turned to him to say, 'Take whatever you want'. My brother politely refused by saying, 'We came here to meet you only; not to take things back'. There was gratitude in their silence, which spoke louder than the words could.

Shafqat Ali Khan, the internationally acclaimed classical singer and the son of Pakistan's pioneer classical singer, Ustad Salamat Ali Khan, the tenth-generation singer of 500 years old Sham Chaurasi School of Classical Music Hoshiarpur, which started in the court of Mughal Emperor Akbar, visited Ludhiana for a classical music event—an event which was being managed by my son. As an ardent fan of him, I attended his event where he asked my son if he could take him to his ancestral home, in Shamchaurasi, Hoshiarpur, and maternal home, in Chaura Bazar, Ludhiana. It was overwhelming to see him making that request with so much of curiosity and affection towards his heritage. So we visited his maternal home first, where he started staring at the buildings in the bazaar. He stood there for quite a while, observing, understanding, and absorbing. Then we did some shopping there and roamed a few streets too. The very next day, we took him to his village Shamchaurasi, Hoshiarpur. In that village, there is a tomb of his great-grandfather, where people come to pay their homage and seek blessings. I witnessed something really unexpected. Shafqat placed his hand on the ground to feel his ancestors, maybe. Then, he took some soil and wrapped it in his handkerchief... Later, we went to his ancestral home, which was a small bricked home. He took a brick, put it in his bag, and broke into tears. He cried a lot and it was very painful to see him like that for me, as I could feel his pain. We shared the same pain.

I completed my graduation in Engineering from Guru Nanak Engineering College, Ludhiana and worked as a Junior Engineer in the Government Housing Department. Now, I am living my retirement life happily. Every day, I miss my village and those streets where I used to play. I miss my friend, Mandhi, his mischief and innocence. I never found that kind of peace ever in my life which I had back then. I have lived a long life and all I have learnt and would like to say to the youth of today is, 'Do not hate the people of India or Pakistan for the wrongdoings of the governments; because the people, in all, are just the same at heart; all are good'.

2
The Red Carpet

SAJJAD KISHWAR
LUDHIANA - RAWALPINDI

THE SPEAKING WINDOW

The sparkling waters of Sutlej seemed tranquil at times until it started becoming flooded with corpses and blood started running in it. But whose blood was it? The Muslims thought it was of Hindus and the Hindus thought it was of Muslims but it belonged to no one but to the humanity itself. The cries of children and women, became silent at once; as soon as they stopped breathing. It is so hard to believe all this even today; as I still can't understand why it all had to happen at all.

Ludhiana was a small but very beautiful city in the Eastern part of Punjab and my birthplace, too. Its real beauty was its people who had value for humanity. They knew care, love, affection, and harmony, not the communal differences. But, the chapter on partition in the history changed everything. It created an ambience of sheer hatred, in which the love for each other got lost, forever.

I was raised with two brothers and a sister, in a well-off joint family. My grandmother owned many properties in different areas of the city. My

The Speaking Window. Sandeep Dutt, Faisal Hayat, and Ritika, Oxford University Press.
© Oxford University Press India 2023. DOI: 10.1093/oso/9789391050733.003.0002

father served in supply depot. I began my schooling at the age of five at the Ewing Christian School, an English medium school, which was the first of its kind, started in 1834, with almost all the British staff members. There was a playground full of swings, slides, and see-saws; all imported from abroad, just like all the furniture of the school. It feels as if it was just yesterday when I used to go to the school on tonga. The way to school was surrounded by long trees on both sides and the fallen red leaves shed on the ground, appeared more of a red carpet. I cherished being there with all my friends, who made my childhood more beautiful.

The dawn of 1947 changed everything I had ever known. The winds of disharmony brought a ferocious storm of long-lasting hatred, which only grew stronger and stronger with time. These memories still leave my eyes teary. I can't forget those painful memories, seeing people setting others' houses on fire, slaughtering each other in the name of religion, and burning people alive; it was all horrifying to watch. It didn't just take lives but it was much more than that. The cries and sobs of the people still haunt me at night.

About ten days before the announcement of the partition, the street next to ours, was invaded by a mob of extremists who killed more than a hundred Muslims. In order to protect them, we opened our homes to them and did whatever we could to protect their women and children. Then, one night partition was announced and we decided to migrate to the newly formed nation, Pakistan. Leaving our home wasn't easy. The walls, of the house, were the canvas of all sweet memories, we ever had. Stepping out of the home, seeing it for the last time, trying to relive every moment and staring at it till it wasn't visible anymore. It wasn't easy for anyone of us whether people were on this side of the border or they were bound by pain; the pain of losing their home, loved ones, and even their motherland. We feared the attack of the extremists after the news of the partition was confirmed, so we decided to leave. While leaving for the camp, which was set up in the open ground, all of a sudden, I realized that we had forgotten to take the guns, which were locked in an almirah. I ran back from the caravan to the street of my home to get the guns but, by the time I reached there, extremists had already got there and on seeing me, one of them shouted, 'Catch him!' I ran for life and misled them into the maze of many streets. As they lost my trail, I re-joined the caravan. In that camp, we built many small tents. I remember my grandfather bringing a goat to provide food for the family for Rs. 5. It felt as if the fate was not done with us yet… my father was taken ill and at the same time, my younger brother, Riaz went missing from the camp. I searched for him madly but all my efforts seemed to be in vain. He was not being found and now my courage had also started giving up. But after hours of struggle, I finally found him in different of the camp.

After approximately a week, we got our turn to board the train from Ludhiana Railway Station. The journey was not as safe as we thought. We had heard about the extremists attacking the trains and the massacre. And, that happened to us too; when we reached the next big station, Jalandhar; extremists attacked our train by throwing a bomb. But by the grace of God, the bomb did not detonate. The Baloch Army was also present in the train which, with the help of the police, controlled the situation. There was so much of suffocation all around and due to some breathing problems, it was very difficult for me to survive that situation but luckily, I did. Later the Baloch Army took control of the train's engine and didn't let it stop anywhere before reaching Wagah, the border of India and Pakistan.

On arriving at Wagah, people welcomed us with open arms and gave us food to eat. No one slept empty stomach that night. From there, we moved to Lahore, where the slogans of 'Pakistan Zindabad!' (Long Live Pakistan!), reached the new sky of the new nation. We were sheltered in Walton Training School, one of the biggest railway training schools in Asia then. Later, my father was offered a job there. But our happiness didn't last long as my grandfather got ill and he told us that his time, with us, had come to an end now. During his illness, I used to visit the graveyard which was nearby our house. I saw headless bodies, some without limbs too. I saw street dogs dragging those bodies and tearing them apart. It was all so traumatic that I used to cry a lot afterwards. I often got reprimanded by my paternal uncle who used to forbid me from going there. I remember him asking me, 'Why do you go there, if you can't see such things!!?!' I had no answer to his questions. A few days later, my grandfather died, and we buried him in the same graveyard by making a shroud of the bed sheets we had. My paternal uncle named that place 'Ganj-E-Muhajir'. I used to visit his grave every day.

When we had to leave our home, Ludhiana, we kids were excited to see 'the new place' but after reaching there, we found nothing but misery only. I started selling matchsticks in front of the Walton Training School. Once my father saw me doing that, and he came to me and said, 'You don't need to do this. You are getting food to eat, you have a place to live, go home!' I stopped selling matchsticks and went back home. I know what he must have felt, as a father. He didn't say many things but whatever he said, surely left a mark on me. After a few months, we shifted to Rawalpindi.

I resumed my studies. After completing my graduation from the Government College, Rawalpindi, I started working for *Pakistan Times*. A very good friend of mine, who was a script editor, always encouraged me to work for PTV, but I used to refuse. After many efforts of his, I then one day went to PTV studio, which was near Army Barrack, Chaklala. I was provided with a script and was told to either memorize the dialogues or the movements. I told them, 'As I have come now, I'll do both'. We started recording and I told them that I'd see the recording by myself and would only work if I were satisfied with my own work. During those times, we didn't have much resources, not even a soundproof room. Donkeys used to pass by the studio many times and caused a disturbance in the recordings, because of which we had to re-record the things.

Shahid Ahmed Shahid, one of the legendary poets and writers of all times, opened the gates of glory for me, by offering me to work in my first drama, which was 'Raizgari'. After that drama, people started recognizing me. Whenever I used to go out in the evening, people used to recognize me, wanted to talk to me, wanted to see me, and honestly, it felt amazing. I savoured every bit of it. Later I got another opportunity of doing another drama and since then, I have never looked back. I worked in many television and radio shows back to back and then there came a long journey of endless fame, money, and success. I was awarded a Life Time Achievement Award twice for my individual contribution to both television and radio. It is a very big thing to achieve such heights in both the fields. My plays are also there in different training academies in India. I hold a record for performing the longest scene of 25 minutes 48 seconds, in just one take, which has not been broken till date, and I don't think it will ever be broken; as nowadays, one scene lasts for only two to three minutes. I have been awarded with Tamgha-E-Imtiaz by the Government of Pakistan, which is the fourth-highest honour given to any civilian based on one's achievements.

Even after all these years, after having almost everything, I still long for my city and my school. Those streets in which I used to play with my friends, especially the school. When the ghosts of the past haunt me again, I lock myself in the room, turn off the lights and cry. I just don't understand why we had to leave our home, friends, heritage, and land. I still remember my friends. Today, when I have all the happiness in the world, I still have so much of pain and sorrow inside me. I often keep on asking myself, why it had happened. I never get an answer to this question. No reason can justify the massacre that took place; cost people not only their lives but their souls which got inked with so much of pain that nothing filled their empty hearts and sowed hatred in the roots of the coming generations.

3
Wounded Flower

PUSHPA
MONTGOMERY - LUDHIANA

THE SPEAKING WINDOW

Memory is such a funny thing. Sometimes we try to recall something too hard but can't remember it and sometimes we try to forget something so desperately but can't erase it. My story is kind of the same. Though I don't re-member much about the beginning yet, the journey, is still fresh in my mind.

Montgomery (now known as Sahiwal), Okara, Punjab, Pakistan, I was born there. My memory doesn't serve me well now, so I don't remember much about it but I can't forget the journey to India; that left scars, not only on my body but on my soul also. We had a joint family where my paternal uncles, my grandmother, my mother, and my siblings, including my two elders brothers, an elder sister, and a six-month-old younger brother, lived happily. My father used to work in Sindh, so he resided there and was not with us. However, he would come to meet us whenever he could make time from his job.

As the partition was announced, our family decided to leave Okara. I was five years old back then. We were taken to a camp first, where people

The Speaking Window. Sandeep Dutt, Faisal Hayat, and Ritika, Oxford University Press.
© Oxford University Press India 2023. DOI: 10.1093/oso/9789391050733.003.0003

were divided into two groups. One group decided to walk in the caravan under the military protection whereas; the other one, which included us too, decided to leave Okara by train, via Firozpur route. It was around 2 at night and everyone was fast asleep; when all of a sudden, silence of the night turned into terrifying screams and cries of the people.

The extremists attacked our train near Raiwind. No mercy was shown to women or children. People were butchered savagely. Girls were robbed of their chastity and mothers were holding dead children in their hands. In all this monstrous act, my paternal uncles and their families were slaughtered too. My grandmother was carrying me in her lap and my mother had my youngest sibling in her lap. When the extremists were approaching my grandmother, I ran to my mother. They killed my grandmother barbarically and threw her out of the train. It all happened in front of my eyes. It filled me with fear and I lost my mother's hand. Then they turned to me and hit me on my head twice with a spear and then on my knee. They threw me on the railway lines among the other corpses. Both of my brothers hid themselves in the corpses carefully.

The very next morning, the survivors were looking for their families, but all they could find were either their cold bodies or their limbs. My brothers, who were hiding among the corpses, started looking for the family members. I was almost invisible among the dead bodies but they recognized my frock and pulled me out. I was smeared in the pool of my own blood. They washed my hands and face. There was a huge pile of corpses all around. We started looking for other members too but our search came to an end very soon on seeing the lifeless bodies of my paternal uncles and their families, along with my grandmother. We couldn't find our mother and sister, so we assumed that they were dead like others. We left that place, wandered here and there, and reached a town where people were more interested in knowing our religion than our well-being. They kept on asking us whether we were Hindus or not. Though we kept on refusing and lied by telling that we were Muslims. Religion, which is supposed to protect us and our soul, our beliefs and faith, goodness and purity, had become the cause of this hell now. It became just a tool in the hands of those who benefitted themselves by using this chaos as a ladder. But, where there were those who raised their swords in the name of God, there were also those who were seemingly sent by God, to save people like us. There were many kind-hearted people who were willing to help us but couldn't; because of the fear of extremists. We wandered on the streets for a few days. During those few days, my brothers tried to abandon me four times, due to my critical condition as they thought that my survival was nearly impossible and they were starving just like me. Imagine a ten- or twelve-year-old kid carrying a wounded five years old; for how long could they? They were also kids only. Less injured physically but they were too wounded mentally, just like me. But every time they tried to leave me behind, they couldn't. After all, how could they? I was their blood and might be, their only family left. And finally, one day, help found us when an old lady invited us to her house. She cleaned my wounds with the boiling water of Neem leaves and gave us bread which we shared and then asked us to leave before the extremists could find out that she was helping us. Then, one kind-hearted Muslim saw us, who knew we were concealing our real identity to protect ourselves. He asked us, 'Say truthfully, are you Hindu kids?' My brother, who was ten years old, still knew that he had to lie and so he did, 'No, we're Muslims'. The man sensed the lie and remained silent. Then, he asked us to follow him, without getting noticed by anyone. He told us that he would take us to a safe place among Hindus. We agreed and followed him. That walk was quite long but not longer than the one that got us there. He took us to a military gate and left. We went inside and the military personnel took us to Firozpur and got me hospitalized there.

A few days later, my brothers who were playing with a rubber tyre, at the railway station, saw some people of our locality from Okara. For the very first time, we had a hope of getting reunited with our lost family. So they decided to live at the station. It also benefitted us in a way to get sufficient food, as it was free there. They came to the hospital to ask for my discharge, but the nurses refused. My brothers, who saved me, carried me all the way long, were now not allowed to take me with them. They started crying and then they decided that they would come at night and take me with them. And, they did. We used to stay at the same station so that we could get to know anything about our mother and sister and finally, exactly after one and a half months, we were reunited with our mother, at the same station. My younger brother was also with her but my elder sister was still missing. My mother disclosed that extremists took the young girls and unfortunately, my sister was also taken. We lost hope of her return.

After a few months, we were reunited with my father and then went to Saharanpur. One year later, after the partition, in 1948, because of the efforts of both countries' governments, many girls who were abducted from their places; got rescued and fortunately, my sister was one of them. This news delighted us all as my whole family finally got united and later went to Firozabad and then to Delhi. I got married in Delhi and then came to Ludhiana in the late 1990s.

I have four daughters, all are married. I had a son too who was really handsome and had no bad habits. He also started his own work. I was looking for a bride for him but one day, he just died. He was healthy and charming. I don't know what went wrong. He was only twenty-five years old. Life has been very tough on me. From the age of five till now, I have lost so many things that it has emptied me. Even after twenty-five years of his death, I still mourn for him. That pain never goes away, never. Only a mother knows the pain of losing a child. How many layers it slips into, how deep it goes, and why it can never heal. If I, after all these years, still mourn for my son, then my motherland has lost millions of her children in the partition, her pain is unimaginable. The pain of all the mothers who lost the lives of their children, at the hands of politics or fate or circumstances, can't be healed.

My brothers and my sister all passed away, and I am the last one in my family, who belonged to Pakistan. All I can say to the youngsters is, I wish you all a happy and successful life! May no one, has to ever face the circumstances which I had to.

4

Nation Keeper

DR. MUHAMMAD RIAZ
PATIALA - GUJAR KHAN

THE SPEAKING WINDOW

A house in Christian Pura, Rawalpindi, Pakistan was bought for Rs. 25,840 in the year 1956. It was not as big as our older house in Patiala, nor it had the scent of our ancestral heritage in it, yet it became our home soon or we can say we made it into one.

Things were changed yet seemed unchanged somehow. We had around forty acres of land there, which we didn't have here anymore. Although many properties were offered to my father many times, he didn't wish to take anything more than he ethically required. The streets of Pindi reminded me of Patiala's, yet they were somehow different. I started studying here in a Government School of Syed Kasran where my father was appointed as a Head Master as he had twenty-two years of experience of serving in the same position in a government school back in Patiala. The journey from this new home to my school was new to me as before I only used to see other children going there but now it was me, all dressed in a neat uniform. The journey to school always started with a

The Speaking Window. Sandeep Dutt, Faisal Hayat, and Ritika, Oxford University Press.
© Oxford University Press India 2023. DOI: 10.1093/oso/9789391050733.003.0004

kiss from my mother, which she never forgot to place on my forehead before I would leave for my school. Still there was something strange about this new home which never gave me the feel of home we used to have. Neither its structure nor the neighbourhood was the same anymore.

Though a few things were still similar even after the partition, yet they were different in their own ways. We were still living in Punjab. It was just that this Punjab was a province of Pakistan, not India. Both cities were rich and renowned, and were having a diverse populace with an old and great heritage in their hearts. There was one more similarity; both were ill-fated. The bigger the cities, the worse were their condition in times when they were supposed to stand strong but fell down to pieces like a sandcastle and so did the lives of their people. And one of such lives was ours.

My father had always made efforts to inculcate values in his pupils, was given a salary of Rs. 250 that time which was enough to provide us a lavish life. We were landlords in our area and were having quite a reputation. If he was a 'Nation Builder', my grandfather was a 'Nation Protector' who served in the Second World War. The vast family tree of our Awan family had been into the service of the nation for generations. Most members of the family were into the armed forces, yet when they were required to save their respective families, most couldn't. And, only a few could make it to Pakistan with their whole family like ours.

After all these years, the younger brother of my father still cries for his family, which he lost at the hands of the frenzy of 1947. He is forced to live with every shred of memory, he has of his wife and children and the beautiful moments of their smiles which he had to watch as they turned into cries and soon into screams. Their voices in his head never let him sleep and all he is left with is a sobbing heart. He laments in front of us, even today, over the cruel circumstances of the partition and how nobody came to save his children and wife when they were being preyed on by such circumstances. He was the only one who was left behind to live with the flashes of them being murdered, the loss of his family and the feeling of helplessness that he felt when he wasn't able to save either them or himself.

My Chachaji (paternal uncle) was a session judge, who spent his life providing justice to people but he couldn't deliver it in a situation when the judge was extremist and the executioner was hateful. The life of a judge is spent in weighing the facts and evidences to draw the truth out of different possibilities so that justice can be served to those who were the victims of the wrong time or wrong intentions. But what if the victim is the judge itself? What if the accused is the time itself? And what if the justice is never served to him who served it to others? In the courtroom of injustice, the law and order is a mere joke when the gavel is in the hands of inhumanity. So was the case of my grandfather who lost both his wife and brother to the acts of extremism. Just like them, countless other families suffered the same. A relative of ours who was an SHO then, too, lost his kids in the attacks, which was why he used to advise my father to train his children to prepare them to fight and protect themselves if need be.

Patiala, a Muslim-dominating region, had royalty in its gestures with a grand heritage. So, when the riots broke out, the level of disaster was also at a great level. There is no doubt in the fact that before the partition, everyone was nice to each other but, the same people turned on each other later and did not remain 'nice' at all. In those days when the difference between days and nights was nullified and time was no longer a consideration to carry out the act of wiping out the existence of humanity, it appeared as if God had left heaven and was no more there to hear the prayers of his children.

One day, my father was in Dhuri when the outraged extremists attacked him but he escaped death with luck that day. As soon as he got back, he told us that migration was the only chance of our survival now. So we did it. He was attacked in the afternoon and by the evening, we had left for Ludhiana by train, which reached there by 7 pm and by midnight, we were at the Amritsar station. We tried reaching for our relatives who were living in different cities and asked them to migrate, but their families were already lost in the journey by then. Nearly forty of our relatives got killed as most of our houses were of influencers which made them an easy target of the attacks.

Once we crossed the border of India and stepped on to our land, Pakistan, it was then when we had a sigh of relief as we knew that we didn't have to see any deaths anymore. The footprints left on the sand are not permanent, one wave is enough to wash them out as if they never existed and no one ever walked. The Radcliff line was that wave and the relationships amongst people based on respect, love, and cooperation were just like those footprints which vanished as it appeared to wash them away. Only the migrants know what they suffered, saw, and survived. This pain was neither understood nor empathized by the residents who didn't have to migrate at all. The attitude of the society towards the migrants was not very kind. As if people were robbed of all the goodness they had and the only thing they could offer was nothing.

We were five brothers and two sisters. I was five at the time of partition but no more a kid after that. My elder brothers had established themselves well there; one started serving as a Director General in Pakistan and the other did a Charter course which in those days only a handful of people had completed in the whole country. Now, it was my turn to make my family proud but I have always been the laziest sibling. After my FSc., I joined Lahore College to complete a degree in the medical stream and I started off my career as a Veterinary Doctor and worked for the Government. I was the only Pakistani who was offered to complete a Meat Expert Course in a foreign country, which I gladly accepted. I came back from there in 1972. I remained an in-charge of Islamabad Zoo, Barani Commission, and also served as the head of Pak's biggest slaughterhouse, Sihala Depo, for six years. I served in Libya for seven years, where 3,500 km^2 of the area was under my command and I did work in Al Sham as well for this job. I was the only Pakistani who got selected to do it there. I have met Col. Gadaffi in person too.

I have been in the positions that one can only dream of, but I have lived that life. I have met 1965 warriors, too. Since my work was such, a bribe was offered to me in six to eight figures, but I never took it because I believe in serving my country with dignity. Moreover, I had lived my whole life like Kings, so materialistic charm never charmed me like it does to many. Riches have been in our heritage for generations and our family members have served in different important positions, like my brother-in-law had remained a personal advisor to Benazir Bhutto in both of her regimes.

My life has been filled with great events and has been a fest of successes that came to me wherever I went but all these victories and achievements cannot fill the hole in my heart that still misses our house back in India. The kind of ambience it had, the kind of people who were in those times, and the sort of happiness that was there in the little things we did, that love, that innocence and friendship and those friends; are all gone. I remember Ram Laal, a Hindu friend of my father, and also, Ashok Kumar, a very dear friend of my brother, whom he visited when he went back to India after partition and he treated him well. I wish if I could, I would visit all the historical places on the other side of the border.

I have been to different places, seen many things, served under different regimes, and lived with different people. That is why; I can say people need to understand that Islam was spread on the basis of its ethics, not by force. Not only Islam but any religion, when used like a tool, then the people who pull the strings of beliefs and take advantage of innocent people, become gods. The fate of a nation doesn't depend on the gold or silver it possesses but on the wisdom of its people in choosing the right representatives. People have lost their path. I believe the only purpose of the mankind is to learn as much as possible.

One must do one's job with dignity and honesty so that one can be remembered even after one's gone.

5

Judgement of Life

JUSTICE JC VERMA
MIANWALI - CHANDIGARH

THE SPEAKING WINDOW

On 18 October 1942, the Indians who had been celebrating Dussehra for hundreds of years with a tradition of setting the effigy of Ravana on fire that signifies the victory of good over evil, set fire again; only this time, it was the effigy of the British Raj. The Indians wanted a new Ram Rajya (a prosperous nation) whose foundation was demanded to be laid on independence. But in this Ramayana, Ravana was not supposed to be defeated in his own home, Lanka, but he was to be chased off Ayodhya on which not Rama but Ravana was ruling. The crowd of thousands emerging at the fairs of Dussehra was on the roads this time as protestors supporting the Quit India Movement. However, my family has not celebrated Dussehra from the said year till now for my father lost his life in that very year in Karachi in the lathicharge that happened.

It seems strange how a class A officer of the 'Railway Claims Tribunal' went to Karachi for a tour, ended up in the Quit India Movement happening at the time, and was killed in lathicharge like many other Indians.

The Speaking Window. Sandeep Dutt, Faisal Hayat, and Ritika, Oxford University Press.
© Oxford University Press India 2023. DOI: 10.1093/oso/9789391050733.003.0005

I was 2.5 years old and we were living in Sukkur in Sindh as he was posted there. My mother told me that a protest for the Quit India Movement was going on in Karachi in October 1942, but what we never got to know was how he got involved in that movement or whether he was involved in that or was led there by the act of fate, or if it was a misunderstanding. To control the mob, the police did lathicharge and it was told that he passed away in it. We were not sure about the whole scenario that led to his death as he went to Karachi on a tour, but it seemed that he was a part of that protest. He was into the services of the British government, so he was granted certain incentives, which were revoked by Britishers, after what seemed like his indulgence in the Quit India Movement. Even his pension, gratuity fund, and other amenities which were to be given to his family after his death were not given because the Britishers assumed him to be a part of an anti-government movement. His years of service and dedication to his work; nothing was taken into consideration. To be honest, what I feel in my heart is that my father supported Mahatma Gandhi with the Quit India Movement; every Indian did. Didn't they?

Only his body was sent to Sukkur, which I remember being kept on the ground, covered in a red cloth with flowers on it with people gathering around him. The impression of that memory never gets blurred.

After his death, we came to Mianwali, the home of my paternal and maternal families and also my birthplace. My grandfather lived and worked as a Hakim (a physician who uses traditional remedies for curing diseases) there. My father was the only one in the family who had a government job in my paternal family and that too was in such a high position which is why his lifestyle was completely different from the rest of the family and relatives. Imagine his status during that time, when today the Railways Claims Tribunal is headed by the high court judge. He was given a complete boggey and special security everywhere he travelled. We had a bungalow in half an acre in Mauhalla Gaushala, which had his name, *Khillu Ram*, written on the nameplate of that *Haveli* (Mansion) in English and Urdu as well. I remember playing in its verandah.

As I was very young when I lost him, so what I know of him was told by my elders. I never got to know what kind of a person my father was, but I learnt about his personality in little glimpses from those around me, to whom he was a son, a brother, a husband, and a father. As a person, he was cordial, supportive, and a nature-lover. He helped his nephews to pursue engineering in Lahore, but unfortunately, he couldn't help his own children in getting the right education. From what is told, I understand he was a good soul.

Besides my father, one more person in our extended family was into government services. My maternal uncle, Gyan ji was in the military and like my father, he had a wide network of resourceful people. He was also friends with Muslims. I remember one of his friends who used to visit our home much often, Mustafa Khan, again a military official. He was way too amusing and talkative for his job! He was 6 feet long and had a well-built body, giving him a dominating persona. However, he was a really great friend to my uncle and above all, a very nice person. He would pick us up and play with us and used to call my mother 'Didi' (a term used to refer to the elder sister).

I remember us having a radio which could be operated with a battery and the spinning gramophone's pin on the record, every track playing such tunes which would spellbind everyone who would hear it and in no time, people could be seen around it. My elder brother had a bicycle which he loved riding. We had goats but no buffaloes or cows. We had land in Bahawalpur of around 100 acres and about 25 acres of land was gifted to us by Britishers because my father had planted trees over a distance of 20 miles on both sides of the road, starting from Chistian Railway station. I reminisce about our lands and roaming there. I can't remind myself of any hand pump in our lands back then, although there were hand pumps in Mianwali.

Mianwali was populated by Hindus and Sikhs inside the city and the Muslims at its outskirts. It may sound weird, but it was not the religion but the occupation of a person which made them live in that part of the city.

The fields for agriculture were at the boundary of the city and all other work, business, occupational, or professional ran inside, which led to such distribution of the population. There was an unexplainable bond and unspeakable understanding that they had, along with mutual respect. I also remember a road leading to the station.

I do remember the Pathans of Mianwali, big in stature, cladded in salwars and kurtas with a turban on their head. They were very fun-loving and light-hearted people. One could hear groups of five to six Pathans singing in the evening on their way back to home after work. People used to find them so fascinating that everyone in the society used to stand at their thresholds to see them.

The ambience in Mianwali was filled with serenity and being a very young child, what I have understood from our surroundings was that there was harmony between Hindus and Muslims. In the past, I don't recall having any temples at Mianwali but yes, there were many Gurudwaras which we kids often used to visit for their tempting prashad. In fact, it may amaze people of the present generation but there was an old Hindu custom where the eldest son of the family would take up Sikhism. Even our oaths used to begin with 'In the name of the Guru …' because we believed in the Sikh Gurus. My maternal grandfather, Takht Ram, was a school headmaster and very religious in his ways. So, before school, he would be the first to unlock the gates of the Gurudwara and do the first prayer.

At the time of the partition, we were three brothers and three sisters in total. My elder sister was married, and her husband was also a railway employee who was posted at a distance of around 1.5 hours by train from Mianwali. My other sister was married in Firozpur, and my elder brother also stayed with her to study. I was about 7 years old, my sister was about 9, and my elder brother was 11; we all three were living with our mother. My grandfather had died a long time ago, but our maternal family was looking after us.

The story of partition is saddening. After partition, our families had conversations about not leaving Pakistan. They often said it was an internal matter of the nation and not a war against external forces, but they didn't realize that the choice was not theirs to make; the decision was already taken. It was not the locals who forced people to migrate with their changed attitude or sarcastic tones; it was something else. People had started their migration journey long before its declaration, out of fear. My maternal family decided to migrate for the very reason everyone else did, but we didn't till September. It was perhaps 27th or 28th September of 1947, when in the morning, Mianwali was attacked by a mob of 10,000 people and surprisingly, there was not even a single familiar face. We woke up to see the city wrapped in flames. From the terrace, we could see the flames reaching up the sky and forming black clouds of smoke. The rioters were Qabaili people. Now the question arises of how my family and I survived.

If it were not for Mustafa Khan, our lives too would have turned to ashes. A day before the attack happened, he came to inform us about the same and requested my mother to stay at his house. However, the situations were such that my mother had a sort of fear in her mind. Sensing her discomfort towards his proposal, Mustafa gave the charge of our safety to a friend of his who was serving as a Major in the Army with him, who promised that he would not let any harm get near us. Five to six Army officials inspected our terrace to conjecture about all the possibilities that could happen and see how we could be saved. On the day of the attack, the Major was in his jeep at the entrance of our street, with his finger on the trigger of an automatic machine gun installed on his jeep, but Mustafa wasn't there. The attacks happened, and the rioters set the houses ablaze. The huge clouds of smoke were clearly visible but our street, which was under military protection, was safe, for now. Soon the extremists reached there and they were about 1500 in number. They offered the Major to let them do what they intended, and they would spare our house, but he speculated that once he set them loose on the street, they would not be able to control this pack of hyenas. Thus, he refused but knew that he needed to do something real quick because they were not going to wait for long and would attack any minute. So, he told us to get ready and get on the Army truck, which would take us straight to the refugee camp. We had no time to pack anything at all, not even our clothes. Everything happened so fast and so suddenly that there was no time to respond.

We were standing at the door for the truck to arrive. The Army officials were inside and so were we. And soon a truck passed, a military truck. The official at the door gave him a signal to halt but instead, it only slowed down momentarily, as if the driver was confused about whether he should or not stop. I ran behind it as it was not stopping and got on it by climbing from behind, but I didn't realize it was the wrong truck! It was a truck carrying corpses. I could not believe what my eyes were bearing witness to. The dead bodies, covered in blood, with scattered limbs around, the wounds on some heads and the expression of pain or fear frozen on their cold faces, scared the hell out of me. I was lying in the middle of the corpses. I felt their eyes gazing at me as if they were trying to penetrate my thoughts, my fears, and my soul. Terrifying, it was. The truck didn't stop anywhere before it arrived at a place where a big mass of land had been dug out, possibly to bury them. We used to hear that people driving the trucks quash children under their tyres, so when it finally stopped, I ran as fast as I could while still drenched in blood. I looked like a zombie, or maybe, I was scarier than that. As I knew where the camp was, I ran straight towards that way. My family probably reached there by the truck which we were waiting for on the same day I reached, but we could not find each other as there were over 1000 people at the camp, which made it difficult for us to find one other. But someone there, who recognized my mother and me, helped us in getting reunited. It took us three days to find each other!

We were grateful to Mustafa, no one in our family got harmed, but we could not express our gratitude to him in person as he was not there where we were taken. The Muslims who attacked us were not from Mianwali. However, we got to know that the day Mianwali was attacked, the radicals of Mianwali went to loot Multan. Maybe, this explains how the cities were being looted by the strangers as told by people in their stories. And maybe, it was not rage or vengeance which made them do so.

I can't remember for how many days we stayed there but we were later taken by goods train to India which in normal scenario used to take eight to nine hours to reach its destination, but that train took five to six days, and the journey itself was not easy at all. We were first escorted by the Pakistani Army till Sargodha, from where the Dogra regiment took over. The train didn't move for four to five days from a station named Lalamusa because some trains were stopped in India too and the routes were jammed. People gathered at the station, certainly not with good intentions, but the Army warned them about the retaliatory consequences. Still, some rioters would shoot at passengers from trees in the dark and injured some of them. Because it was an open train, we were instructed not to raise our heads by the Army still few people died in the firing. I remember some corpses were thrown by the people in a river near Sargodha.

No one was prepared for such a journey that lasted for so many days. No food, no water, and increasing threat outside; nothing was favourable, and the survival was getting tougher and tougher with every passing day. For the days when the train remained there, people would go to the wells to fetch water with the Army escort, but a word got spread that the wells were being poisoned by the extremists. No one knew how true it was, but obviously, no one wanted to take any chances either. Ultimately, the train moved. Before reaching Lahore, there was a forest on the way where the train stopped, and the Army allowed people to use the nearby pond. The pond was filled with dirt, buffaloes, and other animals, but the people who had been thirsty for days didn't mind sharing the water with those animals, nor did those beings mind sharing it with humans. At Lahore's station, we were welcomed by swords and our story could have ended there, but fortunately, the train didn't even pace down before reaching the Atari station. We reached India in the same clothes we left home because we didn't get a chance to pack anything but carried a few currency notes.

As the train entered Atari, it started slowing down. I didn't know if it was going to stop or not, but I was so hungry that I jumped off the moving train to fetch a chapati from a Sikh standing there who was distributing them to the people. I ran towards him and snatched it from his hands, and he hugged me tightly. I can never forget that hug. I felt so much affection and empathy coming from him, and his warmth touched my heart. 'It is for you! It is for you!'—he said, referring to the food I ran to snatch from him. He asked me if I had anyone else in the family, and I told him that I was with my mother. He gave me six to seven chapatis more and bade me goodbye with a soft angelic smile on his face and some tears in his eyes. I can never forget him. How can I? I remember his face. He was tall, had a long beard, with a white turban on his head. It was the face of God himself, cladded in humanity and having kindness in his heart. I can never pay off his debt.

The train then headed to the refugee camp in Agra. However, we got off at Khanna, where my maternal uncle and aunt were living. From their house, my sister, who was married in Firozpur, took us with her. One of my brothers was staying with her already because he was pursuing his education there. Because we didn't stay at the camp, our name was not registered in the list of the refugees here and we were not provided with any government relief, which led to a harder time for my mother, who had the responsibility of four of her children. For earning a livelihood, she had to do menial jobs. In Mianwali, we had at least three servants serving our family at a time, but here, I saw her working as a housemaid in others' houses—all for us—and later worked as a midwife. I have seen my brothers selling groundnuts too while they used to study, only to support my mother. I studied till fourth standard in the Mauhalla Ganga Mandir Bansi Gate, Firozpur.

Even after seeing all those deathlike situations, most of the people in the family hoped to return; thinking it was all just for the time being, but I wish they knew, the time had betrayed them. Soon when the nightmare of partition shaped a new reality, only broken hearts and exploited souls were left to be seen in tears. Convinced we were not provided any Government aid, surprisingly, in 1952, we found out that we were allotted some wetland in a village of Haryana, Saidopur, which we got to know from someone while living in Firozpur. As if the truth hadn't been delayed so much already, one more truth was waiting for us to be uncovered only to make the rest of the relationships bitter. My uncle from Khanna had taken over the possession of the land without our knowledge. It might be for the same reason as to why we didn't get to know about it before. In Pakistan, we had 100 to 150 acres of land, whereas here we were allotted only 30 acres that too gave birth to avarice in someone's heart but with the help of the villagers, we got its possession back. We got shifted there and started over our lives again. As the wetlands are not ideal for cultivation, we employed some labour to work on them and earned our bread and butter from them. Life after partition was a partition in itself. We were four family members living in Saidopur—my mother, along with my sister and brother, and me. Whereas, my eldest brother stayed in Firozpur to complete his studies and later got a job in Delhi, so he moved there. Both of my brothers completed their education.

While walking on the bed of roses, one can barely know the pains of a thorny way. I used to walk bare feet from four to five miles from Saidopur only to study in a school that was that far away. Nonetheless, those walks never seemed more difficult than seeing my mother working so hard. I wish I could do something to ease her pains, so I used to do whatever she used to ask me to do. I started cutting wood from the jungle and then carried it to a nearby town. The little I could earn from the wood which I sold, anna or 2 anna or rupaiya, mattered a lot. Even as a kid, after the school or whenever I would get time, I would go into the woods to get some of it and sell it as people used to burn wood for different heating purposes back then. The axe then got replaced with a plough and the woods with the field, and so did my occupation. I started working as a farmer. Working in a jungle had never been easy and the kind of area in which we used to live, encounter with a wild animal was not surprising; especially the big cats, so a tough body built was important which I did work on and became a wrestler and bodybuilder. But during all that I never left my studies.

If there were difficulties, God had given some ease too. And my ease was in the form of my teachers, who had been very supportive throughout my schooling and helped me pass my 10th grade. I, not only, passed it but also became one of those five students who won the scholarship out of our school's 'scholarship group', which was made to prepare students for getting scholarships. Only seven scholarships were given in four districts of our region, and five of them were won by our school. In order to achieve this, we were provided with a room in the city so that we could go and study there. I remember there was a table and two oil lamps in the room.

However, I had to leave my education in the middle for the lack of proper financial circumstances at home. But the representatives of the colleges of Ambala, DAV College, and SD College, used to look for the students who scored well in their matriculation so that they could have bright students in their college, who could earn a name for themselves.

I got chosen for F.Sc. Medical at DAV College and upon finding out about our financial crisis, they tried to convince my mother by offering free education and books and all I had to pay was for my hostel facility. When I went there to study, they exempted my full fees and everything else, and now when the final decision was stuck on the admission fees only, I wished to share it with my mother. The happier she was on hearing this, the sadder she became when she thought of our financial situation because we couldn't pay my admission fees, too. I too didn't wish to continue my studies.

Nevertheless, a friend of mine, Harish who became a very good doctor, with whom I joined F.Sc. medical before I dropped out, was disappointed in me for wasting my talent, so he requested his father to pay my fees for F.Sc. Medical, without my knowledge. His father came to see my mother and told her that he had paid my fees, but she told him, 'He'll too, like his brothers, pursue distance education'. I didn't go for F.Sc., considering the possible future expenses I had to incur, besides admission fees. Thus, I went for Faculty of Arts instead and took advantage of the relaxation given by the Panjab University to the refugees to attempt F.A. and B.A. through distance education. With the help of guidebooks, I cleared it too. After clearing F.A., I saw an advertisement for the post of clerk in Chandigarh Secretariat and applied for it. I was 17 then. I got the job and was paid Rs. 100 a month! And when I handed my mother Rs. 60 out of it, her joy burst into tears.

Incidentally, I was posted in the office of the then Chief Minister Partap Singh Kairon at Chandigarh, so I shifted to the city in 1957. Even after getting the job, I continued my studies. I completed my B.A. and then law through distance education while working there from Panjab University. My brother, who came with me from Pakistan, was also posted in Chandigarh, so I was staying with him. Time passed easily after that. As soon as I started practicing law in 1964, I resigned from the post of clerk immediately. I was an advocate till 1996 before becoming a high court judge in Chandigarh High Court. I requested for a reposting within a month of my job and went to Rajasthan High Court. I came back after retirement in 2002. After retirement, I headed a few commissions. The chief minister of Haryana had made a provision. I was asked to head the commission, which did enquiry about the ambiguities in the execution provision. I was one among those heads who took the least time in submitting reports. I wanted to practice law again, which I could do only in the high court. I started again but left because the quality of judges at our times was high. Judiciary is different now. Then I became the Chairman of Indian Law Tribunal, and now I am free.

Whenever a delegate used to come from Pakistan, I asked him only one question about Mauhalla Gaushala. I would tell him about my house there and ask him if it is still there. In my heart, I want to go to Pakistan and see it for myself, but a sense of fear holds me back. I can't comment on internal matters of India and Pakistan, but I don't see a bright future ahead for both countries socially if they stick to the same attitude they have for each other today. When people from India go to Pakistan, they are very receptive. The public is very nice except for the politicians. The only thing I want to tell the youth is that learn to fight against the circumstances. If you don't ask for help, you won't get it.

By the time I did my matriculation, I had read countless books, novels of Munshi Premchand. I had read Fickle, Nanak Singh, Gorki, and Karl Marx. I am a communist and what I learnt was that the value of human values over communism. If I had ten cases per day, I did four of them free. I didn't ask for my fee; if people had anything, they gave it else they wouldn't. Now communism has become limited to slogans only.

From roaming in the forest to gathering some wood to holding the gravel, the twists and turns have been sharp but of great significance. The failures in hard times teach a person a lot more than the success in good times; what is more valuable and what must be valued are no easy lessons to learn, but wisdom lies in learning from others' mistakes to avoid the same hardships from falling in our own way.

There is only one thing if I could ever change, which would be the time. I wish I could go back in it and take my mother back here, only to give her the proud moment of seeing how her son has grown up into the man he is today. If I could just give her back the comforts of life she had once when my father was alive. If I could just hold her hand once again and put my head in her lap, and say, how grateful I have been for all her love, for all her patience and hard work, and for everything she ever did for our family and for me.

6

Born Beautiful

Life is pretty strange; it can give you wings to fly and the feel of being invincible but, at the same time, it can chop those wings off, and make you hit the ground in no time. In the carefree days of my childhood, when my parents used to treat me like a princess; I never ever imagined that I had to live like a pauper someday.

Born in Lalamusa, Punjab, Pakistan, I grew up in a multi-cultured environment; for my father was a DSP, so I had seen many places including Sargodha, Hyderabad, Kolachi (now known as Karachi), et cetera, therefore, I had a bunch of friends from these places. My father took early retirement and returned to our hometown Gujrat, Punjab, Pakistan. I have cherished every luxury of life, yet everything was simple, easy, and joyful. And then, the fortune smiled at me; I got married to the man of my dreams. It was all so perfect that even now, I still get short of words while describing that. We moved to Dariyaganj, Delhi, in early 1947, just after a few months of my marriage as my husband being an army officer got

The Speaking Window. Sandeep Dutt, Faisal Hayat, and Ritika, Oxford University Press.
© Oxford University Press India 2023. DOI: 10.1093/oso/9789391050733.003.0006

transferred there. It wasn't much difficult for me to gel well with people as I had relatives there already, including my paternal uncle. The slogans of protest were becoming more and more normal with every passing day and, the rallies and influential speeches had heated up the political environment. Even after all that heat of revolution, it didn't disturb the peace of the city.

And then, after all that struggle, endless sacrifices, and a long battle for existence, there came the fateful day, when the nation got liberated but no one could have ever imagined what it concealed within. The joy of freedom was very much short-lived. No one knows even today, how the sound of celebration turned into the screams and cries of the innocent. I was twenty-two years old back then with a four months old daughter, when it all happened. Streets were red with blood weeks before the partition. The situation got more intensified with communal hatred, which was nothing but a ridiculous misunderstanding. People, who loved each other for years, were now ready to slit each other's throats! The extremists were winning and the humanity was losing incessantly. A mob of extremists attacked our streets a couple of weeks before the partition and killed every Muslim in their way. All the shopkeepers were forced to shut their shops and were out of business, which led to a shortage of food. It was not the only incident, but one among the countless ones which gave a flip to the spark of communal hatred, which grew into a wildfire and burned the entire nation.

Curfew was imposed for a few days and only an hour of relaxation was used to be given in a day during that time. Then, many trucks were sent by the authorities to take all the Muslims, who were stuck there, to a refugee camp that was set up in the Old Fort. We were in them too. In hurry, I only took a packet of dry milk with me for my daughter and left all my jewellery and clothes. I also shared that dry milk with other mothers who were having toddlers with them. It all became so much more difficult because of starvation. The lack of food became the harbinger of death which was waiting with its jaws open and to it, age didn`t matter much. Children were dying because of hunger. Many women were in the final month of their pregnancy and were forced to deliver their babies there. But unfortunately, many new lives didn`t even get a chance to see the world; some died at the time of their birth and some, a few hours later. The memory of that day still gives me chills. The sobbing of those mothers, their mourning, and their cries shook even the coldest of hearts. It all was extremely sorrowful to bear that sight. This came into the notice of Mohammad Ali Jinnah, the leading face of Muslim League, who asked the authorities to help the people, who were stuck in that situation. He then arranged an aircraft that flew from Karachi with the food which was then delivered by trucks and a man used to throw those food packets towards people like one throws bits of bread to animals.

Even the food which was delivered got spoiled due to humidity as that was rainy season. As if the shortage of food was not enough already, the extremists then poisoned the hand pump from which the majority used to satisfy their thirst. Those twenty to twenty-five days of hell, without food to eat, shelter to cover our heads in rains, not only of monsoon but also of sorrows. No words can give justice to the feel of that fear, in which there was, just wait to live or to die.

We, then, were taken to the airport where there was only one flight to Pakistan which was already full. We were asked to wait that lasted for eight long days. Every day we used to watch that flight taking off with a lot of migrants, but us. Meanwhile, the circumstances were becoming more critical with every passing day. So, on the eighth day, we decided to take a train to Pakistan via Amritsar. That journey was also not so easy after all. On our way, our train stopped at Amritsar station where extremists were already present and were not letting our train pass. They demanded a similar train to run from the other side to India, carrying the Hindus and Sikhs who lived in Punjab, Pakistan. We locked the doors, and the feeling of fear swept over us. Despite all that, there were those who tried to help us. People, standing outside on the platform, were throwing dried chickpeas towards us, so that we could eat something. But it wasn't much helpful as most of the chickpeas fell on the floor, got crushed under the feet of the people, and got spoiled. For the first time, I saw hunger winning over everything else and people were fighting with each other to eat the same, wrapped in dust and dirt; having no other choice, I too had to eat the same but soon I felt thirsty and there was no water around. We were stuck in that train, without food and water. Even the air felt heavy and it was so suffocating all of a sudden that in a fraction of second, I lost my consciousness. My husband, who was there with me, got very much scared. He then rushed outside, to fetch some water for me, knowing the risk that it might cost him his life; he went, however. He was trying not to get noticed while searching for water, which sadly, he couldn't find. It was raining and the roads were flooded with water. Disappointed, he had to collect some water from the potholes with filth and algae inside and brought it to me and insisted me to have it, if not for me or him then, for the sake of our daughter. I, who was raised to savour all the delicacies in life, was now forced to have something like that I had to have it. Finally, the train was free to depart after the wait of this long time and we reached Wagah Border. The soldiers of Punjab Regiment there took charge of the train and made us reach Lahore safely. We stayed at a camp there and the people of the city were kind enough to give us food.

We went to our hometown Gujrat, I still remember it was the time of sehri (a meal eaten before the sunrise, by Muslims, in Ramadan), when we reached there on Tonga. My husband was then transferred to Karachi and I stayed with my sister-in-law, in Gujrat. After six months, my husband again got a transfer and this time to Rawalpindi, where we were given a big house in Dheri Hassanabad (at that time, it was known as Chak Dharam Singh). I am blessed with very wonderful children; who made my life even more beautiful. My husband got retired as a Colonel and passed away in 2002 and left me very sweet memories of our life together. I am in my nineties but no one believes that. They think I am in my sixties. Even my doctor compliments me saying, 'I want to look just like you when I will be your age'. I never applied any beauty cream ever! I advise the girls of the new generation not to apply too much of makeup. You see, I am still young and beautiful and have a very sharp memory. You're born beauties, just believe in yourself, not in other people's perspective.

I rest my words just by reminding this generation that we sacrificed only for our next generation but sadly, the youth is disappointing me. May God never put someone's children in such a painful situation that we had gone through! May Allah keep everyone happy and young!

7

Three Goddesses

PRABAL KUMAR SHYAM
SYLHET - GHAZIABAD

THE SPEAKING WINDOW

In the life of a Bengali, the importance of Goddess Durga is immense. She being a divine power, is considered to be the Protector of the universe who puts an end to the evil, she being a mother is considered to be affectionate towards her children and being a woman, points to the immense power concealed in a woman which at times, can change the whole history. And like every Bengali, she is dear to me too, but I also believe that somehow, I am dear to her also. That is why, she came into my life in three different roles symbolizing love, strength, and empowerment. These had been virtues in my life that I needed as she came when I lacked affection, when I lacked courage and also, when I lacked vision.

Starting from the very first role of Goddess Durga in my life; love that I received from the very first and extremely important woman in my life; my mother. She was as beautiful inside as she was outside. She was a living definition of patience, affection, and motherhood. She was a perfect mother who raised and loved me as Yashodha did to Lord Krishna. And

The Speaking Window. Sandeep Dutt, Faisal Hayat, and Ritika, Oxford University Press.
© Oxford University Press India 2023. DOI: 10.1093/oso/9789391050733.003.0007

if I get another chance to be born in another lifetime, I would ask for this life again, just to be her son once again. We had a beautiful relationship that was very unique and strong. I have been a very mischievous kid, but my mother never got angry at me; literally. I used to steal food from home so that I didn't have to share it with any of my siblings, but my mother was clever too, she started hiding the food in different places so that it would not get into my hands. The roads then were not cemented and had potholes in them, so in the rainy season, those potholes remained full of rainwater which used to attract crabs; something I had a weakness for. I loved eating crabs, so I used to jump into those potholes to catch them and most of the time, I would be successful but would get something in complementary too; the leeches! They would get attached to my soft skin and have my blood for their lunch! So, I would run to my mother every time to get rid of them and she would spread salt on them to make them fall off my legs. Nevertheless, this never prevented me from going after crabs.

Apart from that, the village had a forest which was another playground for me where I would go on my Red-Ant-Hunt'. It may sound a little disgusting, but I liked their sour taste, which again was a concern to my mother who would come looking for me and take me back by my ear! A special stick was made just to 'threaten me' into becoming more disciplined. And after every mischief that could get me that stick in reward, I would run from my mother who would chase me till I climbed a tree and then, I would never climb down till she had put that stick away. If not that, I was bribed with honey to come down; as it was something I relished too! But she always kept her word, and this is one of the things I have learnt from her. If she made a promise of giving me honey, she always meant it.

I have introduced you to my mother and now it is time to introduce other important members in my family. Firstly, with all the tricksters; my siblings and to everybody's surprise, the count is a double digit! Ok, not that big of a number, but not that small too. We are ten siblings; seven brothers and three sisters (from the two marriages of my father). And, in true words, we were not so easy to deal with. And now my father, who worked at a Tea Garden, about 18 to 20 miles away from the village and I remember visiting that too, quite often. Despite the size of our family, we were well-off. There were no financial hiccups that we ever had to face during that time. The house we owned was spacious; half of the house was bricked, and half was just like the older mud houses in older times of India. We had two cycles, many cows, three dogs, and ducks as well.

My father was an ardent admirer of *Jatra* (Bengali Theatre), which used to be renowned in that era. So, he would often take the whole family with him whenever he had a plan to watch it. One memory related to this particular *Jatra* trip is really close to my heart. I still laugh while recalling every moment of it. Once we went to watch Jatra like we usually did, just that this one was a little more crowded than usual. We got really late that day as it finished around 2 am. As we headed back home in a truck, after reaching halfway, we realized that my three-year-old brother was missing. My father thought that he was with my mother and my mother thought he was with my father. In this confusion, both didn't notice that he was actually with no one. By the time, they realized and thought of asking the driver to return back, the truck met an accident, fell off sideways, and was not starting again. Now, they had no choice but to get the truck fixed as soon as possible and return back because on foot, the distance was a lot to cover, which wasn't practical. On the other side, my three-year-old brother who was trying to recognize a familiar face in the hundreds of faces in the crowd, was scared and crying. But a family friend saw him there and took him along. On this side, it took them almost an hour or so to fix the truck and by the time, the truck was in a working condition, my uncle, the same family friend who took my brother with him, was coming from the same route and met us there. And finally, my parents had a sigh of relief.

Now that you have met my family, let me take you around my village as well, as I have loved the most after my family. The village Vasudevpur, Sylhet, which comes in present-day Bangladesh, was my birthplace and my paradise. The language spoken there was just as beautiful as the village itself; Sylheti. The region had the comforts of a city and the tranquillity of a village in it; one could experience nature blossoming everywhere. The place could make anyone fall in love with its natural magnetic charm. There was both Hindu and Muslim populace residing with harmony. The celebrations on Eid and *Durgo Pujo* (Durga Puja) were done with the same enthusiasm. Talking about Durga Puja, it was and is still the greatest celebration in Bengal. The preparations would begin months before the procession including the most important part of it; making a huge idol of the Goddess, which has huge eyes, a charming smile, with a trident piercing the heart of the evil under her feet, denoting the victory of the good over the evil. And I was introduced to her glory by my mother who used to explain me everything related to my queries regarding her. Also, every year, a huge pandal was organized near our home where artists would come almost a month prior to the processions in order to make sure everything was ready on time. The fragrance of innumerable incense sticks and the Dhunuchi dance would create a spell-binding ambience all around. I remember our family attending the Durga Puja every year with much enthusiasm and rejoicing spiritually in a way that satisfies the soul.

In Sylhet, there was a school, Nar Singh High School where I studied till grade 7 only. As it was far from my house, I discontinued my education but never stopped learning.

Bengal at that time was not only famous for the Durga Puja but also for some 'special devotees of the Goddess' who I really doubt would have been accepted even by the shadow of Goddess Durga. They were called 'Kapalika' (sorcerers) who used to claim to be Durga devotees and believed in human sacrifices for performing their rituals. Children were the easiest targets for them and in those times, many children got abducted by them just to be sacrificed in their madness. And once, the son of my paternal uncle got abducted but we got to know about his whereabouts somehow and the search parties were sent to get him back. After a cat and mouse chase, when the Kapalika saw no way of escaping, he left the boy on the way while running but he escaped himself. My cousin was safe and back home; that was the only thing that mattered. It could have gotten out of hand, and we might have lost him, but God helped us and that didn't happen, fortunately.

So, my childhood had been a roller coaster of events constituting light moments but when I was 15 or 16, I had to say goodbye to my first love ... My mother passed away, it felt as if time had halted there and nothing was moving anymore, and I was just stuck there. But that was the time, when I thought that I had lost my love, there came the second Goddess in my life who gave me strength. Though the word 'stepmother' has been really notorious, especially in our country but my stepmother redefined the same. After the death of my mother, it was not easy for my father to raise all of us, so he re-married for the sake of his children. And she became the second most important woman in my life after my mother. She loved all children like her own and never even once made us feel that she was our stepmother. She didn't try to replace the memories of my mother but made some of her own. She became the strength of the family when we thought we had lost it all, but she came like a ray of hope and brought backlight to all our lives.

But that year, it wasn't only me who lost his mother but the nation did too. Partition happened and as a result, millions lost their motherland and were forced to migrate. In a way, they also lost their mother who raised them since they came into being and always loved them. Though our area was not much affected by the partition, nor we felt any changes, we came across the fact that Sylhet was now in East Pakistan (current Bangladesh), so we knew we had to leave too. Since Tea Garden of Cachar where my father was employed, was a part of India so finding a new job or the pain of leaving the old one which he loved, was not something that he had to face like many others. Thus, we left Sylhet in 1948 and came to Silchar, Assam. Unlike West Pakistan where genocide was not coming to a halt, here in East; it was peaceful. People migrated but without any chaos.

After migration, for the first ten years, I lived a life of a nomad, but I have no regrets as every single moment led in it, was worth living. I did many things during that. I learnt everything I wanted to learn. Starting from playing Tabla from the nephew of Ustad Alauddin Khan, to the work of tailoring and thus, I started selling dresses for children. I also sold vegetables and fruits. I would just travel around and this freedom of doing what I wanted to give me a unique happiness. I loved living like a hippie. My stepmother, who had had enough of my irresponsible behaviour, once again steered my life's wheel and asked me to take my life seriously. Finally, I realized the value of her advice and joined Civil Defence Army in 1959 in Guwahati, Assam. Her strength gave me the power to better my life.

In 1962, she chose a girl for me and got me married and this was when I met the third role of Goddess Durga; only this time, it was in the form of empowerment. She changed me and made me a better man. Life became much more beautiful after she came. She was matric-pass and wished to have me clear my matriculation too, to which I didn't agree at first, but she was determined and never gave up on me. I attempted that exam in the same year of our marriage but failed. However, my wife still believed in me. She used to make time for my studies, taught me Mathematics on her own, and convinced me to take the exam again as she had faith in me and in 1963, I took that exam again and passed it! She has been very supportive, loving, and caring towards me. Wherever we go, we go together, always. I don't remember even a single situation when we had to live separately, nor do I think we can; at least I cannot! Not everyone gets a soul mate as a life partner but I have been one of those very fortunate people who have one and I have made the most of it. I was transferred to Delhi in 1972 and got retired in 1992. Since my retirement, we have been living in Ghaziabad.

In my life, women have played a really great part! And I thank Goddess Durga for being a part of my life in different forms, and for bestowing me with everything that my life lacked. I believe, if a man stops looking for God in idols rather start looking around himself; he will certainly meet many Gods who help him in their own ways, in different spheres, and have been there for him forever irrespective of their caste, colour, creed, or gender; he is there always; all you need to do is; recognize and also, value him/her.

8

Choiceful Vultures

The common perception people have of 1947's partition is that it happened in the heat of the moment because the then regime wronged its people. The history of the time before partition is glorified with words like brotherhood, harmony, and selfless love, which all the communities residing within the nation shared. There are stories that emphasize over the peace which existed among different religions before the seeds of differences were sown in them. And what is most astonishing is how the partition survivors or the migrants never forget to mention the undying love they miss now, which was so deeply rooted in the people before all of this happened, which, to me, is questionable.

Now, the point I would like to make here is pretty simple. If everything was so well, then how it ended up in a deep blood pool and most importantly, if those stories of friendships were so true, then how come a single move of disharmony was enough to demolish centuries-old bond that millions of people had? Why did people have a change of heart all of a sudden and an era of wars and hatred began, which exists till the present day even after more than seven decades of partition!? How that love fell apart completely when it was required the most and if it was so strong, then where was it when the people were being buried alive? May be, it was not prevailing everywhere after all and my story involves that other bad side of the older times, which isn't the subject of conversation for survivors and, is unknown to the listeners of their tales. Or, there may be a possibility that I was born in an era that had begun to lose all the golden days it had seen before.

I was born in a village whose district was Firozpur, although my ancestral roots are linked to Amritsar. I was born in 1938, the only brother to three sisters who loved me more than anything in the world, and so did

The Speaking Window. Sandeep Dutt, Faisal Hayat, and Ritika, Oxford University Press.
© Oxford University Press India 2023. DOI: 10.1093/oso/9789391050733.003.0008

my parents. My father owned three acres of land and had a wood business which earned our family enough to live a decent life, if not luxurious. My village had Hindu, Muslim, and Sikh residents who were residing together, but there was nothing as such peaceful to their co-existence as usually being told addressing the situation prior to partition. There had been a partition of its own long before it was signed and documented. There had always been questions raised about the need for a separate state for Muslims.

Even within our village, the lives of Muslims were pitiful. There were rivalries among communities; rivalries were so bad that if any Muslim was caught committing any crime, he was thrashed more than someone who was a non-Muslim but committed the same crime. Since the cow is considered a holy animal and worshipped by the Hindus, sacrificing it in the name of religion which is still a ritual among Muslims, was forbidden. There was discrimination and a very little justice for us. It was not that I had no non-Muslim friends; I did, many in fact, at the school I studied. Most of the teachers there, were also non-Muslims. All the children used to play together in spite of disputes between our elders but we were not close to each other. We would get together just to play, and there were no sentiments that made us concerned for each other's well-being.

When the talks of partition were getting heated up, people started picking sides, and soon, there were suggestions on who must and who must not migrate. If suppression and injustice were two dominating aspects of someone's life, they would not give another thought to the chance that promises to take all that misery away. This is how people got in the favour of partition on a large scale and supported the notion of a separate state. In our village, people thought it to be a temporary solution and were in a misconception that after a while, they would return to their respective homes and my family believed the same. Though we came to know through a relative about the partition but no one knew what it really meant for the masses. Therefore, most of them carried no valuables or money with them but some clothes and food. My family too packed some clothes and essentials for the journey, but we did take the jewellery of my mother and sisters with us.

At the first light of day, hundreds of people gathered at the pre-decided spot to start the journey to the other side. A long trail of oxcarts and people on foot could be seen even from a faraway distance. On the way, we got attacked by the tribe which was coming from the other side when we had just reached Firozpur city. People were running here and there in panic, and in no time, it got so much intense that only blood could be seen as far as one's sight could see. People left their belongings right where they were and ran for saving their lives. Mothers took their crying children and ran, men tried to protect their families, and those who got caught were crying for mercy. Everyone lost someone. Daughters were being butchered in the streets after their dignity was disgraced, children were shouting in fear but their cries led no one to put aside their swords and barchis (a kind of lance), a bride was being dragged forcefully by her family to safeguard her as she witnessed her husband being killed. It was all dreadful. Even our family lost two of our relatives who were slaughtered in front of our eyes.

After surviving that massacre, we continued our journey and looked out for any expected dangers on the way. We changed routes and tried to stay off the apparent route to prevent all the likely attacks. And after taking all the precautions, our family finally made it to Bahawalpur, Pakistan, where we stayed for some time and then moved to Chak 51 but after some time, we moved back to Bahawalpur. We were given ration cards, food, and clothes there. Refugees; we were homeless, trying to find a home here. It was a rough road ahead and things were not getting any easier at all. The struggle seemed to extend its horizon more and more for us and we were just stuck into the loop of it.

In those days, the people were being allotted the amount of land as per they had back in India. We, too, were promised the same, which we never got. The Patwari (Land officer) who was supposed to do so, tampered with the documentation and we were never given any piece of land or any help of even a single penny to support ourselves. This was when I realized it was not the communal differences that takes the form of rivalries and, injustice is not a communal thing; it is all an ethical and moral element that people had lost somewhere. Back then, I used to think we were in minority which was why everything that was happening was happening, and no one would help us but after seeing the hardships in Pakistan, I knew it was the mentality and nature of people which has nothing to do with the religion or community which one belongs to. It is a choice of a person how he treats his fellow human being, whether he helps or hinders.

It was 1960 when I got married and got blessed with three daughters and three sons, though two of my daughters passed away at a very early age. The sufferings didn't seem to end. But I did not lose hope or stopped moving forward. I saved some money to invest in starting a business of selling fruits which I still run to support my children. After working hard for years, I was able to buy a plot of half-acre in Lahore in the year 2000, and since then, I have been settled here.

Going back one more time just to relive everything, is not something I wish for. Neither my health nor my heart allows me to do so. But there is one thing I would like to say, in search of a paradise for tomorrow, we must not trample upon the gifts of today. Instead of wishing for a better tomorrow, we must make efforts to make our present better. Differences are natural, even in the same family, we see them a lot; but what we need to do with them matters, we can accept to understand them better instead of fighting them and may be then, we could be able to develop the lost compassion and empathy that the world needs today. No system is perfect, nor are its rulers, or the people but they all can make it better with their absolute devoted efforts. Always.

Muhammad Saddique
Firozpur – Lahore

9

City of Saints

SWARAN NAGPAL
MULTAN - KARNAL
THE SPEAKING WINDOW

A mattock was being hit at the floor of the kitchen very hard, with all the strength its holder had. Every hit was harder than the previous one, and the hole in the chest of the ground started to get bigger and bigger so did the eyes of the seven years old who were seeing things beyond their understanding and imagination. Even one's wildest dreams could not be any wilder than the things that were in the year 1947. After digging the ground, I saw my father bringing something like a small box wrapped in cloth and putting it in that hole which he dug a few moments ago. And it was again filled with sand to cover it.

It was the beginning of the 1940s when I was born in a small town of Multan, known as Bura Mandi, where my father owned a shop that was operated from inside our residence itself. His work brought him fame and earned him the name of 'Lala ji' too, which people used to call him. We, all four brothers and two sisters, were the life and soul of that house. We used to chirp like birds all day long, which kept our parents occupied with

The Speaking Window. Sandeep Dutt, Faisal Hayat, and Ritika, Oxford University Press.
© Oxford University Press India 2023. DOI: 10.1093/oso/9789391050733.003.0009

our little tussles and mischiefs all the time. I used to visit Multan a lot to see the siblings of my father; three brothers and two sisters and also, my maternal family also lived there. Though the city was at some distance from our town, yet the distance never affected my visits. It was a big city, with big markets and especially with a big heart which welcomed its visitors with the Aarti of temples and Adaan of mosques simultaneously. The overlapping sounds coming from both the religious places made it seem like magic itself. Andhi Khoi, was one of the places of my frequent visits, which had a big temple with a very long staircase besides it. My initial education commenced at the Arya Samaaj Mandir School, which had a huge playground opposite it.

'The city of Saints', Multan somehow lacked the saints in it then which is why, the anti-social activities were on the rise. The decorum of the city started to get destroyed almost twenty days before the final announcement of the partition, which sketched a new face of its history. Calculating the chances of the worst-case scenarios after getting to know the horrors of staying in the city, my father decided to send us all to Kapurthala, gave some cash to my mother, where we got us a house rented and my mother took care of us till his arrival. Since our house in Multan was under construction, my father did not wish to leave it in between all that chaotic situation but he could not risk one of our lives too, so he didn't come with us to Kapurthala and remained in Multan all by himself. This is how our family got migrated to India almost fifteen days before the partition without having to face any troubles on the journey.

As the hands of the clock struck 12 at night, the country was set free but also divided. Kapurthala became a part of India and Multan, of Pakistan, which left us thinking about our home at Multan, which was now out of our reach; completely. Riots broke out in the different parts of this newly divided Punjab and news regarding the same was not soothing anyone's heart, especially not my mother's. She was desperately waiting for hearing any word about my father's well-being and her constant prayers were now becoming pleading in front of God. We all were eager to see him too.

The times of sorrow are extremely complex and worrisome. Every granule of sand in the hourglass timer seems to make us count it and at the same time seems to drop at its own pace, yet the pain within seems still; completely immovable but getting deeper inside one's skin like a sharp thorn cutting the skin deep. It was almost the same then.

Somewhere Hindus were running for their lives and somewhere Muslims were. Trucks carrying the migrants were set on fire, passengers on the train were being murdered, families were butchered in their own houses, and drains were left running with blood. My brothers would go in search of my father every day to the station Atari which was the last station between India and Pakistan but would come back with more stories of miseries, violence, and blood. And one day, all of this got way too out of the hands. When trains used to arrive, stations were drowned in the blood of the innocent. So the outrage was natural and circumstantial in people. Unfortunately, my brothers got involved in this extremism and remained a part of the train massacre, which was taking Muslims to Pakistan.

On the other end, it was not getting easier for my father to stay in that place but even all of that could not make him move at his will. A man who had invested all his life savings to build a new home was now supposed to leave it when it was completed to live in it until it became the question of staying alive which forced him to leave. He decided to leave everything there when Ali Yaar, a popular leader in our area, made a public statement about killing Kanhaiya Lal (my father's name). The following day, before the Sunrise, my father took a bag and packed some important stuff. He took the mattock again and started digging at the same spot where he had buried something not so long ago. My paternal and maternal families living in Multan feared for their lives and getting looted, so they had kept their jewellery at our home. My father, before he sent us to Kapurthala, took all the jewellery including ours, and hid that beneath the kitchen floor. But when the house got constructed and it was getting difficult to stay in Multan anymore, he decided to leave for Kapurthala. So, he took some of the jewellery with him and kept the rest buried inside only in the hope of taking it when he would return with his family. He also took along the sewing machine of my mother and a radio of my brother.

Apart from that, the next thing to be done was to make a plan which could help him survive his journey. Since our house had two entrances, one from the front for the shop and the other at the back for the house, it gave him an advantage to escape from the eyes, which could inform about him getting out of his house. He locked every door and window of the house, took the bag which he had packed and left the house from the rear door for the nearby railway station, which was hardly a mile away. I don't know what was crueller; the time or the people. The station

Master taunted my father about leaving his shop for him when he reached there. My father remembered his dialogue, 'Lala ji, dukaan te de jao!' (Lala ji, leave us the shop at least!) and to this sarcastic tone, my father replied, 'Mera ghar bann chukya aa, mein aa jana baccheyan naal wapis' (My house has been constructed and I will be back with family soon). The Station Master smirked at my father and said, 'Hun kon aan dinda tuhanu?!' (Who would allow you to come back now?!). This fuelled the anger of my father, but he knew somewhere that the Station Master was right. He shook his head in disappointment and his curved down neck said the rest. He boarded the train and reached Kapurthala.

And here, our family had no clue about my father. My brothers used to go to the railway station every single day and would check every coach of the train coming from Multan to see if he had arrived, but he didn't; not yet. Days passed, and the hope of his return started to turn into distress and the news of violence only added stress to it; it seemed as if we might never see him again. However, our wait got over and he came back to us. I remember how the glow of joy came back into the dull eyes of my mother who would cry every night in stress which she felt while praying and worrying about him, when she saw him at the door. Our family got reunited finally.

A few days later, we moved to Jalandhar but the narration of the horror stories of partition had just begun. The house we moved in was supposedly owned by a Muslim family before us which migrated to Pakistan, leaving their house just like us but their journey was not as easy as ours. There were talks in the neighbourhood about the killings of their family members. It was told by the neighbours that some of the women of their family were murdered by the extremists in the very house. It was chilling to know that we were living in a house where people were murdered. For the next coming days, we waited for my paternal uncle's family to arrive from Multan. It took continuous ten to twelve days when we used to visit Jalandhar's railway station when finally, we saw them in one of the trains, it was one of the happiest moments to see them reaching safe and sound. Soon, the train started moving and headed to Delhi but their son; my cousin didn't leave with them; he decided to stay with us. After this, my father decided to move to Saharanpur.

My father had been a businessman all his life, back then, he owned a shop and now, he owned nothing, but he had us; his family which had supported it till now and it didn't fail to surprise him this time too. My mother was not educated yet her managerial expertise was not questionable. She had got an account opened back home in the name of my sister-in-law to deposit Rs. 5,000 at that time without telling my father. And it was a big amount back then. And when my father was thinking of the ways of starting some work here, he needed some capital which he didn't know how he was going to arrange. Then my mother told him about the same account and with some paperwork done, we got that money transferred here fortunately, as a branch of the same bank was here too. With that money, my father started a business of soaps which started to flourish slowly but life lived in Saharanpur was short.

It was around two to three years of living a good life in Saharanpur. My father's business was getting profitable at a linear pace but it was good enough for us. We siblings were back to living our normal life and my mother was happy too, seeing her family prospering in front of her. My brothers were helping my father in expanding his business but one of them had joined the Jan Sangh, a political party. Its members including him went on a hunger strike to oppose a government decision and pressure the government into taking back the decision or changing it. Soon many of the party workers got arrested with him but the hunger strike went on for days which turned into weeks. His failing health couldn't weaken his will but did of my father's who could not see him in such conditions any longer. So, on the eighteenth day of his hunger strike and arrest, my father got my brother released somehow and we left Saharanpur overnight. Leaving Saharanpur was important for my brother to recover and not getting back to his older ways. To make him stay away from politics and also the expected threats which my father saw coming in his ways, our family shifted to Karnal where my brothers had already set up our business which soon became much successful and we were able to make our name to the top of the list. In 1955, I got married and since then I have been living here only.

The country has celebrated more than seventy Independence Days till now but what we really need independence from is the hatred which we have carried in our hearts over all these years! We must remember that before being a Hindu or Muslim, Hindustani or Pakistani, we are humans first and humanity teaches acceptance and respect for differences. Bloodshed, wars, and hate have never benefitted anyone but those who wish to fulfil their selfish motives only, and that has nothing to do with goodness.

10

Tangled Kites

FEROZE GUL
DEHRADUN - RAWALPINDI

THE SPEAKING WINDOW

Dehradun, the first thing that strikes the mind after hearing 'Dehradun' is the amazing beauty of this place that is truly bewitching. Sitting at the feet of the Majestic Himalayas, the history of its existence dates back to hundreds of years. Surrounded by beautiful hills and mountain views with tall trees and many lakes and falls, the charisma of the place is unparalleled. The city is my hometown where my childhood was spent. Beauty not only lied in the heart of the city but also in its beat, which was its own people. A mixed population of Hindus and Muslims resided there with the same comfort as that of the place itself, which had a blend of various colours in it, the colours presented together would present a captivating picture of sheer beauty.

My family was one of the residents of Dehradun, however, we were not one of the houses which belonged to the city originally. Since my father was serving as an Architect in the Survey Commission of British India, he was posted in Dehradun during that time. He had designed the building

The Speaking Window. Sandeep Dutt, Faisal Hayat, and Ritika, Oxford University Press.
© Oxford University Press India 2023. DOI: 10.1093/oso/9789391050733.003.0010

of Survey Commission's headquarter in Murree when he was posted there before coming to Dehra, which is now the head office of Survey Commission of Pakistan. He was paid well with an income of Rs. 235 per month. My grandfather, who was a doctor, owned various properties there. My father was very liberal with his thoughts. He had many Hindu friends, some very close ones too including many renowned personalities like D.L. Saigal and his brother K.L. Saigal (the first superstar of Hindi Cinema; a famous singer). My father would often go hunting with him. Except this love for poaching and his work, there was one more thing he always valued and cherished; his family.

Our family was a small one; parents and their three children; including two daughters and a son. My eldest sister was born in Quetta in 1934 when my father was there. When she was eight months old, he got transferred to Meerut. The day they left Quetta, a massive earthquake stroked it, which took the lives of thousands of people in 1935. Five members of our family were just like five different fingers, with different personalities yet united as one. My parents loved us all. My mother was a homemaker and from dawn till dusk, she used to remain occupied with various household chores. My father had his own work but sometimes, he used to help my mother with her work too. They both would make time for us, for studying and playing with us. No compromises were made in respect to the discipline but any activity or mischiefs done by us which required scolding, there was also an expression of love and affection accompanying it.

I have memories of the school which I went to, while I was in Dehradun. The name of the school was AP Mission school where we didn't have the luxury to sit on benches and had to sit on the ground while getting our lessons. Our Urdu Teacher was a Hindu named Girdhari Lal whom we used to call 'Thakur ji'. When we were not able to form the alphabets correctly, he would hold our hands as we wrote and help us by directing our hands in the right direction. There was Kanwar Singh who was our English teacher and Hindi was taught by Sharma ji. Once something venomous bit me on my foot in the class and it got so serious that I had to be taken to a doctor who suggested to amputate my leg to save me, but my mother refused to get it operated on like this. Thus, my father asked his Hindu friend to help me out who was a Vaid (an Indian physician who works with a remedial solution to cure diseases) by profession. He helped us and saved not only me but also kept my leg intact. Like my father, I too had non-Muslim friends. My neighbour and class-fellow, Kuldeep Singh with whom I used to go to school and another class-fellow-cum-neighbour Bhola Ram who often visited my house and flew kites with me on our terrace. We didn't have any intuition about the prevailing situation and how the kites we flew were going to get tangled into each other while they were still high in the sky.

It was the month of Ramadan, 1947. People had started migrating before any official announcement. A group of Sikh migrants was coming from Kohat, Pakistan. My nineteen-year-old cousin who went out to meet his childhood friend crossed paths with these refugees near the Gurudwara who, in no time, turned into murderers and killed him and injured his friend. He survived due to the courage of the locals who could get there in time to save him. Only God knows what kind of situations they had gone through while coming here that made them so cruel. It was an act carried out in pure vengeance. I don't disagree with the fact that there was a chance, that those refugees would have lost their families at the hands of extremists but their reaction to it was neither going to bring back the dead nor would have made them heroes.

No doubt, this loss was huge to our family. As a result, the decision to leave India was taken. I was in class 5 when it was decided that we were migrating, but the whole conundrum was confusing to me as to why were we supposed to go and why were people killing people? Why all of a sudden, the surnames held such importance that they were used to decide who would stay and who would not? Who would live and who would not? It was 4 pm when we reached the railway station. My father who was fond of keeping chickens took them along but the railway authorities didn't allow him to take them with him. Our whole compartment, which was already booked by my father, was accommodating only our family now. I can still recall my mother doing Aftari on the train which stopped nowhere before arriving at Rawalpindi and we decided to get settled there.

The house where we started living was near Bani and a sacred place called 'Mai Veero di Banni' where Hindus would take bath in its holy water.

One day, my father came home and told my mother that his friend Puran Singh had decided to migrate to India, but he was worried for the safety of his young daughter as the circumstances were not safe back then.

My father wanted to help him out for they had been friends for so long. And given the gravity of the situation, his concerns were legitimate. Therefore, he promised him to take care of his daughter so she would remain safe with my family. So, it was decided that when things would get back to normal, he would return for her. My father informed my mother about the possibility of her stay with us until everything fell back in place.

I could see the lines of worry appear on her forehead, but she could understand why he was doing it and what could happen to the young girl if she were to go through the process of migration so she agreed to the proposition without much dissent.

We were all excited to welcome another sister to our family. Some new purchases were made especially for her, like some clothes and utilities were brought for her by my parents. On the other side, we kids were planning about the different games we could play together and how much fun it was going to have her play with us.

Fortunately, my father ran into an old friend from the police department and told him about the whole scenario and the severe concerns he had about the safe departure of Puran Singh. His friend promised the safety of Puran Singh and that of his daughter too. This led to a change of plan we had initially come up with and thus, we never had a chance to know her as she went with her father. Anyway, we were glad to know that she was going to have a safe journey finally. That was the moment when I felt for the first time how much of a rift had come between the Hindu and Muslim communities.

However, there were exceptions too, like my sister who used to exchange letters in Hindi with her old friend Lajjawati after the partition. Every word was being read by the authorities in those days. Secrecy was non-existent back, whether it was in relation to personal matters of the people or anything else. Anyway, these two friends never bothered about it. Their letters kept on crossing the borders every now and then. When Lajjawati's daughter's marriage got fixed, she invited my sister to attend the wedding ceremony, which was taking place in Jalandhar. My sister felt honoured on being invited and she got a little emotional too. Thus, she decided to attend the wedding.

She took her daughter, son, and a friend with her. The year was 1979. She wrote back to her informing about her arrival and the expected date on which she was supposed to reach the Amritsar station. Something disappointing happened. As she prepared to leave for Jalandhar, she got late for the marriage because of her documentation issue. Because she got late and couldn't be there on the said date, Lajjawati kept on searching for her at the station and upon not finding her there, unpleasant thoughts started crossing her mind, which did no good but add to her worries. Lajjawati's son told my sister that she was so worried about my sister's safety that she could not sleep the whole night.

My sister reached two days after the scheduled visit and when she did, she made a call to her best friend from the station and informed her about her safe arrival. Lajjawati reached there as soon as she could. My sister recognized and called Lajjawati who was already looking for her. She heard her name loud and clear and as she turned, she saw that it was my sister who was screaming her name at the top of her voice, so she came running down the stairs for her. They both saw each other, Lajjawati hugged my sister and tears started flowing out of their eyes. Their emotions were understandable as they were seeing each other after a really long time.

Well, she missed the wedding because of her delayed visa process. So, Lajjawati contacted the groom's brother Brijpal Singh who was a renowned Landlord of Garhwal and informed him about her friend's safe arrival in Amritsar. Thus, a lavish dinner party was arranged at a huge hotel called Inderlok for my sister and other relatives. While talking, he told them about his passion for hunting and my sister mentioned mine for the same. So, an invite was sent to me to join him for a thrill there. However, I could not go due to some reasons.

My education remained continued here too. I studied till Matric in Mission & Muslim School, Rawalpindi and served in the food department and got retired in 1995. I got married in 1980 and have four sons and three daughters.

If I conclude the experiences earned in life, I can say that, time was much better in the past, people were sincere, and relations had more value than money. I do recall the memories of India, from the magnetism of Dehradun to the school I went to and the teachers who taught me.

And of course, how can I forget my friends! I am too old to travel now but if I could go, I would try once.

11

Prisoner of Alibeg

BAL KRISHAN GUPTA
MIRPUR - ATLANTA

THE SPEAKING WINDOW

The blood dripping from head, skin starting to peel off from the wrists of hands tied in ropes, the bent lifeless neck, face scarred with injuries, dried lips requesting for water, with the visible red marks left by the whip, and feet with cuts and torn skin, having no ounce of energy to balance were lying in a way as if they would never walk again. The windows of that room were open, to let the chilling Himalayan winds cut through the wounds. He wasn't the only one with such pitiful condition but there were hundreds of youngsters and men bearing the same or even worse torture in the prison of Alibeg. Death seemed merciful but the men had forgotten everything about mercy.

Every night I used to think it to be the last one. I would pray for death to come and put an end to my miseries, but the lines of my hands had a long life written in them. I was destined to witness something more. Even the tears in my eyes had dried after crying for so long, but every time I closed my eyes, the only thing I would see was Mirpur; my beautiful

The Speaking Window. Sandeep Dutt, Faisal Hayat, and Ritika, Oxford University Press.
© Oxford University Press India 2023. DOI: 10.1093/oso/9789391050733.003.0011

home and my blissful life there. The cool mountain breeze and beautiful snow-capped peaks presenting the most mesmerizing Sunsets and Sunrises in the world. The calm stillness in the surroundings was there in the people too. And under the reign of our Maharaja Hari Singh, its people were living happily. My maternal family was wealthier than my paternal family. My maternal grandfather was a Tax Collector of the Maharaja and owned a double-storey house with a big compound at the back where the delicious Tandoori Chapatis were cooked in the Tandoor placed there. We had a big family of fifteen people including my maternal and paternal families, which included my grandparents, siblings, cousins, uncles, and aunts. Mirpur had a high school and a college for boys while only a middle school for girls. I completed my education till grade 5; up to grade 4, I stayed in my paternal house and I started pursuing the next grade while staying in my maternal grandparents' house as my school was closer to their home. The chimes of bells with the Aarti of the Hindu Arya Samaj Temple, occasional countryside trips, the hustle and bustle of fairs of Eid, the Ram-Leela at Dussehra, the tableaus and processions at Krishna Janmashtami, and the celebrations of Gurupurab, were leisure enjoyed by the people of Mirpur.

But all this seemed to be a beautiful dream when the eyes opened to the reality of Alibeg prison. All that could be seen through the prison bars were smelly ragged blankets with the stinking smell of blood and flesh everywhere, walls filled with screams and cries of the 'prisoners' who were then imprisoned in the name of God and were being punished for not being one of them. Around fifteen to twenty young Hindu/Sikh men were being killed every single day in front of us. Some were waiting for their turn to come and some were still praying for help from heavens. Old folks and children were spared by some from their swords or gunshots and so were the women; only to face the worst of situations!

I still get goosebumps just by thinking about that part of my life where witnessing death was an everyday scenario, and due to my helplessness, I couldn't change it then; neither for me nor for anyone else. Who could have ever thought of a Hindu-majority city being invaded in such a brutal way as if the Angel of Death has led rage all by himself? Princely state Jammu and Kashmir was still in a dilemma about taking a decision on what was best for them. The schools and colleges were running like normal days, people were going to work like usual, and things were as smooth as they were before.

In October 1947, Tribal Pathans backed by the Pak Armed Forces attacked Jammu and Kashmir state so the cordial relations among Hindus, Muslims, and Sikhs took a nosedive and suffocated soon. Till 25 November 1947, the city remained surrounded by the Pathans and was turned into a fortress. Nothing could go in or go out. Firing could be heard round the clock. As starvation struck in, understanding perished. The destitute Hindu Refugees from Gujrat and Jhelum sought shelter in Arya Samaj buildings to live off the depleted food items, offered to them in charity. My family too was starving and fearing for its safety. On 25 November 1947, the Pakistani forces along with the Pathans took a victory lap and we all were defeated. There were around 25,000 Hindus and Sikhs in the city then but as soon as the battle was won, approximately 2,500 were killed in the infernos because of the Pak artillery fire. Another 2,500 escaped with the Jammu and Kashmir Army, which was retreating after defeat. Due to shelling and cross-firing, a major part of the city was burning in flames thus causing a major migration in the middle of the night. Houses were burning, streets were engulfed in smoke, and there was blood everywhere; it was all very horrific. The house of my paternal grandparents was burnt to the ground. My grandparents and a paternal Uncle were turned into ashes. The disabled took shelter in an old judicial building and my mother who could not walk was left among those 1,000 people in that Court House. I was a ten-year-old boy who was forced to leave his mother in an unknown environment which was filled with anxiety and all kinds of terrifying thoughts. She hugged me, kissed me, and we left her. With a really heavy heart and teary eyes, I bade her goodbye, wishing in my heart to see her soon and praying to God, for keeping her safe.

Our caravan was very large for the count of refugees was in thousands. Many hopeless people who had left their homes and loved ones were making their way to Jammu. But unfortunately, the massacre had just begun. The Pakistani Armed forces and Pathans attacked us on our way and many people lost their lives in the firing that took place in the dark. By the dawn, 20,000 people were captivated by them. All Hindu and Sikh prisoners were made to march towards Alibeg prison. Out of 20,000 prisoners, half of them were killed on the way and over 5,000 young girls and women were abducted including my two maternal aunts and some distant cousins. Only around 5,000 people could make it to the Alibeg prison alive just to be tortured like animals for an unknown period. I saw Hindu and Sikh men being hued with swords or getting shot to death; some of them were my uncles ... On seeing what was ahead, a large number of women consumed poison to commit mass suicide as they could not bear a sight of a man disgracing their bodies like they saw being done to others before. It took us three long days to reach there, which to us were three days of hell but the real hell awaited us.

Alibeg prison was a broken-old building with a large tomb-like structure in the centre and some small ones along on its sides. It was winter and there was a deadly chill in the winds, which made the look of that place scarier. On its main entrance, there was some space that looked like a foot cleaning pool and we realized that the Alibeg prison was actually a Gurudwara Sahib, which was distorted during the invasion and then used as a prison. A Sikh holy shrine was converted into a slaughterhouse. We were kept in rooms that were used as prison cells and were given 0.5 oz of wheat flour per person. By the end of December, about 2,000 people had lost their lives at the hands of the prison guards, more than 1,000 were sick including children and elderly who were dying of poor health conditions caused by malnutrition and food poisoning. Men were randomly killed, and women kept on going missing. No Sikhs were left alive. I had to watch my two out of four cousins dying due to starvation after their mother and my aunt was kidnapped. There seemed no end to these atrocities but it seemed as if the end of our lives was just around the corner.

January 1948, the International Committee of the Red Cross (ICRC) arrived at Alibeg prison to spoil the celebrations of its hunting party. It firstly stopped the killings and then started the rescue mission to get the people out of there. By April 1948, the said 'prisoners' from this deadly prison were taken to the refugee camp set up in Kurukshetra via train through Wagah border. Out of 20,000 prisoners, only 1,600 refugees including children, widows, and old survived, which later on became known as the 1,600 survivors of Mirpur Massacre in the government documents. My brother and I were two of them. My father died when I was 3 and I used to miss him a lot. But after seeing all this, I am glad he was not there; imagining him dying in front of me like the other people would have been much more painful.

My uncle who survived took us to Jammu. After almost four years, in 1954, we were informed that the Red Cross had found my mother and she was reunited with us without any further delay. I can never describe the feeling of feeling her arms around me once again, after years of separation. I was happy to see her alive and with us but found it hard to believe it. It was no less than a miracle. At least my brother and I were not orphans; we had our mother who promised us not to leave us ever again. I resumed my education and started my schooling again. I went to college later and went to study at Ranchi's Engineering College. I got married in Jammu in 1967 and immigrated to the United States in 1971. I got an MS in 1975 from New York University and worked as a design engineer and senior mechanical engineer from 1971 to 2006 in the United States. I got retired in 2006 and have been living in Atlanta, Georgia with my wife ever since. My daughter went to Harvard University and my son to Stanford University Medical College, and both are now settled in the United States itself. I always wanted to tell the truth about what exactly happened in 1947 in Mirpur, so I thought of penning down my whole experience. It wasn't easy certainly, re-living those memories again … but I was determined to do it so as to get myself out of them. In 2012, I got my book published in the United States about my imprisonment in Alibeg by the name 'Forgotten Atrocities: Memoirs of a survivor of the 1947 partition of India', which was translated into Hindi in India and Urdu in London. In 2006, one of my maternal uncles, who was eighty years of age at that time, visited Mirpur again. And what he told us is heartbreaking. He said that the whole area has now been submerged into the seventh largest dam in the world, Mangal Dam. And a new Mirpur with new infrastructure and new people has been established, which is now the capital of *that side of Kashmir*. I have seen deaths, been through atrocities, and have seen people killing one another, yet here I stand to say that the youth of both countries must forget the sufferings of their forefathers and stop sowing hatred for the generations to come. If their forefathers who lived in their own time were here, they would never be able to recognize the place they ever called 'home' nor they would have ever wanted the love they lived in, to perish like this. Both countries are neighbours and good neighbours take care of each other. This is what their culture and religion teach them.

12

Love Migrants

JANNAT BIBI
HEEND - SARGODHA

THE SPEAKING WINDOW

It was THE BIG DAY of my life. My joy knew no limits as life was about to unfold a new chapter. I was dressed in my best to look as beautiful as I could. The exuberance and euphoria in the ambience increased by many folds with the auspicious presence of all those who came together to shower their blessings on me; regardless of their different customs and traditions related to 'Nikah' (wedding ceremony in Muslims) and not only this, they helped my family financially in making the necessary arrangements of marriage.

I was taken to the special seating meant for the bride, which had a flower curtain hanging before it. I remember, my hands, soaked in the aroma of mehandi (design made on hands consisting of a paste of the leaves of Henna plant), the Quranic verses being read to seek the blessings of the Almighty, the marriage vows being taken and the customary words, 'Qubool hai' (I do!) being said. That was the happiest day of my

The Speaking Window. Sandeep Dutt, Faisal Hayat, and Ritika, Oxford University Press.
© Oxford University Press India 2023. DOI: 10.1093/oso/9789391050733.003.0012

life. I was very young, innocent, and ready to enter into a new phase of my life.

'Heend' in Uttar Pradesh was not much developed at the time but yes, it was a beautiful place with a diversified set of religions. While there were different religions, Hinduism had the highest number of followers. The bond among people was strong, and we shared meals with each other except beef, which Hindus did not consume. Majority of people were into agriculture for the sake of earning their livelihood and so was the case with my family. Apart from agriculture, we were also involved in cattle farming. My father was a respected figure among people. He was a happy man who had three sons and two daughters. Like any other father, he also had dreams and aspirations for his children. We owned ten to twelve acres of land too. In that place, everybody knew everybody and all of us were aware of each other's struggles, so everyone tried to make things easier for each other. This made those times and place special. My childhood was beautiful and so was my teenage. I was in my teenage when my marriage got fixed with a man who was the only Muslim to own a shop in the town.

For many years that came after my marriage, I was happily married, had a caring husband, and was content with my life. His general store was doing good business. Everything was perfect till the violence consumed all the peace we had. In the year 1947, many people lost their lives at the hands of extremists who targeted everyone who ill-fatedly fell in their way. It was the Nambardar of our village whom we called 'Mukhiya' who brought us the news of the partition. It hit us like a thunderbolt. The news was received with disbelief and almost everyone questioned its authenticity of it. No one wanted to migrate, so we stayed like everyone else. But soon we realized how real the partition was, when our village was invaded by the extremists. These attacks created dismay and perturbation among people and most of the families made up their minds to migrate for the sake of their children's future which then, seemed quite uncertain. My in-laws' family was also in the favour of migration but my parents were not. On one side, my husband was expecting me to back him with his decision. On the other side, my father was also concerned about me and wanted me to stay. It was a tug-of-war and I felt like I was at the centre of it, being stretched from both ends. Both were important to me, but none was listening. The stress got higher when I was at my father's home and he did not allow my husband to take me with him. Eventually, he left me at my father's house and went with his family. Meanwhile, my younger brother who was working in the fields one day, got attacked by the extremists. No mercy was shown to him and he was butchered in broad daylight. This incident hit my family like a thunderbolt. Yet, my father stood by his decision and did not migrate. On the other side, my husband's family and other relatives from the in-laws' family had already migrated.

I was married, with a two-year-old son in my arms at my father's home; house-arrested. My husband was with his family there, trying to settle down the things which were turned upside down while figuring out a way to reach me. There were two nations in between us. The differences just grew bigger. I was missing him, but I could not do anything. Nonetheless, he did. He did not forget me and came back, searching for me everywhere, in the refugee camps and every other possible place he could think of. He thought my father might have changed his mind after the death of his own son. And then he came to the same place where he had left me and found me there. For a moment, I thought I was dreaming but it was real. He had come back for me.

He had already seen the conditions of the newly shaped nation. He knew it was not going to be a bed full of roses there but here we had our own house, our own lands, own lives, and then, he had me. He also knew my father was not moving from his decision by any means so he stayed; he stayed for me, for his son, and for his family. For the next ten years, we remained in India. We had everything that we needed but there was a problem. If my father was happy, my in-laws were not. And, how could they? Their son was not with them and it was not just a different city that he was staying in, it was a different country, all together. In the beginning, the Pakistani Authorities used to issue permits to keep a track of the people coming in and out of the country. The visa procedure was introduced much later. So, my husband used to visit his family whenever he could. From our side of the family, only my brother who was serving in the military, migrated to Karachi, Pakistan. Time started its healing process and things got better over the years, but many things had changed. The brotherhood and harmony among different communities were not the same anymore. The brutality shown in riots left that bond scarred which never faded away.

After a decade, my husband felt the urge to reunite with his family. He wished to migrate. But even after all these years, my family's response to his decision was not any different. Again, my father was not being much supportive towards me getting migrated. Years ago, when I requested him, he stayed with me, and now it was my turn to stay with him. So, we decided to leave without telling anybody. We knew we could not take anything with us, it would only raise the eye-brow of doubt at us. Therefore, when we left, we took nothing but food with us. We had a bullock cart, a shop, and agricultural lands but we didn't sell anything; we just left. We took an off-road route to escape the eyes of the known and unknown. We started the journey to Agra and spent two days travelling before we reached there. Then we went to Delhi from where we boarded a train to Lahore and went to Piplan from there and finally, we reached home, Sargodha, Pakistan.

My husband's family was already here and so were his relatives. They all welcomed us wholeheartedly. We were not allotted any land here, so my husband had to make things work on his own, but we didn't lose hope. He started working as a labourer. And with time, our situations got better as we had each other to depend upon. My husband passed away in 2001. He gave me a good life. I have eight grandchildren and have seen my next four generations! I am happy with my life.

At this point, if I look back, I can see things which we had struggled for and now we are in a better position. We only had a cot with us when we came to Pakistan but now, we have good food to eat, a house for shelter, and a family to live for. I keep on telling my grandchildren about my life earlier so that they remember how many hardships we went through to have what we have now. I have not seen my own relatives since I have come here. Only the relatives of my daughter-in-law visit India often and they tell me that my family is doing fine there but I miss them. I wish to visit there again once more to visit the grave of my parents and see my siblings. I want to feel the same cool breeze, the shades of those trees, and the home, where I spent my childhood. I wish I could relive all that again and if I could, I would.

13

Home Nankana Sahib

HARNAM SINGH
NANKANA SAHIB - AMRITSAR

THE SPEAKING WINDOW

'If you get to know anything about my brother Shahid, do write back. I'll be waiting.'

Words may not do justice to the expression of grief in it, but they do reflect it … at least a part of it. So many people lost track of their family members, friends, relatives, and many loved ones who they wouldn't recognize anymore if they had to. So many letters were written to those who could possibly know or help find them in the hope that they could see them once again, could hold them once again. The partition of 1947, which saw genocide at its peak with countless abductions and suffered unmeasurable loss during the biggest population swap in the history of migration, crushed thousands of spirits. It finally put an end to prolonged wait for the people who were either expected to be dead or went missing. Such was the massacre that general population became so accustomed to seeing the dead that they felt fortunate upon getting dead bodies of their relatives to give them a proper funeral. The others felt devastated upon

The Speaking Window. Sandeep Dutt, Faisal Hayat, and Ritika, Oxford University Press.
© Oxford University Press India 2023. DOI: 10.1093/oso/9789391050733.003.0013

seeing scattered limbs of their family members and friends, while the most unfortunate ones didn't even know whether to mourn or wait for the missing. One such family was of Shahid whose brother wrote a similar letter to my family after the partition, hoping for us to help find him.

Shahid was a Muslim and his family was one among the only three to four families of village Chak 3/53 which were involved in the occupation of blacksmithing. His brother mentioned in the letter that he was certain of him going to Master Kartar, a Sikh and teacher of Shahid, who migrated to India after the partition. Shahid did not want to leave his Master for he had taught him practically everything. Well acquainted with his brother's defiance who feared for his well-being because the circumstances were already unforgiving during those times. So naturally, he requested for our help to find him and we decided to revert positively to his request. After many exhausting efforts, at last, we found him in Talwan town near Jalandhar. Upon finding him, we requested him to go back to his family which was worried sick for him but to our surprise, he denied it. He wanted to remain there with his Master but this could have landed him in a big trouble so by hook or crook, we took him to Noor Mahal station and then to the border village called Hoshiar Nagar where a person from our native village was already residing. From there, a letter was sent to his brother ensuring his safety with details of our whereabouts. His brother reached Hoshiar Nagar a few days later and took Shahid with him. Till the very end, he was requesting us to let him stay but was there really a choice we could make under such circumstances?

I served in the post offices of Punjab for all my life. I would see people exchanging light and dark moments of their lives through letters or telegrams. This continued even after the partition when letters were seen addressed across the border, but these acts of love vanished sooner than I had anticipated due to the inconvenience we had to deal with because of the authorities which kept a close eye on every single word shared across the border. Letters were not the only things that were shared among people, they shared affection too, especially in my village Chak 3/53, Tehsil Nankana Sahib. Though a small place yet, it had everything to offer, from fresh food to rejuvenating breeze, favourable agricultural conditions, beautiful canals, and not to forget the peaceful surroundings where pieces were done to share; not to be a dessert on the platter served for a conflict.

It was a Sikh-majority region with only two Hindu families and three to four Muslim families, and almost the same handful of Blacksmiths' families; it was a place worth living a life in. Our village had a school but we didn't study there beyond fourth grade due to unavailability of classes succeeding it, so after this last grade, children were sent to a middle school in the nearby town, Bucheki. It was situated at a distance of 5 kilometres and we used to cover the distance on foot. But, it was all worth it considering the kind of education and quality of teachers the school had to offer. There, slate and chalks were replaced with notebooks and pens. I still remember one of my teachers who taught us agriculture. His name was Milkha Singh. I studied Urdu and English, and completed my eighth standard in the year 1947.

One of the best things about olden times, which is a rare phenomenon nowadays, was the joint family system where the children were homeschooled for morality, patience, acceptance, and empathy. May be that was one of the reasons why relationships were so valued during those times, while blood seems to be 'thinner' than water now. I was raised in one of such large families. My parents had three sons and five daughters, whom they had brought up with a lot of care and love till a tragedy hit our family like a lightning bolt. I was in fifth standard when my father died. I don't remember how many days or months it took for us to accept it and then to move on and make a habit of living with it. A home where my father used to come after his day's work in the fields was left with an emptiness created by his absence. Nothing of him was left. No more hugs, no more scolding, no more advices, no more waiting for him to get home and bring us something and no more of him. When someone dies, there's just an absence. Everything that you never cared to notice before reminds you of that person whom you couldn't even say sorry to before he left or how much you loved him. The new things or people make their place in our lives, distract us from the emptiness that hollows our hearts but even they can never fill it. The worst part of it was seeing my mother, who had to keep a strong face in front of us for our sake, for the sake of staying strong for herself but even she, in her time alone, shed countless tears and went to sleep while still sobbing.

I have really good memories of him. I remember him taking us to monthly fairs organized on every New Moon day and the yearly fair, which held on the birthday of Guru Nanak Dev Ji, the first Guru of Sikhs.

We never missed this fair. He often took us to Nankana Sahib Gurudwara where we would bow down to pay our obeisance towards the Shri Guru Granth Sahib and listened to the soothing Satsang. We would, then, go to savour the delicious langar before exploring the fair. He used to buy us toys and sweets. Also, he would take us to various rides and when anyone of us got tired, we would sit on his shoulders, from where the best view of the fair could be relished. I can also recall one time, my sister complained about me annoying her. Hearing this, he got so furious that I got a bashing from his hands! Despite this, he was not an inconsiderate parent. He might have expressed his love lesser than others but he was the one who cared enough to, later, inquire about my well-being from my mother. And, he was the same father who used to take me for the long walks in the fields, played with me, and took care of me.

Our family-owned some cattle and had a hundred acres of land on which my paternal uncles and my father used to work hard to grow various crops. Since our area was relatively on the higher side of production in terms of rice crop, we used to grow that more and used to sell it in the grain markets of Nankana Sahib, Jaranwala, and Bucheki, as well. Our house was quite spacious despite the large family which is accommodated. We were well-off and happy with what we had. My childhood has been the greatest time period of my life. Childhood has its perks; no responsibilities, no worries, no liabilities, and absolutely no tension about the future. The best part of our childhood was that the whole day was spent thinking about the different games we could play or in planning mischiefs. I used to go with my friends and siblings to the canal and sometimes to the bank of the river Chenab to swim. And when the night dawned upon us, we used to play hide and seek in the haystacks. The one seeking us would get fed up at the end, would simply return home and go to sleep while the hiders would wait long enough to be found but would return to their homes eventually when they would realize no one was coming to look for them. This was the story of every single day, but no one would stop playing. Haha! Those were the days!

As the year 1947 started, everybody knew that the sun of great British Empire was soon going to set in India, but nobody knew that it would leave us with a darkness of hatred for the generations to come. From the month of March/April, situations got so tensed that at night, the village was strictly kept under watch to avoid any unwelcoming situation. It kept going on till August when the military marched to a neighbouring village with Muslim majority and asked the non-Muslim population to gather in a single place. Non-Muslims from nearby villages were also instructed to accompany them. A few people from our village, including my brother, went there to find out what exactly was going on. The officials told them that a plan for carrying out a vicious attack on these villages was being chalked out, the kind of attack which would be uglier than any we had heard or seen before. They had come to inform us about the same and also to advise us about leaving the village. The people of our village came back with that threatening news and an emergency meeting was called. After due deliberation, the decision of migrating to India from Pakistan was taken. Our entire village was deserted overnight, with only Muslim families left behind who also helped us in our safe departure. However, for some reason, one of the daughters of a Hindu family could not leave with us at that time but no trace of her could be found later. God knows what had happened to her!

The night we left was a tough one. It was raining heavily. The short window of time to make our departure and the fear of something bad looming upon us, forced people to leave several of their belongings there only. The general consensus was that the migration was temporary in nature and we would be back after a few days as the partition and the severity of the decision of migration were not considered at that time. The road ahead was long, dangerous, and we were all scared to death. On the way, a lady was bitten by a snake and died on the spot. Her body was thrown into a canal as there was no time for preparing for a cremation; so many lives were at stake and any delay could have put everyone in grave danger. Though it was a tough call yet it had to be made.

The first place after crossing our village was a village with a majority of Sikhs living in it. When the people there got acquainted with our reason for leaving our village, they turned us into a source of laughing stock and simply turned a blind eye towards the danger which was on its way to annihilate everything. It was a confirmation received through a radio broadcast that led them to believe us and they too, decided to migrate by joining our caravan. We spent the night there till those villagers packed whatever they could think of taking with them, and prepared their ox-carts. No one from our village had any ox-cart with them and carried on the further journey on foot. The very next morning, we set our course to Ludianwala where we spent another night. Helplessness spreads like cancer and makes a person desperate to get rid of it so much so that the difference between right and wrong matters no more. My sister was hungry and was asking for food constantly. I saw people in that village preparing food while packing their things so I went to them to ask for a loaf of bread for my sister. But they refused and disrespected me a lot. In a rage, I stole five to six pieces of bread and ran from there. I went straight to my sister and fed her with it. I don't know how people become so difficult to deal with in difficult times, especially when they are going through the same pain as you. No one has any right to mock at the misery of others; time takes unpredictable turns. If I am being tested today, tomorrow it can be you. And we should remember, if we can't make things easier for others, we have no right to make it worse either.

The following day, we resumed our journey to reach Lahore, but the story was about to take a sharp turn. During our journey, we were attacked twice that too in just one day! We were able to escape the first deadly attempt but the second time, it was fiercer. And this one, not only made us stumble but fall too. Eight people from our caravan died in it before the army showed up to scatter the extremists and save the rest of us all. We were taken to Lahore in military protection and further, no attack happened and finally, we reached Lahore where we spent a night. We found some Taro root there which we all cooked and ate. Now the journey to India began where three soldiers joined us to ensure the prevention from any further attacks and that we would be able to cross the border safely. After a strenuous journey for seven days, we reached Khalra at last!

We had a few relatives in Ibban Kalan so from Khalra, we decided to go to Ibban. This side or that side, the story was no different; neither in the terms of cruelty nor inhumanity. On reaching there, we got to know that the people of Ibban had looted the migrants who were coming from Tarn Taran but they shared the loot with us. Now, I am not sure, what to call it! On one side, people were being selfish and vicious to others and on the other side, the same people were helping people of their own community. And the basis for their balance of justice was easy for them to figure out; religion. If their own, then a friend; if not theirs, then a foe. But weren't they the same? Or, their humanity towards us made them seem different? From Ibban Kalan, we moved to Nizampur where we stayed for the next fifteen to twenty days before we finally settled down in Malowal. The authorities did allot us some land just like other migrants but apparently, it was not sufficient for us. There we had a hundred acres of land and here, we got only 1/5th of what we had before. And it was not easy to claim it! It took a long struggle to get twenty acres of land in our name.

The initial days were very tough for my family as a whole, and individually for me as well. I wished to pursue my studies further for which no one was being supportive. So, I ran from home with a threat of not coming back ever. In those days, my elder brother, who started working as a bus conductor, saw me at the bus stand. He came to me and I narrated the whole story. He convinced me, reminded me of my responsibilities and made me realize how childish it was to run away like this, and then took me back home. He also talked to the family and finally, I was admitted to a school in Tarsikka, from where I did my Matriculation. Soon, I started working at a railway workshop in Jalandhar but in a few years, the government closed it and I had to move to Firozpur where I worked as a Signal Man for the railways. Then, one day I got to know about the vacancy available for the position of Patwari (a government official who keeps records regarding the ownership of land) and I decided to apply for it. I appeared for the exams. I remember how I bought a sheet for writing my exam with my hands full of dirt due to work. And when the result was out, my name was not on the list. I was infuriated. I went to the officer who had a hard time believing my story and he simply asked me, 'Why should I care?' I told him it was impossible for me to fail the exam as I was certain that I had gotten at least 90 out of 100. He was a little surprised at my claims and then smiled. He ordered to bring all the exam sheets and to his surprise, mine was unchecked. My sheet was bigger in size because I had bought it from outside, it was covered in some dust too as my hands were dirty when I wrote my paper. As a result, it was easy to recognize that sheet out of all which were surprisingly wrapped inside my sheet. Imagine, they used my sheet as a cover for their papers! Then, he got it checked at the spot and it turned out my claims were more than just castles in the air. I got the job and worked there for four years. Later, I was appointed as a rent collector. And after some time, I joined the post office of Firozpur and then of Ludhiana and at last, got shifted to Amritsar and got retired in 1995.

India and Pakistan are two nations now but my generation doesn't look at them that way. There was a time when travelling from Amritsar to Lahore, either via air or road, meant travelling between two cities but now Lahore is a city in another nation for which one has to go through a long tiring visa process which is difficult to attain, at times. Despite this, I had visited there eight times! My last visit was in 2015. And amazingly, each time, the people of my village were there to greet me on my arrival and to take me to my village. During my very first visit, when I crossed the threshold of my house where now a Muslim family lives, all the memories came rushing back to me. I could hear the laughter, the tears, every single moment that we spent there. 'Have you buried any gold in the house anywhere?'—a voice interrupted my thoughts and the tears of long-lost memories turned to the tears of laughter! It was one of the family members, curiously asking if we had left any gold in our house when we migrated. I laughed so hard! Oh! That was hilarious!

Eight times!? Why eight times? I am asked sometimes if all those trips were for business purposes. It becomes very hard for them to understand why these many times? The answer is pretty simple actually. How many times do you visit home, if you live somewhere else? As many times you miss it, I guess.

14
Death Is Peace

MUHAMMAD YAQUB
FIROZPUR - BHALWAL

THE SPEAKING WINDOW

108 is considered a very sacred number in many religions of the Indian sub-continent, especially Hindus. And interestingly, my village had 108 families living in total, which had a dominating number of Hindus while the second highest number was of Sikhs, a few that followed Islam. My village, known as Bhai ka Jumba fell under the district Firozpur, had a pacific ambience, with green grass and a saffron sky painted over it. There was no school in the village so the students had to walk for miles to study in a school which was in a nearby town. This was one of the reasons why people took the least interest in education. Besides, my father, being a labourer, could hardly earn much. With a little piece of land and a few cattle he owned, he was able to feed his small family that included my mother, my sister, and me.

Though, the village had less resources, yet it had something of more importance… peace of mind. There were disputes sometimes but nothing such serious that they could take the shape of rivalries. I was fifteen years

The Speaking Window. Sandeep Dutt, Faisal Hayat, and Ritika, Oxford University Press.
© Oxford University Press India 2023. DOI: 10.1093/oso/9789391050733.003.0014

old at the time of partition. There were talks about the clashes in the opinions of the big leaders, but no one expected them to become big enough to stretch a permanent line that would divide the country into two parts. Unlike other villages and cities, there was no official announcement made in our village. However, the news was brought about by two soldiers from the nearby camp.

Two armed soldiers who belonged to a nearby village, Chak Multani, left their camp and came to inform us about the partition. Nobody forced us to leave but they advised us to migrate and move with their tribe, which was at a canal situated close to us, to avoid any life-threatening situations. It was a time of distress and needed us to come up with a decision that was about to change everything. Without wasting any time, we decided to leave. We joined their tribe and decided to travel further via train. The closest railway station was in Bathinda, which was twelve miles away so we had to cover this distance on foot. The leader of that tribe had binoculars with him, which helped him see over long distances. He used to alert us from any upcoming danger but even he could not have foreseen what came next. Our journey to Bathinda was not a pleasant one. While on the way, we were attacked by the extremists who abducted nineteen young girls.

The Nambardar of the area, who everyone referred to as 'Bhai Saab' out of respect, was a really nice person. So was the case with his wife, who was quite active politically and thus powerful, too. When they heard the news of the abduction and what transpired on the way, they decided to help us. His wife had a lot of support from people as well as from the administration. She somehow managed to exert pressure on the extremists who had to surrender all the girls later on. His husband provided wheat and Garbanzo seeds which were enough to feed sixty to seventy people. And, we made our way to the railway station of Bathinda. It was a big railway station and could facilitate seven trains at a time. From there, the trains travelled to Kasur, Khushab, Bhalwal, and Sargodha. We took one to Kasur. The station was flooded with people.

Our train was under the military protection with a handful of soldiers; six in front and six at the back, which provided us a sense of safety. I still remember the driver of the train was hesitant to start off the engine, before the soldiers got into an argument with him and he had to surrender. Bhai Saab and his wife came to see us off and stood there till the train left the station. There were mixed emotions felt by everyone, whether it was Bhai Saab, his wife, or us who boarded the train. We felt happy that the journey was safe and so were the girls whose fate could have been catastrophic. Simultaneously, there was a feeling of sorrow to see us leaving like this. At last, we reached Kasur safely, but the real journey had just begun. We had nothing at all; no money, no work, nothing. We had to fill our bellies at Langars and Darbars. We spent nights at a graveyard. In the beginning, we were not charged for travelling in the local transport as people there knew we were migrants and couldn't afford to pay for our travel charges. We went to many cities where we could find a place to settle down. We went to Okara, Khushab, and many other places. Being one of the refugees of the largest human migration of the world, we found a home in many places like; railway yards, refugee camps, mosques, Gurudwaras, deserted houses, and graveyards; after we were alienated from our own home in Firozpur. At last, we went to Lyallpur (now better known as Faisalabad) and settled there for we had a few relatives there.

My mother was expecting a child when we were in Lyallpur and our family welcomed my brother, followed by my sister, who opened their eyes in a new home with a new nationality, Pakistani. I tried getting some government jobs but when I saw there was no hope of getting one, I started working as a labourer and after some years, I got married. After a few years of my marriage, my parents passed away.

The Government of Pakistan allotted us a piece of land that we never received due to lack of knowledge, and was occupied by the higher officials who were, ironically, responsible for providing it to us. In Bathinda, we had twenty-one acres of land. The Government of India informed us several times about it because the authorities needed to take a decision on it. Unfortunately, we had lost the papers of that property in the process of migration, nor we had enough money to go back and do something about it, so we could not get anything out of it, either. In 1970, I got a house built in Chak 18 with my own savings. Now, I have two children and nine grandchildren.

I have witnessed brutality of partition on both sides. Some memories are still so fresh; they do not let me sleep at night. Extremists on both sides, slaughtered people in cold blood and dumped their bodies in wells. The wells which were supposed to have water became graves of the people with birds and rodents feeding on them.

Despite spending my whole life in poverty, I, personally, have no regrets about migrating here, or having hard feelings towards anyone or anything. Now, I am just counting my days which I feel, are numbered. I am just waiting for the Angel of Death to bring me serenity and hopefully in my afterlife, I will rest in peace.

15

Spinning Wheel

AMAR KAUR
LAHORE - HOSHIARPUR

THE SPEAKING WINDOW

In a typical Indian society, where girls were raised with a strenuous training of being a brilliant house-maid who worked for free all their life, remained available 24×7, were supposed to perfect the art of being a clapping monkey running on endless power batteries, taught in the classes of 'how to keep the husband happy' with an ultimate goal of achieving motherhood yet were considered a sack of liabilities there, my fate chose a different way out for me. As it is said, a right person met at the right time in one's life can really make a difference and a wrong one can create differences. To my luck and surprise, I met the former one. I was married but still independent, working, and happy. I am Amar Kaur and like my name, I have lived many things in eternal.

I was born in a village of Hoshiarpur, named Khanpur where I spent the first sixteen years of my life, got my education till class 5 while being nurtured in an environment full of harmony and peace with various communities who were residents there. Moreover, being the only sister of two

The Speaking Window. Sandeep Dutt, Faisal Hayat, and Ritika, Oxford University Press.
© Oxford University Press India 2023. DOI: 10.1093/oso/9789391050733.003.0015

brothers, I was highly adored. At the age of 16, a life-changing decision awaited me which flipped my world upside down … marriage! I got married to a small-scale businessman in Rawalpindi because my father had made a promise to the groom's father a long time ago. Despite this being an arranged marriage, my family was not so happy about it for we held a higher status in the society comparatively. But if you ask me, it was one of the important decisions in my life that, by God's grace, steered it on a beautiful track.

The family of my in-laws was living in Rawalpindi, but my husband was doing his cotton business in Icchra, Lahore so I also went there after my marriage, but we often visited Pindi. A right life partner can really make you a better person and my right man was in my life. He made my life more beautiful, not by showering gifts on me but with cooperation, respect, understanding, trust, and equality; all gift-wrapped in love and affection that he had for me. He gave me the opportunity to walk with him shoulder to shoulder in every walk of life and trusted my wisdom when it came to making important decisions. While he was busy in his day-to-day business of cotton, I used to twist the same cotton on the spindle of the spinning wheel to form a cotton yarn and then later turn the same yarn into carpets. There was cooperation; not compromise, respect; not dominance and love but not with the material, which is why it was a real relationship the kind a husband-wife should have. And I am thankful to God for not making my husband with the clay of male chauvinism but with every ounce of a humane trait.

To have a place where all are considered one and differences don't matter, where peace prevails, and empathy lies in all, is a distant dream now but back then, it was Lahore, standing tall with all its greatness. The strength of the Lahori Gate, the charm of the Anarkali Bazaar, the sense of silence and respect at the Samadhi of Maharaja Ranjit Singh, and the beauty of Shalimar Garden with its mesmerizing fragrances, Lahore had been charming and full of positive spirit. Out of these, Anarkali Bazaar was on my topmost, most oftenly visited places. And what made this city touch one's soul was its neighbourhood. The house opposite to ours was friendly and so was their next door but the house next to ours was a little more special as it was of Bashira, my best friend. We would chit-chat all day, sometimes through our windows while working and sometimes visiting each other. We would sing and chat while spinning, learn and teach

each other new embroidery designs, sew together, and visit the market together. We were stitching a new and beautiful design on the frame of our friendship. I had it both; love and friendship but sweet things last for a short span of time.

It was when my husband and I were planning to expand our business and get a bigger house built in Lahore itself so that we could bring my in-laws' family here and would live together with the blessings and love of our elders. But little that we knew then that we might have to leave our own place too. Though I had learned many techniques and designs of embroidery and sewing but the dreams we were weaving on the spinning wheel of life from the time of our marriage, never got fulfilled. After nine years of life lived in a heaven-like Lahore, suddenly the flames of hell started burning everything we ever knew. Six months before partition, the humans turned into demons and their souls fuelled in hatred burnt everything formed with love. Dusk became the harbinger of death which came untimely to most of the people. Despite all of this, we stayed there for almost six months and needless to say, it was not easy at all. If it weren't for our Muslim neighbours, we wouldn't have ever survived there for that long. We started sleeping on the terrace of our house and our neighbours gave us the sense of security in those fearful days. They were supportive and understanding enough to be caring towards us. People had started to migrate long before 15 August 1947 and we knew it too, yet my husband decided to stay. He used to say, 'How can anyone leave one's own house not just full of belongings; but also has countless memories in it of its dwellers!' He thought things had gone on a rough patch, but they would be back the way they were in some time but soon he realized that the whole selfish system of extremism was insensitive; there was no place for emotions or may it be emotional but certainly for itself only and its unforgiving nature would be fatal to his loved ones. I was twenty-five, young and a woman. That was enough for the vultures outside to feast on me just like they did on those abducted women whose only fault was their religion. Therefore, he decided to migrate, but it was for me only and not him.

It came to our knowledge that our Pindi family, along with other relatives, was migrating. Thus, my husband thought it to be a perfect and safe opportunity to cross border as they could protect me if it was required. Bullock carts and trucks carried us and our luggage. We walked for days to reach a nearby city, Amritsar. Fortunately, our caravan did not become a target of ill elements of the society. After reaching Amritsar, we took shelter in a refugee camp for a few days and then my father-in-law took us to Shergarh, Hoshiarpur where some of his relatives lived.

And like one complete rotation of a spinning wheel, I too dramatically landed at the place where my story began; Khanpur, which unfortunately had drastically changed. When I left Khanpur after my marriage, it was a place of tranquillity and civility but with my latest arrival, I found it in jeopardy only, circumscribed in fear and lost in blood. The differences which existed forever but never offended others' interest, now possessing them became a sin all of a sudden. Shlokas or Azaan either became a life-line or a ticket to hell. The same place where I grew up became so unrecognizable to me as if I had never known it. The Muslim families of our village were scared to death. Some had moved, some were moving, and some were still there but knew they had to go. Moreover, I found out that my family was protecting one of them. The family was drowned in grief. There was neither stopping their tears nor any end to their sufferings. It was so painful to see them like this. The whole night their daughters kept crying and sobbing in my arms and their tears were tearing my heart apart. And the very next morning, the family left our house taking only a hope to live, leaving everything else behind.

However, I was still in a long wait for my husband who had not arrived yet nor we had any clue about his wellbeing. And the frightening stories of Pindi and Lahore being a slaughterhouse were not bringing any comforting thoughts of him in my mind. After long days of wait, he finally made it to us, safe and sound. Unfortunately, many of our relatives either were butchered or went missing about whom we never got to know till now. Only God knows what had happened to them.

After migration, poverty struck us hard. I and my husband moved to Amritsar and started to work in a cotton mill there. We were working really hard to make both ends meet. Days of struggle changed into months and months into years. There were times when we used to recall the days of our flourishing business, which we were about to expand, the house which we were supposed to build for our family and the life which we had planned to live in the coming years; all of these things seem to bring sorrow only but they reminded us about our cooperation and co-ordination with each other too. We had faith that we could still achieve it as we were still together. In the early 1960s, my husband got an opportunity to go to Jordon in search of better employment opportunities and once again, Khanpur invited me to stay there. In 1991, he passed away with only one unfulfilled wish in his heart; to walk in the streets of Lahore once again which if it were in my control, I would have taken him there. Today, I live with my children. I have three daughters and two sons.

It took only one fateful line stretched along the lives of millions who despite sharing the same heritage, values, culture, and choices, aren't friends anymore. I was born and brought up with Muslims. Being a Sikh, I never felt my identity being in crisis nor found theirs dominating. As kids, the only difference we could count was the number of candies one had, or the maximum count of marbles one owned. May be that's why, our parents too who grew up in the same atmosphere maintained the same level of dignity in their adulthood and showed us how relationships are to be valued and relished.

Talking of values, which today only seem bookish, were actually imparted to children long ago. Honesty, Consciousness, Empathy, and Humanity; these were not mere words mentioned in the storybooks of children but were really there in people. I remember when my husband came here after migration, he could not bring many things with him as he was travelling all by himself so he came with the few things he could carry. The family living in front of our house, which migrated to Tarn Taran much later, decided to carry along our possessions with them while packing theirs. In fact, our Muslim neighbours helped them pack our things and escorted them to the border of India in order to make sure of their safe arrival. When they reached Tarn Taran, they sent us a letter and asked us to take our valuables which we, too, went to take back and expressed our gratitude towards them. In the time of robberies, riots, and murders, many people had forgotten their years of relationships, filled in so much of rage that all they were thinking was of harming others and those who didn't get involve in the butchery, were not in the favour of giving a helping hand. In such tough times, there were people like our neighbours who were trying to restore faith in goodness and humanity.

I find it really amusing how people on both sides wish for peace yet aren't even near to it till now. My granddaughter, Manpreet Kaur, is a filmmaker and has worked with people from both sides. She tells me stories of her meetings with Lahoriye, how people are good at heart there and want peace and the same story is with the people living this side. How can they wish for peace when it is a piece they are fighting for? And then they complain of returning empty-handed.

16

Lost Friendships

ABDUL RASHID
AMRITSAR - SHEIKHUPURA

THE SPEAKING WINDOW

My village was just ten miles away from the holy city of Amritsar, which had a magical tranquillity in it, where the winds whistled the enchanting stories of the courage and the sacrifices made and how a culture embraced people coming from different parts of society with open arms irrespective of their religion or societal standard. The Golden Temple is an epitome of the same message conveyed hundreds of years ago by its founder, the fifth Guru of Sikhs, Guru Arjan Dev ji who allowed a Muslim to lay the founding stone of the biggest Sikh shrine and the last Guru of the Sikhs, Guru Gobind Singh ji who named five lower-caste Hindus as Panj Pyare. The very thought of oneness was deeply rooted in the soil of my village that the major community of Sikhs treated the minority group of Muslims like a family.

The tales of brotherhood of Hindus, Sikhs, and Muslims were not a fluke, nor were they ghost tales which are told by the old folks just to make their successors believe in the goodness which never existed. There

The Speaking Window. Sandeep Dutt, Faisal Hayat, and Ritika, Oxford University Press.
© Oxford University Press India 2023. DOI: 10.1093/oso/9789391050733.003.0016

were only a handful of Islamic families, which were hardly five to seven in number, but were treated with equality, equity, and mutual respect. Not many people had been fortunate enough to grow up in such surroundings, which exemplified the bond between two communities so well and lived it every day, especially when one is a minor group. People find it hard to believe when I say there were no rivalries between the two but as I explained earlier that the village was blessed with the grace of the Almighty and more importantly, they imbibed the teachings of the Gurus in their lives, which is why humanity was valued more than anything else.

Our village had a school but because of the lack of awareness about the education and its importance, most families never used to send their wards to the school, including ours, which had four sons and a daughter. Yet our learning and teachings were carried out in a unique way by our elders, which included learning about ethics and morality. The people of my village might not be literate, but they were educated well in unity and fellowship, which are more important to make a nation over the group of chaotic kingdoms or states which forget that they all are branches of a giant tree; and are not the tree themselves.

During those times, no matter if anyone belonged to higher or lower class, people used to grow different vegetables in their home only, no matter how big or small piece of land they owned. They used to visit each other to double the joys and halve the sorrows, not to criticize or demean others. They genuinely cared for each other and never used to think twice before helping someone in growing one's life. I am not firing arrows in the dark when I say this. My family received one such favour once. Having a horse was considered a symbol of royalty. My father was a farmer who owned a little land and some cattle. He used to take the land on lease to grow crops so the financial situation of our family was not very sound. At that time, the young boys of the village used to have a horse as a symbol of their good status which is why my grandfather's friends suggested him to get one his son as well to which he refused considering family's economic health. So, one of his Sikh friends gave him one of his horses. And, the story of the fellowship doesn't end here, it was generational.

My father became really good friends with Shingara Singh and soon enough, they were more of brothers to each other than just best friends. They were together in everything, in whatever good and bad they faced. They shared the responsibilities for each other's mistakes and took risks together. They were inseparable. They also started a business together. They used to travel to far-flung places for trading. Even when the situations started getting a bit serious over the issue of independence which was just around the corner and the partition which became a subject of day-to-day debate, they still carried on visiting such places without their families' knowledge or consent for business purposes. I remember how Shingara Singh's mother came running in worried sick to our house and was shouting how irresponsible both had been. She asked our family to get some news about their whereabouts and if they were alive or not! She was quite furious, and everyone got worried as not every village exhibited harmony like ours. There were unsettling incidents arising from conflicts people had there. Finally, a Sikh girl of our village who had been married in the village Farooqabad, which they were visiting at the time, paid a visit to our house and brought their news with her as she had seen my father in her village. My grandfather immediately went there and brought them back safely. That village is now in Pakistan but then it was one of the villages which were not safe anymore due to the constant lootings and killings.

The idea of the partition seemed absurd when the word was first spread about it and reached us. The places were set to be divided on the basis of Hindu/Sikh and Muslim majority. The Muslims had to leave those places where they were in minority. Though the Authorities confirmed that no one had to migrate against one's wish; yet the circumstances were such that staying was not an option. I was eighteen years old when I was witnessing all this and to what I understood of it was that it was a result of a big political failure in which people had to suffer ultimately, something even the regime could not prevent from happening. The news of partition did not change a thing in people's attitude in our village. They were still together, holding a common opinion against the decision of the Government and willing to do whatever they could to protect their families, which in their view included their Muslim neighbours also.

Sometimes, things change in a click flick and do not go as planned. One day, Shingara Singh came to our house to inform us that the extremists of the neighbouring village had been planning to attack our village the following day with the intention to kill all the Muslim families. Without wasting any time, an emergency meeting was called at our home. All the Muslim families decided to migrate and agreed to meet at the midnight hour again at our home and leave from there. We didn't carry much but food was something that constituted the majority of what we did. In order to ensure a safe passage, it was important that no one knew whether we left or not so we decided to leave from the backside of the house instead of the main gate and for that, we broke the wall at the back and helped everyone in getting out of the house. Shingara Singh and many other friends of my father helped everyone to pack our food and other essentials and get out of there. No one wanted to leave, nor anyone asked for it but there we were. We had to so no one would get hurt 'cause of us as we all knew beforehand that extremists would not have stopped till they took innocent lives.

We travelled till we reached Khilchian, a Muslim-majority village where a camp was set up for gathering migrants. It was five miles away and had a railway track nearby. It was very dark and seeing so many people moving towards the camp together, there was a good chance for them to mistake us as extremists, so we waited by the track till dawn and when the first ray of sunlight appeared that brought the daylight and a clearer view, we entered the village and stayed there for an unexpected number of twenty-seven days. The time was going to take a really hard test of our will it seemed as if it had just begun with its test. The first among these was starvation. We ran out of food sooner than we expected it to last. We were given only half of a chapati to eat over the course of a whole day. It was becoming more and more difficult for us. Even the strength of the elders was starting to give up so one can imagine how hard it must have been for kids and infants. When it went too far, my father and paternal Uncle, Laal Din, decided to go back to the village and ask for help. Knowing the danger, they were about to step into, they went anyways and found themselves knocking the door of Shingara Singh in the middle of the night.

At first, Shingara Singh got suspicious but the moment he realized it was my father, he took both of them in and asked how he could help them. My father explained the whole scenario to him and told him how worse it had been lately. He woke up his sisters and mother to prepare food for us. They made us paranthas greased with desi ghee and packed with pickle. He insisted my father to carry as much wheat as he could carry. With all that food and wheat which my uncle and father carried on their heads and walked five miles, they risked their lives and that of his best friend just to fill our bellies.

After twenty-seven days of starvation, the military arrived. It was difficult to earn the trust of people for them at first but eventually, people put their faith in the officers who extended a helping hand and from there, we began our journey to Pakistan on foot. We stayed a night in a village called Juburji at first and then by 9 pm, we reached Padhana, which falls in Pakistan's territory and then moved towards village Hudiara. It was established in the name of Islam, so we expected people to be kind and welcoming towards us, knowing what we went through but the reaction we got was quite the opposite of it. They did not even show a stitch of compassion towards us, they called us 'Muhajir' and turned their backs towards our sufferings. This test of patience and tolerance was about to get even more bitter.

Those three days spent in the village Hudiara were the most challenging days of our lives. It had been raining torrentially for three consecutive days. While floods were feared to occur on one side, on the other side, we had no shelter to shield ourselves from the fury of nature. Drenched to bones, we were void of essential amenities like clothes, a place to cover our heads, and there was not even a single person who was willing to show a little support towards our cause. This made me wonder about Shingara Singh who was not one of us but still remained with us till the time he could and those who were our own, turned a blind eye towards us. No matter how unfair it seems, we were not getting any help from anyone. Finally, after three days, we reached the Walton camp, set up in Lahore where we stayed for a day, and were then sent to Shorkot. For seven days and seven nights, we stayed at the railway station of Shorkot, seeing people arriving and leaving in panic. From there, we decided to leave for Sargodha and then finally to Chak 27 after some time as we had a few relatives there.

Then the final test of a long struggle began. I started working as a labourer initially but soon I realized the importance of education, thus, I joined a government school in Lahore. As my grandfather had already promised my Nikah with a daughter of one of my relatives, I got married when I was in grade 9. I used to call her 'Baso' lovingly. She was responsible for making me a happier man. The first five children I had died at a very young age. I never understood how much more sufferings I was destined to go through but now, I am a proud father of two sons and two daughters. In 1966, I started off as a teacher at Government High School and continued doing well at my job. During that time, I completed my F.A. (Faculty of Arts). After getting retired, I moved to Shiekhupura. Now, one of my sons is a teacher and the other one is a supervisor at the veterinary hospital in Lahore. Nowadays, I am living well on my pension.

Like all other migrants, we were too allotted some land in Pakistan. I never got a chance to go back but my father did get that. After a few years, to claim the land of nine acres which we had in India, my father went back to Amritsar for eight days. And when he got back, he would keep on talking about how well the people there treated him. It was an overwhelming experience for him as if he had never left and nothing had changed.

I wish I could go back once again to feel the same breeze brushing my face gently and whispering the same old stories which I once, listened to as a child. I wish to experience how the past chimes with the present and if it is still the same in its extraordinary manner. I wish to experience the same warmth which my father received when he visited there. I want to roam in the same streets again and see if I am able to find my friends, who were Sikhs and didn't have to leave the village like us and if they would be able to recognize me. I want to see how much a line stretched on a map to divide a nation, has been successful in drawing the same in the hearts of the people living there and here.

17

Sighted Soldier

SHYAM LAL KANOJIA
LAHORE - MEERUT

THE SPEAKING WINDOW

Millions of Indians served in the Army of the Undivided India, but their loyalty remained a vessel to the 'Union Jack'. In my family, my uncle and father served as British Indian soldiers. But I, on the contrary, served the Indian Army, after its independence. The only difference in the service of the two generations was that where my father was a soldier of the Undivided India; there I had been serving in the Army of free India, but my uncle who served in both, not just marched from the slavery of the British Empire to the fresh air of independence as a soldier but also as a refugee of the fateful partition. May be for this reason, he can tell whether we lost or won, at least, more than I can. Being the inhabitants of Lahore, we were addressed as 'Lahoriye', which is in Pakistan but now we are known as the people of Meerut, India.

I don't know how to explain how my home was but may be this popular saying could help me do that: 'Jine Lahore nai vekhya O Jamya-e-ni!' (He, who has not seen Lahore, has not been born!) Among some famous

The Speaking Window. Sandeep Dutt, Faisal Hayat, and Ritika, Oxford University Press.
© Oxford University Press India 2023. DOI: 10.1093/oso/9789391050733.003.0017

places of Lahore were, the beautiful, Anarkali Bazaar, which was the most famous, attractive, and crowded market in the city, Shrine of Mian Mir, Data Darbar, Qila Gujar Singh, and Shima Pahari. These were a few of the splendid places of Lahore whose glimpses are still fresh in my memory. A greatly Hindu-Sikh populated city back then with five railway stations and almost double the entrances in total, savoured the title of a 'big city'. All houses were painted with the same colours. The only other common thing among people was 'Punjabi—the language and the culture', which was enough to unite them.

Being born in a joint family teaches a person the art of establishing coordination among different threads of thoughts. The same teaching which began within a family was the basis of the social norms which put people together like pearls in the thread of a necklace. In my case, my family included Uncles and Aunts with their children. There were fifteen members in total and it was quite a big family. Though we had a house of our own in Lahore, yet we lived in the Army quarters, for my father and uncle served in the military, in the eighth Punjab regiment, Mian Mir Cantonment, near Topkhana, in Lahore. That time had its own grace. There was our Urdu teacher whom we called, 'Mullaji'. He was one of the finest teachers at the Centre school and undoubtedly, was loved and respected by all. During those times, people valued relationships so much and that too, not only in the family but also in their neighbourhood; such was the charm of Lahore.

During that time, people would leave their whole house under the care of their neighbours when they used to be away from their home, whether for a trip or any important ceremony; such was the trust they had in each other. I consider myself very much fortunate to be able to see such brotherhood. The present generation is not so lucky enough to experience such love, unfortunately. May be, that's why it becomes very hard on their part to understand as to why their ancestors yearned for what they had lost.

The windows of the neighbours which remain shut now, out of rage or hate, were medium for conversations of love then, despite the apparent differences in cultures of people, just like the window which remained open for us and that window was of 'Bhau' this is what we used to call him. He was one of our Muslim neighbours with whom we had cordial relations. He loved our family and was always at our beck and call.

Benevolent, solicitous, cooperative, cordial, empathetic, acquiescent, and he had everything a great soul has. Our families' traditions, rituals, eating habits, and festivals were completely peculiar to our respective heritage. Nevertheless, our bond was beyond our religions. His family was family to ours, and ours to theirs. There was no festival or celebration when we didn't share each other's joys. Even our family gatherings had us helping each other out. I remember him driving a bus full of our relatives, in my uncle's marriage.

We didn't just share the merriest moments, our Muslim neighbours stood by us even in our gloomiest times. When our family faced eleven deaths during the span of six months including my father's... they didn't let us feel that we were from two different communities and stood beside us throughout our hardships. When the partition left us with no choice but to leave, the feeling of severance was apparent in their eyes. They were concerned, worried, and perturbed. They were heartbroken and literally wept with us in our grief. The humanistic bond that we shared was beyond the understanding of those who divided us into two nations!

The decision to migrate to India was not easy for anyone of us to take or accept; it wasn't ours to make either. It's not easy to get uprooted from your native place and shift to a completely strange land. I was around ten years old when we left Lahore. Since my father and Uncle were in Army, we were helped by the military in getting shifted from Lahore to Amritsar. We travelled in a special train which was carrying only the military personnel and their families, which made our journey far easier and safer than others. The ladies and children of our family arrived in Amritsar earlier and the males came later in another train. It was days before 15 August, when I, along with my mother and uncle, arrived in Amritsar.

Amritsar station had its own scary stories to tell, which were painted in every nook and corner of it. Trains were carrying only dead and with terrifying notes written on them with blood. The people who had come to receive their relatives were taking the slain bodies back to give them a proper funeral. It was not only the trains which were coming to India were butchered, the trains which left for Pakistan were too carrying only the deceased. Gandhi said, 'An eye for an eye would make the whole world blind', and everyone was blinded by a pointless abomination that only brought despair to people.

Fearing an epidemic breakout, all the dead bodies were thrown straight into the river. After our whole family got united at Amritsar Railway Station, we moved from Amritsar to Ambala. And then after we moved to Fatehgarh Sahib where we faced intricacies in communication. From the language spoken there to the sense of dressing, everything was so different that we felt alienated. Hence, we moved to Meerut on the eve of Choti Diwali. From that day onwards, Meerut became our hometown. The time we had spent as refugees was full of hardships. At times, we were forced to eat the cornflour, which had mites in it.

However, life goes on and we kept on doing whatsoever work we could find. And finally, I was able to join the military like my father. With time, the scattered pieces started falling into place and life came back on track. This place has been our home since then, but still the memories of my home find me lost in its sweetness and give me nostalgia. My love for Lahore is still imperishable.

If the youth can learn something from my story, it is love. This is what I got, all I learned, and this is what kept our family stronger. I can only advise them to give as much as love to everyone around them. This world has been burning in the fires of hatred and it is only love that can save it. Love every human being, every religion, and every creature created by God. Respect your elders and keep them with you in every pace of your life; doesn't matter whether you are succeeding or losing. Grow by taking the unprivileged, the needy, and the helpless with you. Your success should be collective, dedicated to all those who need it, dedicated to your motherland, and dedicated to your country. A life lived like that is the only life that's worth living.

18

Ink of Peace

KHURSHEEDA NAQUVI
KARNAL - RAWALPINDI

THE SPEAKING WINDOW

Being a Teacher, I have enjoyed every part of my job. It gave me the freedom to learn, which I never stopped, and it also helped me in sharing the same knowledge with the young minds that were waiting to direct their thoughts in the right direction. To be a good teacher, one needs to be a keen observer and remain open to all the available sources from where one can gather as much knowledge as possible, something I have been doing since my childhood. And my first teacher had been my own family.

Though, our ancestors were originally from Amroha, a city in Uttar Pradesh, I was born and brought up in the city of Karnal, a district in Haryana state (at present) which was majorly a Hindu-populated region yet minorities never felt discriminated with. The people were close to each other and had known each other for generations. There was every-thing that a good city should have. I was born in the family of a Reader of the then Deputy Commissioner of Karnal, among six brothers and two sisters. The street, in which our house was located, had a huge shrine

The Speaking Window. Sandeep Dutt, Faisal Hayat, and Ritika, Oxford University Press.
© Oxford University Press India 2023. DOI: 10.1093/oso/9789391050733.003.0018

in the name of '*Bu Ali Shah Qalandar*'. People from distant places every year would visit this holy shrine and pray for their wishes to be fulfilled. Especially in the month of Ramadan, from the 10th day to day 12 of that month, thousands of pilgrims could be seen seeking the blessings of the saint. Small stalls of eatables and other items would be organized during that span of time, and the people singing Qawwali and playing different instruments could be heard and seen creating a mesmerizing spiritual environment there. And amazingly, the Hindu families like those living in the same street as ours, would never feel odd or express any kind of objection to it. So, the lesson of understanding and acceptance deep imbibed in my blood; I have learnt it from there.

In my family, I would see my elder sibling going to school every day and my mother would remain occupied with her household chores and taking care of me. When they would come back, my mother would prepare them something to eat and then we would play till night. My father used to remain busy with his work most of the time, he was very dedicated to his work, and his job would provide him the opportunity to come in touch with many influential people, with whom he developed and maintained good relationships. He was very much into politics also, which is why and how, he had close relations with Liaquat Ali Khan and many other important people. But the thing he loved other than his job was, books! He was fond of books so much that he owned a huge collection of them which we all siblings used to mess around too. With my siblings, I learnt cooperation and the value of brotherhood. However, there was a very important lesson, yet to be learnt.

Things were quite well till the news of the partition broke out, which did not result in peace for sure. The news started the wave of disharmony and that disharmony gave a fillip to the already increasing differences. But no one could have ever thought of what followed next. Riots broke out and genocide began. As the murders became a common scenario, our parents had strictly forbidden us to leave the house, at any cost. I remember on the occasion of Eid that year, there was a lot of stress all around. The extremists were threatening the people. My uncle was not at home and had gone for his Eid prayer. My aunt, in rage, went out with a gun that belonged to my uncle. She went into the street and openly challenged the extremists. But thankfully, nothing happened. When my uncle came back, and got to know about all this, he got really worried about his family, and he made my aunt understand, how dangerous it was and how worse it could get. Something she immediately realized and assured that she won't put everything at stake like that again.

The count of incidents kept on increasing and when it became very much riskier to stay there any longer, my father decided to migrate. He asked us to pack our bags and be prepared for a long journey. My father owned a gun which in that time of need, he sold for Rs. 2,000 and made every possible effort to make our journey safe. Because he had good relations with Liaquat Ali Khan, so it was easier for him to arrange for military protection. Thus, we travelled in a military truck. We were two families who were supposed to travel together; ours and of my maternal uncle's. There were two trucks departing in the space of twenty-four hours, so it was decided that our maternal uncle's family would travel in the first one and take my brother along and our family would leave via second truck, which was supposed to depart the next day of the first one's departure. My sister was just six months old then.

The next day, we bade farewell to our relatives and sent my brother with them and prayed for their safe journey. But on its way to Gurdaspur, that truck was attacked by the extremists several times. Consequently, my maternal uncle, his wife, and children got killed, whereas my brother got severely injured. It was an irreplaceable loss to us. Despite knowing all about it, we still continued our journey and reached Lahore safely. There in Lahore, my father got a job in Bait-Ul-Maal because of his previous experience, which helped us settle a few things. We were allotted a house in Krishna Nagar where we lived for a while and then later, we moved to Pindigheb, near Fateh Jang. But after some time, we shifted for the third time; this time, it was to Campbellpur, which is now known as Attock. After living there for years, we finally got shifted to Rawalpindi where my father bought a house in Saddar.

Life in Saddar was stable than before. I was able to continue my education. I joined CB College, when the war of 1965 was at its peak. I completed my graduation in Arts in 1970 and B.Ed. two years later and after that, I started working as a government teacher. Then, I got married in 1977. My husband passed away in 2005. I have a daughter who is married now. After serving for more than thirty years, I am retired now. Our relatives, from Amroha, still come to visit us. I have faced much struggles and hardships in my whole life. I have given everything what this country demanded. But now, I just want to live my life with my grandchildren.

For almost three decades, a four-walled classroom, with a blackboard and white chalks, countless lessons on the board, erasing the mistakes and rewriting texts for enabling pupils to understand better, this is all what has been my life for all these years. Yet, I wish if it were so easy to erase the flaws of the Rulers in the past too, just with a duster and rewrite the history with a pen filled with the ink of peace.

19

The Salvation Story

SAI RAMTE SHAH CHISTI
MULTAN - LUDHIANA

THE SPEAKING WINDOW

The joy of feeling the little fingers trying to hold your hand, watching the little smile spreading across the face, the first time when he calls 'Mumma' or 'Dadda', watching those little feet trying to make a balance for the first time and seeing a life being nurtured in front of your eyes just leaves you in awe. For twelve-long years my parents yearned for this happiness but couldn't get it. There was no place left where they had not prayed to get the blessing of having a child. Science and faith both had no magic left in them anymore that could fill the heart of my mother which longed for motherhood. After all these years, they had been disappointed but not hopeless. And finally, their prayers were answered.

One day, a *Fakir* visited our village. My grandmother made him food and sought his blessings for my mother who had only one wish in her heart. Overwhelmed with the hospitality of the family, and feeling their pain of not having a successor, the Fakir said, 'Soon, she will give birth to

The Speaking Window. Sandeep Dutt, Faisal Hayat, and Ritika, Oxford University Press.
© Oxford University Press India 2023. DOI: 10.1093/oso/9789391050733.003.0019

a son whose youth will witness him as a warrior and with the declining age, he will turn into a *Fakir* like me'.

In 1910, I was born. And like he said, I became a revolutionary. I lived many lives in my lifetime and I would like to begin it from the beginning when I was Malkeet Singh, a name given by my family. I was born to Jathedar Gurmukh Singh Rahi, a cloth merchant by occupation and a freedom fighter by choice. He had actively participated in the freedom struggle and had been my role model. Our family was well off in the village. We had a cloth shop and were into the business of bricks too. I studied till eighth standard and was inclined towards the philosophy of Lenin. My village Rohira, Malerkotla, despite being a Muslim village, was never indifferent to families like ours. It was more of a huge family. I used to address everyone as uncle and aunt there and all the children were like siblings to each other.

With the speeding time, the efforts made to free the country got speeded up as well. In the early 1920s, the fight for the freedom struggle got more intensified with many movements taking place in different parts of the country. In one of such proud movements, my father was a participant too. The voices raising slogans turned into cries in no time. It was 1924, when my father was one of the supporters of Jaito Morcha, which was undertaken against Britishers for removing the king of Nabha, Ripudaman Singh from his throne for voicing his opinion against the government's atrocities. When nothing worked to cease the protest, the government ordered the army to open fire, and the consequences were not pleasant. My father was one of the martyrs of that movement, but this incident inspired me to follow the path my father walked on.

Since I jumped into the revolutionary struggle actively, my family landed into trouble for that. The police harassed them. Because of that, we left our village and resettled in the village Pamal, near Ludhiana. The family got much concerned about my activities, so my grandfather got me married, thinking I might leave my life as a comrade but to my luck, my wife, Pritam Kaur supported me rather stopping me. This led me further on the path of revolution.

The journey of me as Malkeet Singh turned into being comrade Dukhiya as soon as I began my journey as a rebellion. I started giving speeches which included Punjabi and Urdu couplets. Since my pen name was Dukhiya, so I was better known by that name. In Maharashtra, a secret conference of all revolutionaries was called, which was attended by Bhagat Singh, Chander Shekhar Azad, and Ajay Ghosh, the organizer. I was there too. The time when I was supposed to be there for my first-born who was about to open his eyes into the world, I was attending that meeting, making efforts for his future, a free future.

I remember many important moments of that meeting including the speeches of everyone but what struck me the most were the words of Teja Singh Sultantar. He was a great revolutionary who was on the run for around fifteen years. He rose and said, 'The Independence won't come through speeches but through the barrel of gun'. Yes, indeed, it was the barrel of guns, and not the words.

The Britishers grew suspicious about it and started inquiring about the conference. Somehow almost all the participants were in the circle of their doubt. Hence, their houses were searched to get a clue, and so was mine. I couldn't return so I approached Teja Singh and requested for shelter. He didn't know me, so the mistrust was natural. However, after thoroughly enquiring about me, he agreed to it. I was made a companion of Teja Singh's brother Major Singh. Our job was to decimate the British or our own traitors as per the given information.

So, we remained underground and carried on with our work. Took lives of the foes and kept the fire of revolution burning. We were on the run for years, lived in many places, and travelled a lot. However, we got caught once and that too because of a backstabber. During our escape, we stayed at the confidant's home in village Baathdi, Himachal Pradesh. It was one of the safe houses of ours. But he came out as a traitor. He mixed something in our food, which made us fall unconscious in no time and then he called the police to get his reward and got us imprisoned in Multan Jail. The Rulers were foreign, so could never be trusted but our own people came out as backstabbers too. It was because of them that people like us were behind the bars, many were tortured, and many more were martyred. Sometimes, I think it was not them who betrayed us, it was us. Our own people sold their loyalty to betray their own brothers.

Like me, hundreds and millions were working for the revolution. Where there were hopes building upon and people were preparing for the big moment to happen there, a news broke a million hearts, Bhagat Singh, Sukhdev, and Raj Guru kissed their noose and sacrificed their lives. A new fire ignited the broken hearts of the youth and the way was paved to Azad

Hind Fauj (Indian National Army) of Subhash Chander Bose. World War II and the uncontrolled fire of revolution forced Britain to give up its authority over the nation but even while leaving, they played their last move; partition. A permanent rift that was only going to get deeper in the hearts of people. Carved in blood, the newly free nations, were now shackled in enmity. It was all the work of the Devil who wore the face of God and toyed with the faith. But there were some who lifted the fallen humanity on their shoulders and didn't stop helping others in getting their wounds healed, no matter how much injured they were. Killings were done on both sides but there were some saviours too. Hindus and Sikhs helped Muslims in India and Muslims helped Hindus and Sikhs in Pakistan.

When the country celebrated Independence, I was imprisoned in Multan Jail. Our jail celebrated the Independence by hoisting the national flag of Pakistan, but a few of us were sad, and there was a reason to be too. As the sorrow of partition consumed all the joy of freedom and to some, their home was now in a different nation and they needed to migrate. Then later, after some months, freedom fighters were released by both the countries and I came back to India.

Then people said, 'Comrade if you want to become rich then you should change your way'. But being a communist, even after the partition, I kept fighting against injustice. I have held many labour protests. I fought the election as well but lost by a small margin of votes.

I have been to jail more than twenty times, fifteen years in total, half of which I spent before the partition and eight years after that too. I have always been proud of that but not when it happened in 1960. In that year, when I was protesting for the rights of labours, I was falsely accused of the death of a labour. I was prisoned and went to jail on 4 November 1960. But this time, it was for all wrong reasons and for all false charges, which was nothing to be proud of.

It may be harder to walk on the path of truth but it becomes a walk to remember. It was 15 August 1968, on the occasion of Independence Day, a small event was organized in the Patiala Jail where the CM of Punjab, Lachhman Singh Gill was invited as a chief guest. We were about fifteen people who were participating in a play called 'Qatil Kaun?' After which, I recited a poem based on oppressed women, which left our chief guest's eyes teary. He got up, came to stage, very much emotional, and then something incredible happened. He not just ordered my release but also reduced the sentences of all jail mates by two years. I earned my freedom back and coincidentally on the day of Independence Day! Now finally, I could return home.

My sentence was longer than the jail time I served of eight years, after which I was released. I came home. My wife didn't know about it at all. So I thought to play a prank. After all these years of grave issues and serious moments, a light moment was required too. As soon as I reached back home, I asked her to pack everything. She was shocked to see me, but she could not celebrate the joy of my return. Before she could understand anything, I lied about having fled from prison and told her for the same reason, we could not stay there anymore, and she bought it! Hahaha! It was funny. The expressions on her face were so intense that I still remember them. Before the joke could turn any meaner, I started laughing and told her the truth. She got a little annoyed for terrifying her in such a way but then she laughed too. And, she was happy to have me back.

I was in Mumbai as well for some time. I worked in Jhansi Ki Rani, Buzdil, and Kali Ghata. When a movie based on Bhagat Singh's life, *Shaheed*, was in making, which was later released in 1964, I was contacted to help describe the details about Lahore Jail. I had many brief meetings with Manoj Kumar, who was playing the lead role. Once casually, he asked me that 'We just fake killing people on screen, but as you have killed people in real, can you describe that how heart beat sounds like while dying?' I told him that when an innocent is killed, his heartbeat is filled with fear but when a person, who has committed sin towards someone, is killed, he senses his death beforehand and the feeling of regret overtakes his heart. I have witnessed only the latter one.

I have had experienced the life of a warrior, which at times protected others but also took lives, so my humanity and evil remained with me side by side. So, I had lived as a human and a Devil, as well. But then it was time, to live as a saint. I have had crossed paths with spirituality which has taken me to my salvation. In 1972, my spiritual journey began, which took me to God that I believe I have found too. And since then, I have never looked back. And this led me to a new life and I became Vaid Sai Ramte Shah Chist, also known as Lambe Daade Wali Sarkar.

Some say, life is a song, all one has to do is get its notes right. Some say, it is a colourful journey and one needs to see which colour one wishes to have to create a masterpiece out of it. But I say, it is a big question mark, a question on one's existence to which one must find the answer. For me, I have had my existence with different names but one soul.

This is how Malkeet Singh became Comrade Dukhiya and then Vaid Sai Ramte Shah Chisti. I believe, courage is needed to be a revolutionary and also for choosing the way of spirituality. It's time you need to ask yourself; how brave are you?

20
Fate of Father

MUHAMMAD SIDDIQUE
KAPURTHALA - LAHORE

THE SPEAKING WINDOW

Maa: a small word for the biggest sweetheart in the whole universe who has a paradise of her own in her home, where the sweet humming of her lullabies and the tempting smell of spices from her kitchen spreads joy in the air, where she fills every heart she touches with her warm fuzzy hug and a big smile. She plays with you in rains, sings with you all your favourite numbers, be your support system when you feel alone, and helps to lighten you up with her delicious delicacies and empathetic talks. She loves you with all her heart even when you don't love her back, at times. We all know how mothers are, possessive and protective, but truly amazing.

But can anyone imagine the same sort of compassion, patience, tolerance, and affection from a father who tends to be more of a coconut in most cases, hard from outside but a big softy from the inside? Who secretly loves you and, is there for you even when he has a hard time in expressing himself? Well, I certainly cannot say about others, but my father

The Speaking Window. Sandeep Dutt, Faisal Hayat, and Ritika, Oxford University Press.
© Oxford University Press India 2023. DOI: 10.1093/oso/9789391050733.003.0020

was like that. He played the role of both parents alone after my mother passed away but there was never a day when we would think about, 'If we had her … ' He was there to give motherly affection to a very young me and my sister. Also, he was there to be a supportive father when she was gone. With a sprinkle of motherhood, he embraced his fatherhood to raise two children after the death of his wife.

My father was a farmer with no land, so he used to grow crops by taking land on lease. He earned his living out of the few cattle he had and the land he used to take on lease to grow crops as we had none of our own. But even after working hard all day long, he still used to make time for us and be with us. My sister and I were born and brought up in the village Phulewal which was 6 to 7 km from Sidhan Wali, district Kapurthala. It was a village with all Islamic families; no Hindu/Sikh or any other community resided there, even in minority. Although they were in majority in the neighbouring villages but we had no communal conflicts with anyone. The family of my grandmother used to live in one such village where Muslims were in minority. The people of our village and my grandmother's village would visit each other, not only for business purposes but also personal friendly visits were paid time to time whether it were festivals or other social ceremonies, they used to attend them.

Like that of Eid, which I specifically remember not just because we would get sumptuous treats made especially on that particular day but also, the display of brotherhood which was at exhibition made it special. I remember people visiting each other's homes to wish each other. The beautifully decorated bazaar used to have special varieties to offer that day. The stunning New Moon rising over the mosque and the Salat-al-Eidan after Ramadan gave Eid a beautiful feel. And it all became more special with a caring father and a sweet sister. I used to thank God for keeping our small family under his grace.

However, soon the same New Moon turned blood red and witnessed a new horrific eclipse on the humanity. Darkness, suddenly, crept upon everything we ever knew remained a part of. As soon as the news of the partition got confirmed, there came along a strange frenzy that engulfed the mind of the people and they became a pawn of sick minds who wanted nothing but destruction. Our village had only Muslim families so it was far safer than those which had Muslims in minority and the incident that happened in the family of my grandmother was one of the alarming messages sent in the utmost prevalent cruelty.

It all started with threats initially which nobody took seriously. The areas in which Muslims were in minority were being targeted. People were threatened by the extremists. To prove the words were no empty threats, soon the attacks were undertaken. People were not killed, they were being slaughtered like animals as if it was some sport and killing was fun. And before we knew it, death was at our thresholds too. The brother of my grandmother was caught by extremists who did not care about sparing his life. No mercy was shown, he was a Muslim, and that was enough to put an end to his life. Our family could not even bid their last goodbyes to him. His body was cut into pieces and buried by them. Our family was devasted. Being concerned about the rest of the family, our relatives moved to our village as they felt safer here. Carrying out an attack in a Muslim-majority area could backfire, so it was better here.

Our village might have never had a conflict, whether within or outside but there were some rogue social elements. Our village had always been a victim of looting, committed by some notorious criminal groups. And when the situations got such critical, it became easier for them to carry out their crimes. For a criminal to commit another crime to cover one, is not a problem. Who knows, they might have been a part of that massacre too? People were dying already and that too at a large scale; keeping a record of who killed whom was practically impossible. And for criminals, dead bodies and abandoned mansions were no less than gold mines. The graph of looting was moving parallel to the speeding death rate at that time.

Our village was still somehow untouchable and secure. So, when nothing worked, then another attempt was made to penetrate the perimeter. One day, the village was raided by the police. The officers stormed into every single home with all the force they had and accused people of keeping arms illegally. Every home was being searched thoroughly. There were uniforms moving all around and no nook and corner were left untouched. People were being disrespected and their self-respect was being sabotaged. But how could they find something which was not even there, and they discovered it in no time? Later we got to know that someone had falsely reported to the cops about villagers keeping arms illegally with intent to create violence. Embarrassed at their behaviour, they left soon enough but that day we knew, it was time to move to Pakistan. It was not safe anymore. We were being framed and next time we might not be so lucky to survive through.

I was 12 then and fearful. Even the comfort of my father was not enough that day. I could sense his fear and it was more terrifying. My father discussed this with our relatives and it was decided that we all would leave the following day. My grandmother who looked spry despite her old age, made all the preparations that night. She packed all the family possessions safely in a sack and prepared food for the exhausting journey ahead of us. It was unbelievable how strikingly demanding time had become. It never had much to offer yet we were happy but now, it wanted everything from us. The home we had was not big, still it was home to us. That house had the essence of my mother, affection of my father, and little games of me and my sister. It was where my father used to return back every single day after his strenuous work and still used to play with us. He used to make us meal and then lie down with us under the starry night, making patterns with us and telling us bedtime stories. It is awful really to feel unsafe in the very place which had kept you safe forever.

By morning, the whole village was ready to join us on the journey. One of my maternal Aunts lived in Kabirpur, a village in our own district Kapurthala which was on our way. So, my father decided to stay there for some time. Thus, my father took us there and planned out the further journey. The rivers were the ones dividing India and Pakistan mainly. They were the fastest way to cross the border, but the misery of others had become a profitable business for some. The boatmen there knew how desperate people were to get on the other side, so they increased the fare of the ferry, which no doubt not everyone could afford like our family. It was a very difficult time. I had never seen my father so helpless; he was trying everything he could to get us all out of it and make us feel safe again. He was feeling so weak, but he could not afford his children to see his teary eyes. I cannot recall his words, but I can still feel their emotions. I remember him holding my hand so tight that I could feel the fear of losing me or my sister in him. He was trying to keep him collected in front of us and even in that condition, he was still trying to comfort us.

When the money for the ferry was not arranged, we decided to carry on the journey by road. Eight days or shall I say eight long days full of fear and a constant struggle for life. It felt as if the time had lost its speed, and it was making us count every second. Though we were not alone in our journey. In fact, a huge caravan was there, which we were a part of, but the attacks were not coming to halt. Even huge caravans were on a target and only dead bodies were left, which were later looted by the vultures that were looking only for gold and cash. If anyone was by any chance alive in the heap of bodies, s/he was not aided by them. They were, either left to wait for their death which came painfully slow or were killed instantly and, on those occasions, it was made sure that the person was dead. Fortunately, our caravan was not attacked, not even once, and finally after eight days, we stepped into a border hoisting green flag with a crescent and a star in white in its centre, which gave us a hope of light after the dark days we had experienced.

After arriving in Pakistan, we were given permits and people started scattering to various places. We too, did the same. We went to my maternal Aunt's home in Badami Bagh where we stayed for a few days before shifting to Shahpur. The wells of Shahpur didn't have water in them, but blood. They were filled with the dead bodies of Sikhs and the pinching smell of their rotten bodies. Neither the sight nor the smell was bearable. Their eyes wide open, bodies hued, and clothes soaked in blood, was a haunting sight. After staying there for a few days, we shifted to a village named, Doori and got settled there. Even after migration, the murders were not coming to an end. People kept on killing each other out of revenge and hatred. Since the borders back then were not sealed like today, people from both sides used to cross it and carried on their bloodbath. A Sikh from Chaidu village used to cross the border at night and kill Muslims on this side. He used to take back their heads to show off, but one shall reap what one has sown. The same thing happened to him when he crossed the border one night and a Muslim killed him the same way.

Sometimes, when we have something in abundance and that too for free, we never value it until it's gone. I might never have understood the meaning of harmony, brotherhood, or the kind of peace we had back in our home till I experienced the ambience in this new village where we shifted at last. People were not welcoming here. They did not make it easier at all. We got negligible support from them and we struggled a lot. I started working with my father as a labourer and tried my best to support him. My sister had to leave her childhood behind and she got indulged in the household chores. She did everything she could to help me and my father. My father who had never been afraid of hard work, worked here too. He was at peace with this thought that at least, all of us were together. There were families who had lost so much.

After working as a labour for a long time, I finally got a job at Water and Power Development Authority (WAPDA) in 1961 where I served for forty years. Soon after getting a job, I got married. It was in 1963, when my Nikah was read and my wife brought her graces into my life. She became another pillar of support and made me a proud father of four beautiful daughters and three noble sons whom I was able to provide the formal education of which I am very much proud. Today, all my sons are working independently; one is into business, one is in WAPDA, and the other one is a Homeopathic doctor. I am happy that I was able to make them capable enough that they could stand on their feet.

It is unfortunate to see that the value of the lives which were sacrificed for the freedom of a nation and then countless more which were taken to divide it in the name of it, hold negligible value in the eyes of today's youth to which the Independence Day is just another holiday or a day to exploit their right to express their thoughts. In the name of celebration, they take out their bikes, organize rallies, and with their silencer's exhaust removed, produce an obnoxiously loud sound, and call it 'freedom'. For breathing in this air which is free from the smoke of slavery today, it is the same old people responsible whom they either blame or hold responsible for bad decisions. But whether they like it or not, they must understand that their elders were not perfect and might have made mistakes, but they too are not making it any better. Like someone said, 'You might be given a cactus, but you don't have to sit on it'. Before questioning the older generations, they must raise the same finger towards themselves to ask what they did to make it any better, to make a difference.

And now, to answer the most common question which every migrant is asked, 'If given an opportunity would you like to go back?'—in the hope of a common answer of 'yes, I wish to go back'. I would like to answer this most common question with an uncommon answer which might raise many eyebrows; it's a no! No, I would not like to go back even if I ever have a chance. I have two very rational reasons behind that. First, my aging health, which won't allow me and second, and the most dominant reason, I don't wish to. It has given me enough pain already. Neither do I wish to feel the same pain all over again by visiting it, nor do I wish to add more to it. So, no, I won't.

21

The Persistent Princess

KUSUMLATA SHARMA
MAGHIANA - DELHI

THE SPEAKING WINDOW

The moment a daughter wraps her tiny fingers around the finger of her father and smiles at him, a bond of trust and friendship establishes between the two of them. It is, then, upon him to either nurture a daughter in a way that he teaches her to rise after she had fallen or just be a father who has a checklist of responsibilities to be fulfilled on his part. It is not God who writes the fate of daughters but a father. He is someone who shapes her persona and empowers her to write her own destiny. It is him who becomes a pillar of strength when she thinks she doesn't stand a chance in front of the world. It is him who makes her realize that she doesn't need anyone to look up to; and is wise enough to rely upon herself. He can do all of this for her daughter or shackle her potential with societal norms.

I have been a daughter, a wife, a daughter-in-law, a mother, and a widow but whenever I forgot the strength of a woman, it was the role I played as a daughter that helped me realize my true potential. Obviously, it is no secret why being a daughter has brought me so much of courage; because

The Speaking Window. Sandeep Dutt, Faisal Hayat, and Ritika, Oxford University Press.
© Oxford University Press India 2023. DOI: 10.1093/oso/9789391050733.003.0021

behind my present self who knows how to get up again after getting knocked down by life, it is my father who has never stopped believing in me ever since I stepped into this world.

I was born with a silver spoon in my mouth for I belonged to one of the biggest aristocratic families of Lahore at that time. I share my birthplace with my grandfather who was born in Tulamba, Tehsil Shorkot. We had a huge business in Sindh and Punjab. We had a cotton factory in Khanpur Katora, near Karachi, which was handled by my father. This is why he was living in Karachi with my mother. We had a wire factory in Shahdara, Lahore, which was an industrial area across the river Ravi and it was under the care of my eldest paternal uncle, Pandit Ram Pyare Lal Jaitley who was also a public figure. He was also a General Manager of a bomb factory. He was loved by people for his benevolent nature. He would never refuse anyone who came to him seeking work. My other paternal uncle, Har Bhagwan Jaitley was a renowned radio singer in Lahore. There were Shahabuddin quarters in that industrial area where our Lahore's factory was located. Our joint family was residing in a huge palace-like house with a dozen of servants to serve us.

In my own family, I only had a brother as my sibling but I did have many cousins as my paternal uncle had six children. All of us children were residing in Lahore for we were pursuing our education from there. I studied at Rai Bahadur Sohan Lal High School, Shahdara till fifth class. We were taken to school by the servants who used to take us back home, too. After coming back from school, we would have our lunch and in the evening, we all cousins would play together. Our family was one of the few families of its time which owned a car. We had two horse carts as well with horsemen.

In Shahdara, Hindus and Muslims studied together and were taught by the teachers who came from every kind of faith. Lahore had such comfort in its environment that students from abroad used to come and study at Punjab University. We used to go for an evening walk at the Tomb of Jahangir, which was near to our home. Our area was a Hindu-majority region, but no Muslim family ever felt discomfort in that. Every festival was celebrated together. We used to go to the fair of Goddess Sheetala every Monday. Lahore had the best zoo I have ever seen in my life. Apart from attending fairs and feasts, I was fond of movies too. I have watched a lot of movies I can remember. Ram Rajya, Zeenat, Bharat Milap, Man ki

Jeet, Prithvi Vallabh, Devdas, etc., were some of the movies I watched in Lahore. At that time, people knew how to live life to the fullest and wealth had nothing to do with it. Every house had its own cattle. In winters, I used to visit my father in Khanpur Katora. My father had been really respectful towards his elder brother. My grandfather and eldest paternal uncle used to travel by air as well by a family car, but my father neither travelled by air nor by car out of respect towards his father and elder brother. This brotherly sentiment of my father might never be understood by the generation of today.

Since many of our relatives and my maternal family were living in Maghiana, our family decided to make a house there for everybody to live together. Thus, we purchased a boarding hostel and converted it into a huge bungalow with more than twenty rooms where we moved in, in the year 1947. We all siblings used to study in Lahore and now that the family had decided to shift to Maghiana, we were supposed to continue our education there but one Government decision shifted everyone's world upside down.

Because of all the disturbances happening in 1947, my paternal uncle went to Khanpur to look for future business possibilities but when he came back to Maghiana, my grandfather noticed his deteriorating health. So, my grandfather took him to Mathura Das Hospital, Lahore where a heartbreaking news awaited us. The doctors informed us that he was suffering from a serious heart disease. We had just got him admitted there, when he had a heart failure and, he could not be saved. Our family had not even recovered from it, when another dirty trick of fate awaited us. When he died, Lahore was under curfew due to the riots. So, we had to cremate my paternal uncle in Lahore itself. After this, we all came back to Maghiana to our newly constructed house as we needed to help each other overcome the huge loss we had to bear. But little that we knew, that the house which our elders had got built with so much of affection and desire, was about to be taken away from us.

Because our area was a Muslim-majority area and our elders feared for our safety, so my father rented a house near my maternal grandmother's house as other relatives were also living in that area. This was done so all family members could live in close proximity, because nobody knew what shape the riots were to take. To avoid any kind of risks, there were many protection measures taken by our elders. Big iron gates were built on all sides of the house with electric fencing. I still remember women of our house were given poison and were instructed to keep the children with them all the time because rather than dying at the hands of extremists, it was better to take their lives and of their children.

Despite being rich, we never had any ammunition with us because not even once did such a situation arose when we had to be concerned about our safety like this. It had always been peaceful but soon riots broke out in Maghiana. The cries of women and children were heard all night. The noises of extremists, setting up houses on fire, filled the sky. Then one day, in early September, all the influential families in Maghiana decided to go to the Deputy Collector of the city to request him to take some action. However, there was a different story being written there altogether. When we went there, we weren't allowed to come back. We only went there to talk, not with an intention to pack and leave everything.

We were taken to a ration depot and were instructed to live there till their next orders because we were told that it was too dangerous to head back and we might get killed. We made a small hearth of bricks to cook food for ourselves. All of a sudden, the landlords were homeless now. As the saying goes, 'riches have wings', fits in our situation perfectly. The houses of our families including ours, my paternal aunt's, and of my grandmother, were really big. We were rich enough that our coming generations didn't need to work all their life, if they didn't want to. But now, the situation was different. The only clothes I had were those which I was wearing. I borrowed a dress from a classmate who had brought three pairs and was kind enough to lend me one as she came after us. Our comfortable beds with soft velvet blankets which were now replaced with a hard-rocky ground. It was painful for my father to see us all in such conditions as he had provided us with all kinds of comforts of life. So to make up for the sudden change, he used to become a 'bed' for us. He would take us in his arms as we went to sleep.

After spending a few days at that depot, we were evacuated. For a moment, we thought that we would be sent back finally but there was no going back. We were told that we were being taken to the station and from there, we would leave for India. It was no less than a bolt from the blue sky, but the circumstances were so tensed, we didn't have a choice. We were not even given a chance to get our belongings. We had gold beyond imagination, and money, too, which could have helped us; we had silverware and goldware in abundance and many other priceless and valuable possessions, but we left empty-handed. As soon as we got out of that depot, the extremists attacked us and looted all the gold from the women. They snatched the jewellery from their body, leaving them injured. Considering the whole situation, my mother asked me to hand over my earrings to one extremist without any struggle so that they don't snatch them directly from my ears, leaving them hurt. As the railway station was not much far, we went there by foot.

Since we had left our homes, only bad things had been happening to us and I saw fear on those faces which had never known that feeling before. The train which left before us was full of Hindus and had been left in a huge pool of blood. Everyone on it was killed and all it carried in it were the corpses, with death written on it in red. We all were terrified when another train came and stopped in front of us. Going back was not an option and boarding the train, which could become a coffin for the dead was also a great risk to take. Nonetheless, the moment we left our houses and stepped into that police station, the fate had made a choice for us already and now, we could do nothing more but accept it, so we all boarded the train. The train was completely blacked out when it was made sure that everybody boarded it. All the windows and doors were closed and locked, we were asked to remain under our seats and make no noise at all. I was 11 then, and even today, it gives me goosebumps when I think about it. It felt as if there was a hide-and-seek game going on with a monster who already knew where I was hiding and was waiting for me to get out of my hideout. Somehow, nothing happened. We could see the Indian flag hoisted at Atari station and we knew it was over. Back home, we never had to wait for food, and we had relished the most delicious cuisines but now, for the first time ever, we felt what hunger was, we felt the importance of food that was being distributed in a little quantity.

After reaching Atari station, the first place we moved to was Jalandhar where we reached an area called '*Sheikhon ki Basti*' which was a prosperous Muslim region and all families residing there were noble and affluent. As the people here got to know about the Hindu and Sikh families getting murdered in Pakistan, the families here suffered the same fate. Vengeance gave motive to people to take lives in their 'righteousness', in order to serve justice but what they forgot during that was, neither those whom they lost could come back with their acts of revenge nor there was any difference left now between those whom they hated for murdering their families or relatives, and them. The roads of Jalandhar were filled with the cold rotting corpses, which served as a feast for the crows and vultures. Drops of blood were scattered on the walls of the houses. There was only a staunch smell of death all around.

We stayed in Jalandhar till we lost another member of our family, the son of my paternal uncle who went to the canal for a bath which became his last and got drowned in it. The grief in the family seemed to get its roots deeper and deeper. The loss of my paternal uncle and then our house was still fresh as a wound when we lost my cousin too. It broke the heart of our family and killed its spirit in some way too. It was decided to leave Jalandhar but where were we supposed to go? Seeking that answer, my father came to me, took me in his lap; I could see tears in his eyes, but he didn't cry. He smiled at me, kissed my forehead, and asked me, 'Where do you want to go? We would go there.' It was a father asking his eleven-year-old daughter in a hope that she might point him in a direction that he was looking for. At that moment, if I could recall any place's name, it was Kurukshetra. Since childhood, I had heard the stories of Mahabharata, the war between Pandavas and Kauravas, and of Bhagwat Gita. All these had been fascinating stories to me. Thus, we moved there. My father was appointed as a Commander of a Refugee Camp as he was an educated fellow. Later, he appointed all of my brothers and relatives for different jobs.

Meanwhile, three of our servants came looking for us and found us one by one. One came from the house we left in Lahore, another came from the house we had in Khanpur Katora and then came our driver. They all came carrying some of our clothes, utensils, and some valuable possessions. It was unbelievable seeing them again in those times when people had forgotten the humanity and its values. At the time, when loyalty and friendship didn't exist anymore, even those who could help each other shut their doors to fellow humans. All three of them came, risking their life, searching for our family, and travelled this far just to give us our belongings. If there were these three who remained loyal to our family even when we were no longer their Masters, there were those who betrayed us too.

Our maternal aunt's family, living in Massan, was also a high-born like us. They had a lot of gold and, much wealth too. But neither their gold nor their wealth could save them from what was about to happen to them. When the situations there got so critical that their lives were at stake, they knew they had to leave but were not able to find a way before their servants suggested a way out. They assured them that they would escort them to the border and would protect them no matter what. They all didn't have much choice, so they agreed. They packed everything they could carry and left the rest there. After a few miles of their journey, their own servants who promised to escort them safely turned into robbers and looted them, and if that was not all, they started killing everyone. They killed the whole family but the sister-in-law of my maternal aunt who had her son with her. When the inhumanity knows no limit and evil takes the throne, it is the end of all goodness which has ever prevailed in the world before. Before they could hold her, she asked the boy to run away. One of them went after the boy while the rest killed the faith in humanity. They tore off her clothes, disgraced her faith, and left her without a shred of any fabric on her scratched skin which they feasted on just like the vultures eating the corpses and carcasses. The same hands which served her for years, the family who had given everything to them, shelter, food, and a better life; they not only backstabbed it but also annihilated their dignity and faith. The whole time, they remained deaf to her screams and brutalized her. And finally, when they had satisfied their lust, they left her there, to die.

The boy who was being chased by one of their servants ran into a herd of cattle and tried to hide there but was found. As he was about to kill that innocent, his own son who was standing right beside him, witnessing his father becoming a butcher, said, 'Abba ise mat maaro, mere saath kal school kaun jayega? (Don't kill him, Father. With whom will I go to school tomorrow?!)' Those words shook him to the core and all of a sudden, he realized what he had done and what he was about to do. He decided not to kill him and thought of raising him as his own son, so he took both his son and that kid to his home. It was a dark stormy night. The thunder of clouds felt like nothing less than a lion roaring in the forest, and soon it began to rain. The bare body of the woman who was recently raped, was now lying there, lifeless, in the rain. But she was not dead. She gained a little consciousness only to find herself in an unbearable pain. She didn't even have the energy to scream for help, nor could she walk, but she had to find her son and that thought gave her some strength. She could see a house nearby. She crawled her way to it where she was sheltered and helped. Later when the military helped evacuate that area, she was taken to a military camp. Somehow, her son got to know about her whereabouts and one night ran from the house of that servant to search for her mother. The two of them got reunited in the camp and finally made it to India and reunited with us.

My father wanted his family to settle, so he asked my paternal uncle who was a radio singer to go to Mumbai in search of a job and he himself went to Rohtak, in search of a new job or business opportunities. I was living with my grandparents in Kurukshetra then. Afterwards, my father's friend who was also a partner in the Cotton factory we had, started buying land and properties in Sonipat. My father thought that as we had known each other for a long time, we should live together so, all of us moved to Sonipat. There, my father started the work of property brokerage. He was worried about my education as well. He wanted me to study. But soon, he realized that there were no good options available for education. Therefore, he decided to get me home-schooled and for that he contacted a teacher in Delhi and asked if he could move to Sonipat to teach me. My father was willing to make arrangements for his family as well so that he didn't have to stay away from them but that was not required as he agreed to travel from Delhi to Sonipat every day, only to teach me. Just in a month, one more girl joined, and we started sharing the fee. Shortly we were now three girls studying together. Then my father felt the need for a girls' school, so he opened one real soon by the name of Adarsh Kanya Mahavidyalaya with a sole motive of educating girls. Those who were un-privileged and came from poor background were taught free of cost and even the books and stationery were provided to them. Though my father's name is Ram Narayan Jaitely, here everyone started calling him, 'Mama Ji'(a term used for maternal uncle) and shortly the school became famous by the name of 'Mamaji Ka school' (Mama Ji's school). Many girls from Panipat, Narela, and even from Delhi used to come there to study. That school has provided many service class women to Delhi-NCR.

It was 1954 when I got married to an army officer who, at that time, was appointed in Ambala and my in-laws' family was living in Chandigarh. My father-in-law was working in Public Work Department, who not just contributed to the construction of Chandigarh but was also one of those few people who migrated to Chandigarh in its early phases. I had been to many places in India with my husband as he would get transferred to different places and sometimes, I also used to accompany him. Then finally, we came to Delhi in 1969. Everything was working very nicely. My husband, Mr. Sharma, was a great athlete and was working in National Stadium of Delhi. On 10 December 1972, the annual day was being celebrated in National Stadium and my husband won first prize in ten different games. He came to home very happy but all of a sudden, he died of a heart failure. He left me alone with four children. It was as if an earthquake shook my life and left it scattered in pieces.

A married woman is much respected but only as long as her husband is alive. As she steps into the zone of a widow, the same society changes towards her. I was in the grief of my husband's loss, when my in-laws became the first ones to snap me out of my sleep. My father-in-law was a kind man who had always treated me like his own daughter but after the death of my husband, things changed. They expected my father to take care of his widow daughter and nurture four children as now their son was gone forever. My father was an open-minded person and was not in the favour of a woman being burdened with the useless societal norms which come with a baggage of shame and responsibilities only. He never discriminated between his son and daughter and raised me like he had raised his son. He knew the road for me was about to get tougher, so he came to me one day, handed me a form, and told me that I would have to give an exam. I was a little bit unsure about it as my in-laws were conservative and I knew that they wouldn't like it. But my father said to me, 'What would you do now? How will you raise your children? Do study further and go for a job so that you won't have to beg anyone for anything!' As I had stopped studying after marriage, it was difficult for me, but I studied harder, gave the exam, and secured 75% marks. Then, I got a job in a foreign post office, where imported parcels used to be examined for customs duties.

One day my mother-in-law came to me and said 'You should stop doing job and come back to us, to Chandigarh' I told her that it was impossible for me to do so as my children were studying in a school in Delhi. She again asked me, 'Are you sure you wouldn't come?'—this time in a way, she was not going to take no for an answer. In my reply, I questioned her, 'If my husband could go to wars to serve his country, to raise his children then why can't I do a job to educate them and give them a good life?'

The next day my in-laws left me. After a few years, when it was getting difficult to look after the children and do the job at the same time, as my daughter was also in her teens, my father suggested us to move to Sonipat and travel to Delhi daily to do my job. And that is what I did. We moved to Sonipat and my children got their education from there only. In my twenty-three years of service, I travelled to Delhi every single day by a passenger train for fourteen years. In the meantime, my eldest daughter also started doing a job in Delhi so for a short period of time, my daughter and I used to travel together. Soon my elder son too got a job in Delhi and asked me to stay with him so that I didn't have to travel every day. I came with him and have been living here since then. All my children are well-settled now. The years of patience and hard work paid off but I couldn't have done it without my father who had been standing like a rock by my side all my life. If it weren't for him, I couldn't have done all this at all. That is why I said before that the fate of a daughter is written by her father, not God. Either he can make her capable enough and hand her over the pen to write her own destiny or can snatch the same and make her crippled for all life.

I do miss my home back in Lahore every day, its streets, the movie theatre, the lifestyle we had there, the air travels of my paternal uncle and the way my father maintained his respect, the evening walks, and the huge gardens in our house. I miss all of it.

What I want to tell this generation is that life is all about ups and downs. When water flows from the mountains, many difficulties come in its way, in the form of rocks, stones, and unexpected turns and falls, but it keeps on moving until it forms a river and finally reaches the ocean. Similarly, one must keep on moving in life through it all and must never stop.

22

Ways of God

TALIB HUSSAIN
JALANDHAR - SHEIKHUPURA
THE SPEAKING WINDOW

Even when the Prophet Mohammad (S.A.W.) was forced to leave his home Mecca, he knew he had to go as he had no other choice. No words could describe his pain and feelings. Not only have I read and heard about this countless times, but I had also felt the same sentiments that he might have felt when I, too, had to leave my home.

I am asked: 'Why do you keep on recalling the same old house, you had?' 'Why you get stuck in the memories of the same place?' 'Are you not happy here?' 'It's past. It's gone. Forget it.'—Can I? Should I?

When people move abroad, they are either forced by their will or circumstances. In both cases, one doesn't fear for the life of the loved ones. One is not forced to leave everything earned before, you can always come back to it. And even if we move to a new house, we do not have to leave our belongings behind. It's not about all the valuables you have which had material value attached to them, else you could later buy them with your money, but it was the emotions attached to them, the memories they

The Speaking Window. Sandeep Dutt, Faisal Hayat, and Ritika, Oxford University Press.
© Oxford University Press India 2023. DOI: 10.1093/oso/9789391050733.003.0022

come with, and the token of remembrance that one misses. A child won't miss her neighbour's doll but of her own, no matter how valuable it was or not. The little things in life, no matter how much we ignore, they consume the most room in our mind. You may walk through your street every day, come back to the same house, pet your dog, and then wake up the next day to live the same routine but you would miss the same house, the same street, the same walls again, when you know you can't have them back; like the Punjab I lived in.

Punjab is divided into four regions, the plains lie between the five rivers: Doaba, Malwa, Majha, and Poadh. Doaba is the plains between the rivers Beas and Sutlej, which my village, Hajipur, tehsil Sultanpur of district Jalandhar was a part of. It was a Muslim-majority region. Thus we were known as 'Doabis'. Its neighbouring villages, like Sultanpur had Hindus and Sikhs in a majority but this communal distribution never caused any rift in us. I grew up in a joint family with the affection and care of my grandparents, strict but sweet paternal uncle, loving parents, naughty but two adoring brothers, and a cute sister. I had many friends; Hindus, Muslims, and Sikhs. Back then, the relationships were valued more as compared to today, whereas now their importance is lost somewhere in the quest for materialistic happiness.

My father used to work in China and wrote letters to us from time to time. My friends who used to help their fathers in work or wait for their return in the evening to spend some time with them. I missed doing those things but whenever my father visited us, he would bring us all gifts and tried to spend as much time with us as he could.

Our elders got to know about the partition and many villages and cities were divided; some remained the part of the older India with a new face and some became a part of the new nation, Pakistan. We didn't have to migrate at first because our region was about to be the part of Pakistan but later, the same decision was revised, and we were informed that we had to migrate now as the village was not going to be the part of Pakistan anymore. And with that, the terrors of extremism came with full force and haunted the lives of Muslim residents but fortunately, no harm was done.

Soon the elders started thinking about having a safe way to migrate as the attacks were at peak. Every migrant was a target despite their age or colour, except their religion, and from which side they were coming or going to, decided their life expectancy. The hard banging knocks on the doors were not welcoming in those days. And one evening, our door was knocked on too. It was the time of the evening. The elders were having their deep discussion related to migration. The air felt so heavy in all of that stress. We all siblings were grouped in a room and were doing the usual stuff, playing and teasing each other but we too could sense all that tension around. And then there was an unexpected knock at the door. It was my father. He had returned from China. His arrival was a blessing at that time. I remember how we all ran to him to hug him and he ensured us that he was not going anywhere this time. He was there to stay, but were we?

Not everyone became our foe in Hindus and Sikhs. There were my friends and their families who genuinely wanted to help us and offered too but at a wrong place and wrong time. The village was already attacked so many times by the extremists by then which had made the Muslim families lose faith in the people they knew, even when they were aware of the fact that they were not involved in those attacks, yet a shred of doubt was being entertained in their mind which dominated their trust formed over the years. My friends' families came to our house when my elders were planning out a safe passage to get out of our village with other families. They extended a hand to help us and also offered to escort us the whole way till we reached Pakistan. But a few Muslim families got suspicious of their overwhelming generosity and decided not to take any help from any Hindu or Sikh, smelling a trap that was never there. Lack of faith, at the times of need and fear of losing something of our own which we care about, can make a person so cynical that every helping hand, even if offering a medicine to cure one's disease, may seem like poison.

We had a few relatives in Sheikhupura, Pakistan so we decided to go there. We grabbed eatables and some other things which we thought were useful or valuable and left. People took swords, axes, and gandasas (a wide single-edged dagger, also called the elephant knife) to protect themselves in case an attack happened. Thus, a long caravan with thousands of people on foot and bullock carts could be seen the very next day. The armed men were leading the tribe, the children and women were kept in the middle, and then again, a large group of armed men safeguarded the caravan at the back. People were prepared for the worst if they had to face which they did, just not in the form of what they had prepared for. And this foe they had to fight with was not a mortal being, it was starvation.

A grave situation was at hands, waiting to be dealt with as soon as possible, people were dying of hunger and then it got so worse that people were forced to kill the cattle they brought with them to satisfy their hunger which too, did not last for much time. The whole journey was carried out on foot. After arriving in Amritsar, we were joined by ten to twelve soldiers for our protection as the city was already facing riots. By the time we reached Pakistan, the count of the refugees in our caravan had reached up to one and a half lac. The word 'refugee' or 'mujahir' in itself is not so insulting but rather pitiful. It is when sarcasm and hatred are sprinkled on it, it takes the form of an abuse. This is what happened with us, too. On reaching Pakistan, we were not expecting people to stand in our honour and greet us with garlands in their hands for us. But, we certainly did not expect such cold behaviour too, which they showered upon us. Being a migrant, we had already fought for our lives and now, we had to prepare ourselves for a new war for getting our rights. Even on seeing a beggar who roams in the street, asking for food and some water, people choose to help him, but we were treated much worse than him, I guess. We were not provided with any kind of help just because we were 'Mujahirs' as that is what we were called and that too in a very disrespectful way.

Imagine the plight of a person who had just lost his own home, his motherland, and was forced to take up on a journey to a new place where he seeks shelter after facing a lot of hardships already. And then, on reaching there, his hardships and problems do not cease but are doubled. How does that feel? As if all the things we went through were for nothing? We were being punished for something we had no control over.

After coming to Pakistan, the first place we went to was Sheikhupura as our relatives were living there already. The place where we stayed then was of a Sikh named Gulab Singh, which is still under our possession. Before the partition, only a handful of Muslim families lived in Sheikhupura. It was a region predominately inhabited by Sikhs but it was occupied by Muslims after the partition. We were aware of this region not only because of our relatives but also because people from our village used to visit it before.

The Government here in Pakistan was dealing with many things at the same time. There were pressing social and economic issues and the most immediate one was resettling those who had come from India. It was announced that we would be given some land depending upon the amount of land we owned back home. But in contrast, we were given just one acre of land per person here. And in our tribe, the same amount of land was allocated to everyone, whether that someone was a landlord or a pauper. In 1952, we were given the claim of our land in India. When we settled here, I continued studying at a Madrassa and after some time, I started working as a labour. I got married twice in my life and have three sons now who are busy in their respective jobs. They consult me when they need some advice. Here I can proudly say that in my whole life, I never tried to mint money by doing wrong deeds. The more or the less I served my family, it was done with my hard work.

I am a believer in God and my learning at the Madrassa has imparted to me the knowledge of the Holy Quran, which I remember by heart. I remember it so well that I recite the whole of it in Taraweeh, every year during the month of Ramadan. I have never missed the fasts during Ramadan in the past sixty to sixty-five years, not even once. I had been elected as the Chairman of the Union Council of my own area thrice. I believe God has his own ways of testing his followers and to help them realize what they miss in their life in order to make it better. And, he only gives us that much of pain, as much as we can bear.

No doubt, if I am asked about the life I had lived, I always say that life back in India was simpler, easier, and much different than what I have led here. During that time, the fare to travel from Sargodha to Sheikhupura was merely eight annas which is more than Rs. 700 now. Unlike the people here who refused to accept us, there was no such nuisance in my village. People valued relationships back in the day when even my own children did not talk to me, whereas I used to wait for my father to return home to talk to him. I miss that family in which there were so many people around me to take care of me and love me. Today's reality is completely different from the one I lived earlier, which I truly crave for. If I could, I would have gone back and remained there only in the same house where I used to live before, where I was born.

If the young people really wish to learn something from my story, then I would like to tell them that the freedom they have today was not earned in a day, so they must realize its importance as soon as possible. Everything is important to do in life to achieve success and it is good to see them being so focused towards their goals but what is more important is the means or the way in which they want to achieve it. Failure is not when they fail to achieve what they aspire for, it is when they do not even try and surrender in front of their fears. And, it is also then when they take wrong ways to get what they want by any means and the latter one can't be undone so they should choose wisely. In the race of having bigger and bigger achievements, they must not miss out on the smaller and more important things in life including the time they have with their parents and children. This mortal life comes into being with an end to it too, and the regret for the lost lives is not going to bring them back. Visiting the graves of the dead and decorating them with flowers and marble will neither bring new life in the cold corpses nor will help anyone get rid of their pain.

23

Hands Held Up

CHARAN DAS
LAHORE - GLASGOW

THE SPEAKING WINDOW

A father playing with his kid, carrying him on his shoulders, while the kid plays with his father's hair, giving him a new hairstyle. The mother holds the finger of her daughter who has grown enough to walk all by herself now and is pointing to a balloon seller who is giving a gas balloon to another kid. And a five-year-old me, watching them, trying to hold his parents' hand but is left just waving his hand in the air as no one is around. Suddenly everything gets blurry as if the colours, the balloons, and their faces everything has mingled into each other and there is nothing left. Gone, just like that. And I am left standing in the pitch of emptiness where no one can hear me out.

The sky above us was still accompanied by the Sun and its light, and its sweet winged friends during the day time and with beautiful stars, twinkling by the Moon at night, even he is never alone but I was, a kid gazing the sky, and lost in it, and thinking whom to look up to and whose hand to hold. Feeling a lot of pain, not knowing how to express it, whom

The Speaking Window. Sandeep Dutt, Faisal Hayat, and Ritika, Oxford University Press.
© Oxford University Press India 2023. DOI: 10.1093/oso/9789391050733.003.0023

to approach and what to say, the little boy in me had a saddening grief that buried all his smiles inside.

My father had a huge business in Lahore. He was a big cloth merchant who used to bring cloth from Burma and sell it in Lahore. The business was a huge success and it was all because of him. His business sense, ability to strategize, decision-making skills, and a strong stomach for thrilling ventures, made him a big businessman. His younger brother was the second in command and helped him expanding his dream. He had a family who supported him, a beautiful wife who loved him, a daughter and a son who were his life, and the blissful hands of his parents on his head; what more could he ask for? When life became a dream and dreams started to weave a new beautiful reality, to live the same, he grew short of life. My parents were travelling somewhere when fate took them from us. The family was informed that neither my father nor my mother had survived.

How would you tell the children that they would never see their parents again? Or, were they all alone now? Kids don't understand death, but they can feel the absence and that's what I and my elder sister felt. However, our paternal family was trying to remain strong for us and were supportive too. However, they were not our parents. My paternal uncle and my grandmother raised both of us and remained with us almost at every step, yet their love and affection were never enough to curb the feeling of being lost and alone. But then there he was! A doctor to my ailing emotions. Sometimes, what love breaks, only friendship can heal. Niaz, who was Neza to me, was my companion in my loneliness. He was my best pal! A comfort in my discomfort. We would talk and play and then play more and more. At least for some time, I was able to smile, laugh, and live a little too when he was around.

I never went to school. It is not like that my family didn't want me to pursue my education further. We were well settled, so going to school and then getting a job, was never really a plan. The family had a business left by my father and was then being run by my uncle. It was something which I was supposed to do too when I grew up, so no stress was given to my schooling. Moreover, in those times, getting education was not as important as it is today. Besides, my father's death brought a huge financial loss too. He was the only one who was handling everything and made it run smoothly. After his death, the business had lost its soul.

It had been tough on all of us. The graph of the business, which had hit a new peak under my father's guidance, had now started declining, and so was the graph of love at home. My paternal uncle's wife was not very fond of me. Now when the responsibilities of me and my sister fell upon everyone in the family, a change in her attitude could be seen. I longed for a mother, but she remained my aunt. Thus, we never got along.

Nonetheless, the hands the world refused to hold, were held by God and he never let me fall again. At the age of 20, I got married to a girl from Okara whose father, Sardar Ram Singh was a big landlord there. She changed my life. The support and love, I always longed for, she filled that void. She had been sensitive towards me and very understanding. Her constant support helped me get through everything, always.

Since I started working at a very young age, so I had visited various areas of the British Punjab. I worked hard to establish myself in a position where I didn't have to depend upon anyone anymore. My wife was also finding it difficult to get tuned with my paternal family. Therefore, we were already thinking about getting out of that place and starting a new life somewhere else. I started a flour mill in Eastern side of Punjab, which now falls in India, so I had started living there while my wife stayed back in Lahore with my family. I used to visit home once in a month.

Already stuck in the family feuds for such a long time, there came a new feud that tore the whole country apart. In March 1947, all the harmony and peace ever known was washed away in the recent rains, which showered blood and brought tears. Disturbing violent occurrences started to take place which knew no calm and were not being stopped. Due to all this, I was concerned about the safety of my wife; neither the family nor circumstances around then, were favourable anymore. I decided to go back and take her with me. We didn't pack everything but only a few things and left Lahore, thinking to return once the conditions would become liveable again. But nothing was going to return back to normal and what was becoming normal was not normal at all. The violent occurrences, killings, and abductions were hitting a new number every day. We were lucky to get out of Lahore in time. But, we could never go back.

Later that year, my father-in-law brought our rest of the household goods to us. We also got to know that many of the members of my paternal family made it to India, but some didn't. I didn't get in touch with any of them later. Afterwards, we came to Ludhiana where my elder sister Kaushalya was living with her in-laws, in the hope of starting things over for the better. Though it was not easy, and many difficulties awaited us yet, I had faith.

I could not get any claim for our lands back home as they were in my paternal uncle's name, so I had to start over from scratch. I learned the work of tailoring and later, of repairing watches too. Soon, I opened up a watch repairing shop which helped me save some amount to invest in the business of hosiery. In the field of hosiery, it is not easy to set foot for many reasons. One of the dominating reasons, the big fish in the industries used to eat up the smaller ones so that no one later becomes their competition. I was determined to make the mare go, so I didn't lose hope. I have had great communication skills, which helped me build a good network. I became the contractor of the hosiery goods and from there, I never looked back. I used to get contracts and I would get the work done. All our financial crunches got vanished soon and things got better.

In 1948, the birth of my first son brought new happiness to my life and at that moment, I felt that I had a family of my own now. I was raised without my parents, so I knew how exactly their absence felt like. I wanted to give everything to my child and I wanted him to feel that I would be there with him at every step of his life. Soon, other little members joined the family and I became the father of four sons but, my fourth son passed away at the age of five due to fever. His death was really hard to bear for us all. But God blessed us with a daughter after that and I felt our family was complete now. One of my sons got settled in Glasgow, Scotland and in 1986, I moved there with my wife. And since then, I didn't have to work anymore and have only enjoyed life with my caring son who loves his parents very much.

I am living in Glasgow, with Lahore in my heart which was the best place ever during the time when the times were good. People were good and so were their intentions. The festivals, the fairs, the enthusiasm, the people, the streets with the windows open for the neighbours to talk, and when the colours were vibrant, united to form a beautiful rainbow; not divided. That was Lahore, which now exists in the heart of a Scottish Indian.

24

Spoils of War

MUHAMMAD HANEEF
AMRITSAR - NANKANA SAHIB

THE SPEAKING WINDOW

The reflections, in the waters of Ravi, of the tossing Sun, and the crescent Moon with glittering stars at night presented a strikingly delightful view. The hearts were as pure as the waters of Ravi, which reflected no malice but truthfulness. But the same hearts were soon divided, and so were the waters, since they knew they could not control the flow of the rivers, so they decided whose quench this water would satisfy and whose not? The bank of the Ravi where the children of the Hindus, Muslims, and Sikhs used to play together, swim together, and smile together, transformed into their own graveyard, as soon as the time itself turned into a deceiver.

People blame the then-dominating political figures and/or the Britishers for the fate the nation suffered and why wouldn't they? After a long struggle to get rid of slavery and gain a democratic future, the very first decision taken by the Authorities didn't involve the people who were the most affected by it. Neither their opinion nor their will mattered in the decision which flipped their entire life, their identity, even the name

The Speaking Window. Sandeep Dutt, Faisal Hayat, and Ritika, Oxford University Press.
© Oxford University Press India 2023. DOI: 10.1093/oso/9789391050733.003.0024

of their own nation! People had faith in their leaders who were supposed to lead them to a new way, not part their ways.

My village was near the river Ravi whose Tehsil was Ajnala, district Amritsar, where Sikhs were in majority, with a very few houses of Muslims. The people of the village had cordial relations and were co-operative and helpful by nature. The Sikhs were good with their Muslim neighbours. People used to have intimate relationships. I remember a Sikh-Khatri shopkeeper who used to call my parents, 'chacha-chachi' (paternal uncle-aunt). The whole village was like a giant family with its member having different views, beliefs, and visions yet the one thing that bound them together was the concern for each other.

I was born in a family of a farmer with three brothers and four sisters. Two of my siblings died at an early age. My father owned some cattle, which were well taken care of. They were even fed before us as my parents were of the view that the cattle too work for us, even harder than us, so it becomes our duty to feed them first and take care of them.

I can recall there was a school in the village. Our neighbours advised my father to get me admitted to that school but my father required me to work with him in the fields. I remember my mother giving us lunch packed in a bundle of cloth which we used to carry to the fields where we used to play and have lunch together with my father. I remember how my mother used to narrate her whole day to my father and he would listen to it as if it were some tales from ancient times which fascinated him as a child. We, siblings, used to play around the scarecrow, imitate it, and make faces. I don't know whether we were trying to scare off each other or the birds.

Years passed, I grew up learning the agricultural skills taught by my father along with the teachings he used to give me to make me understand the mysteries of life. A farmer understands the value of his land, he knows the hunger and starvation that comes along if the crops don't grow or get ruined because of the weather. He knows the value of his cattle which helps him in cultivating the same crops which fill hundreds and thousands of bellies. Thus, the attachment with its land and cattle comes naturally to him and leaving them, causes the same pain that comes with leaving a dear one behind.

The year 1947 came just like all the other years but with a lot more enthusiasm and a big hope. From the beginning of the year, the talks of getting freedom were growing with each passing day. The speeches of the leaders were giving hope to the people. Everybody was having dreams of the most awaited day and what one would do afterwards. There were talks about separate state, which were favoured by some and discouraged by others, but no one knew it for sure what would happen. When the partition was officially announced, there were villages like ours where no official announcement was made, so we didn't come to know about it at first. Later, we would hear about the critical condition of the big cities including Amritsar, Lahore, Rawalpindi, etc., where the count of dead in riots was hitting a bigger number every day. Amritsar was in bad shape. The whole city had been turned into a big cemetery.

If our lives weren't at stake, we would have never left the land where our ancestors lived for their whole life, and were buried. Three notorious extremists from the nearby village came to our village once; only to murder all the Muslims. When they were convinced by the people that all the Muslims of the village were leaving already, so there was no point in killing them, they agreed and returned back. This changed our decision of staying and we decided to move to Pakistan as soon as possible. We took some essentials, food, and four to five cows along. We arrived at the bank of the river as the ferries took people to the other side. We saw that only a single ferry was there on which everyone got on except my uncle and me. It was not able to carry the whole luggage which we had brought, so we both decided to stay back and wait for the boat to come back. We thought about going back once but it was too dangerous, so we stayed there only.

The fate never fails to surprise you; one way or another, things bounce back in a way that disturbs the balance of the scale of life. Somewhat same thing happened to us which we could never understand, neither then nor now. After a long wait, we were happy to see the sight of the ferry as finally, we could go to our family. As the ferryman arrived and we were about to get on the ferry, he refused to take us for no apparent reason. When all attempts to reason with him failed, I got so outraged that I was about to kill him but my uncle calmed me down and handled the situation by reminding me that he was also a Muslim brother and may be, he was afraid of what he had seen on the way or on the other side of the river. And with that, he rowed back.

I was 18, impatient and short-tempered, and at that time, all I knew was I had to see my family anyhow. It didn't matter what it took to see them, I was willing to do anything. For eight days, we remained stuck in there. Neither could we go back nor could we cross the river without a boat. Even the other ferrymen didn't want to take people to the other side as they were terrified for their own lives. After eight days, a different ferryman came and finally we began our journey and I could now think of reuniting with my family. At last, we got to see our family who was eagerly waiting for us on the other side and had not lost hope of seeing us again.

After our family got united, we roamed in many cities, in different camps before we went to Nankana Sahib, a Sikh dominant region where even after the partition, many families stayed back and did not leave. I still remember, it was the time of storms and floods. It seemed as if the man and the nature had a race of being more ferocious than the other. One was drowned in one's pride; the other was determined to drown the same pride. We had no shelter. There were showers and an alert about the possibility of floods. We decided to request the Station House Officer (S.H.O.) to provide us with some shelter temporarily till the rains stopped and the weather became fine enough to travel further. The S.H.O. was a Sikh and he helped us without further ado. We stayed there for the next week or so. It was all so exhausting, both mentally and physically. We were roaming here and there in search of a suitable place to settle down, but we had lost all hopes. Only my paternal uncle who had been courageous enough from the beginning of this journey and led us all till here, kept strong. We kept on asking people about different camps, which led us to different cities like Faisalabad and finally, we came to Chak 11, Shahkot and settled there.

By then, everyone's condition had been worsening especially, that of the cattle, which had not had enough food and were worn out and starving because of the long journey. In Chak 11, the Sikhs of the village had already migrated to India, and only the Christian families were left. Those Christian families were so selfless and helpful that the more I admire them, the less it seems. They shared everything with us. They shared their homes, their food, and their warmth. They were very empathetic towards us. We got to know that the Muslims had already plundered the village. Even its leftover cotton, which they called 'Maal-e-Ghanimat', meaning the spoils of the war, was also stolen. This terminology was used because their residents used to grow cotton which they had left in abundance when they migrated. When the looters came back, the Christians protected us and did not let any harm happen to us. They also did not let them loot the houses rather they collected everything from all empty houses and distributed them among the migrants equally. We have been in their debt ever since. They opened their doors for us when everywhere else, most of the people were shutting us out.

After that, I started doing farming but three times, my cattle could not survive for some reason and were wasted. As a result, I was forced to work as a labourer to collect enough money and buy some cattle again. After five years of the partition, I got married. I had five children but two of them died at a very young age. None of them is literate but is taught the values mentioned in the Holy Quran. The Pakistani Government also had promised us some land, out of which we got only one acre, whereas we used to have eight to nine acres back there.

Most of my life has passed now but this kaleidoscope of memories keeps flashing something back all the time in which I often find myself being lost. Although it has never been easy for me or my family, yet I have no regrets in life. If I had to choose, I would consider the life back in my village because my childhood was spent there and my ancestors have lived all their lives in that place. Moreover, women were respected more during those times as compared to nowadays, where they are objectified and exploited. No one used to stop us from exploring the world; we were free to roam at our own will, unlike the children of today. We all would share talks and food, without caring about the caste of a person. I remember my mother's delicious cuisines and her way of scolding us; also the field where we all used to play, the butterfly chase, the smell of newly blossomed flowers, and singing of the sparrows.

Here, every year, hundreds of pilgrimages visit our village as well after visiting Nankana Sahib for a reason. The village has preserved its history till date. From their houses to the school, everything is as it used to be. The school still has the foundation plate and the enrolment register, which have been the footprints left on the pages of history by its dwellers.

Our neighbours visit India very often as their family members served in the Army from Jalandhar but we never got a chance to visit even once, and now, my aging body doesn't support my will to visit even if I would get a chance.

I know I won't be buried with my ancestors as this RedCliff line stretches beyond death.

25
Daughter of Knight

ANIMA SHYAM
SYLHET - GHAZIABAD

THE SPEAKING WINDOW

The world has always been cruel and mean towards women since its dawn but once she recognizes the strength within her and wields the courage she has, she becomes ready to take charge of anything and in that case, even fear can't scare her off. Her will is enough to help her march forward and her fearless attitude is enough to protect her. Once she knows she is complete in herself, she needs no one to come and rescue her. It is then she becomes the knight to rescue those in need. Just like my mother who had to live alone for years, took care of her kids without her husband in a place where she was living in minority. She not only took care of herself but also raised her three sons and took the responsibilities of the household all by herself. It is her bravery, wisdom, and perseverance, which I believe I too have inherited by learning from her at every step since childhood.

I was born in 1936, in a village named Isha Grai, Thana Balaganj of the district Sylhet where my father had a grocery shop. Our family was also into agriculture and fisheries. We owned cattle too. We had around

The Speaking Window. Sandeep Dutt, Faisal Hayat, and Ritika, Oxford University Press.
© Oxford University Press India 2023. DOI: 10.1093/oso/9789391050733.003.0025

twenty-five to thirty cows. Apart from that, we owned an ox-cart and a boat along with many valuable possessions which we had inherited. For the fisheries, we owned two large ponds to farm fish; one was in front of our house and the other was at the back. We were one of the well-known landlords in our area and had a cordial relationship with everyone. We were seven siblings who were living under the shade of the affection and love of their parents.

The village was a natural beauty. Since boats were the main mode of transportation, it looked much more beautiful altogether. Imagine the boats rowing into the sunset and the small waves of water they made while making their way through it, these were the kind of views that captivated us on a regular basis. Especially those boats in spring carrying flowers, there is no comparison to such sights with anything in the world. There was tranquillity all around. There was a school too where I studied till class 3, but then got homeschooled till class 5 because it was far from the house. But my parents have been very cooperative and serious about our education, so they made arrangements to get me homeschooled. The village was mainly populated by Hindus, and Muslims used to live in nearby villages but that was never an obstacle in establishing relations amongst them. People were not only involved with each other because of their business purposes but also because they cared for each other in a way that in today's selfish world is difficult to understand. Like my father who had a Muslim friend named Suraaj Miyan who was more like a family member to us; so close to us.

In 1947, when the country got divided, we got to know that our area was now a part of East Pakistan (current Bangladesh) but there was no apparent haste in people to migrate. No threats or killings happened, nor were people forced by each other to leave unlike in West Pakistan. The attitude of the people in and around the village remained intact and nothing caused any disturbance in the peace we had always been so proud of. Though we decided to migrate, but the decision was a choice, not a compulsion. The interesting thing about the migration of my family is that the whole family didn't leave overnight; it took us almost thirteen years.

It all began in October 1947, when my paternal uncle first decided to leave and asked us to join him, but we didn't agree, and he left us alone. He took some money with him and moved to Hojai, Assam. Then in 1949, our family sent my brother to him so that he could continue his further education and also, would be able to help and support my uncle. After that, we sisters were sent there as well; it was the year 1952. After migrating, I resumed my studies and also tried my hand at the work of art. I tried learning embroidery, which I enjoyed doing a lot and it helped me develop my creativity. I also started learning typing. Though my parents and three brothers were still back in the village, we were not worried about their safety at all as there were no stressful situations arising during that time that could make us wonder or worry about our or their well-being.

After approximately three to four years, my father came to Assam but he was alone. My mother was very courageous. Since she didn't want to migrate till my father established himself in Assam, and risked losing our existing lands and business, so our parents decided that my mother would stay with my three brothers in the village until my father set up something in Assam to nurture the family. And therefore, she was left alone with her sons who were young and needed care. As my uncle was into tailoring in those days, so my father joined him in the same. My parents remained apart for our well-being for around three to four years which was a really long time. It had been years since we had seen her, heard her voice, and felt her hand on our head. In those four years, she took care of not only herself but also my brothers who were with her and while taking good care of the agriculture and fisheries business. And then, there came a time when my father felt that he had established something productive and could take care of everything like before so he went back to take the rest of the family. We were all really happy and eagerly waiting for them, but no one knew we had to wait a few more days due to something that had never happened before.

By the time, my father went to take my mother and brothers with him, we were the only Hindu family left in our village. Now the villagers didn't want them to move and urged them to stay there but when they saw my father didn't change his mind, they did something which no one saw coming, house arrest. My family, which now included my father, my mother, and my three younger brothers, were a captive in our own house. On the other hand, here in Assam, we had no clue of what was happening back home, but no one was worried about their unusual delay because we were thinking that something important must have come up and they would return soon. There my parents were planning their next move and thinking of a safe passage to escape which came in the form of Suraaj Mian. That man helped my family escape at midnight and they all were able to cross the border without any more problems. Before leaving, my father sold off all his lands and left his things to Suraaj Mian who paid some amount of money by asking his son who was living in London and some he arranged on his own. It was such a happy moment when we all saw our mother after so long and finally, the family got reunited. By the time I saw my mother again, I had already passed my tenth grade and I told her that I was the only female in the class of forty-one which she had been so proud of.

My paternal uncle always longed for the same house and environment which we had in Sylhet and wished to live that life again. But he was not the kind of man who just wished for things to happen; he was a man who made things happen. He painted the dream that he had for years with the colours of reality and worked hard day and night just to earn enough to buy a land in the rural part of Hojai. He recreated everything there whatsoever we had in our hometown back in East Pakistan (current Bangladesh). He got the exact same house built where we were all born, farmed fish in the same sort of ponds like we had before and worked on cultivating the same fields. It appeared as if he had got a Sylhet of his own in Assam, so we never had to miss anything.

In 1962, I got married in Guwahati and since then, I have been to many places in India with my husband because of his job before getting settled down in Ghaziabad. I have three daughters and a son. And like my mother, I have tried to tackle every situation in my life with the same wisdom and strength she always had. I have always looked up to her and have never been afraid of anything in my life. And for giving me this fearless attitude in inheritance, I will always be grateful to her.

26

Unwanted Strangers

BASHEER AHMED
AMRITSAR - SHAKARGARH
THE SPEAKING WINDOW

Time ages everything and that age has its own time to live and then to end too. The wheel of the time when turns around, it brings both the sweet and the sour memories around but which of the two we live with, is a choice, not fate. People think that the rift caused among the older folks was just a matter of a few fateful incidents which were portrayed in a wrong way to turn brothers against brothers but not everyone had witnessed that change or for the matter, lived to see it. Millions of families were shifted from one side to the other and, only a few who chose to stay back were the ones who, indeed, saw not only what changed but also the cracks which deepened with time and people who they couldn't recognize from the past.

Kaleke was one of the villages in the Amritsar district, which had a mixed population of Hindus, Sikhs, and Muslims whose families were friends with each other and were residing in peace. Everyone stood shoulder to shoulder with each other through thick and thin, especially

The Speaking Window. Sandeep Dutt, Faisal Hayat, and Ritika, Oxford University Press.
© Oxford University Press India 2023. DOI: 10.1093/oso/9789391050733.003.0026

the Sikhs. Some people are gifted with the heart that is big enough to accommodate the whole world in it and they had one too. Be it glee or gloom, glory or vanquishment, they were the first ones to extend a helping hand. There was a village in the school but my parents who were more into agriculture, didn't show much interest in sending any of their eight children; two sons and six daughters, there.

Partition was certain but what was not as certain was the direction of the concertina wire being uncoiled. There was a dilemma in every mind about which portion of the land would be a part of which side. The decision on some cities was lucid but obscurity was looming on a few like in the one we belonged to. Amritsar and Gurdaspur were one of those places where the distribution of the people on the basis of religion was difficult and complicated. There were places with only Muslims and some with only Hindus, some even had only Sikh population but then there were those too where the count of the three was close enough or almost the same, so the decision related to them was still about to come. So many families stayed back, thinking these areas would be a part of Pakistan but later, it turned out to be untrue and those cities remained part of India.

Our family was stuck in the same perplexity, so we stayed. The people of our area didn't want any Muslim family to leave, so they backed our decision of not leaving the village. Even when the circumstances were very critical around our village, they did not let any harm fall in our way. Families like ours remained in their homes during those days but not even once were we threatened or made to ponder about our decision to stay. Days passed, every new date on the calendar started bringing more and more grieving news. There came times when we found it hard to see through what was going on. This made us realize we might need to reconsider about staying back. The grief we all felt during the partition was about to become more painful with its after-effects which spared no one.

'Hey, long time no see! Where have you been!? Ammi was asking about you'. In usual days this was answered with, 'Of course, brother. Let's go!' But that day, something unusual happened. The warm welcoming question was greeted with a cold death stare and left unanswered as people walked away from the one seeking an answer. The same people who were living like brothers not so long ago, suddenly stopped talking to each other. I wonder, 'What changed everything?' Every moment we spent after the partition in the very village where I stayed for the past sixteen years of my life, was turning into an unfamiliar experience which appeared to be cold and full of an uncomforting feeling.

After the partition, when people started arriving in the villages from the other side, they did not only bring their painful journey with them but they also brought the blames engulfed with sorrow and anger within. The Sikhs and Hindus were killed by Muslims and the Muslims were killed by the Hindus and Sikhs. It was evident that the victims failed to see it was not the religion they had to blame but the sick-mindedness of those who perpetuated agony amongst people, using religion as a tool to hide their own impure intentions.

And the families like us who were families to the villagers before, became unwanted strangers whom they wanted no more there for they had sympathy for the people of their own community who suffered because of our community. Sounds unjust? Surely it was. We were not the ones who did it but we were being punished for it. Those ten months after the partition became more and more difficult with each passing day. When we decided to stay back, it was not only because of our home but also out of the love we had for each other, the kind of ambience we grew up in, for the memories we had made and the time we had cherished together. But when the sweet memories start to get replaced with sour ones, it is a signal that we should let go off what are hanging on to. So we did. No one ever asked us to migrate, neither before nor later but now, there was no reason for us to stay. The wounds were still fresh for people who had migrated from Pakistan to our village and the sight of a community that butchered their people was not helping their cause in any way. The deep hole in their hearts caused by the partition was not getting filled, but was letting the hatred get under their skin.

We were five to seven families, who after ten months of the partition, stepped out of our homes to migrate to Pakistan as there were no reasons anymore to stay back. The people we thought were ours were now of the survivors who didn't like us. One of my uncles was serving in the military at the post of a Subedar who helped us migrate in a military truck, so safety wasn't a concern. We carried no luggage with us for space was an issue. As the engine of the truck roared and our home started appearing farther and farther, all the memories of past times came rushing back to my mind. Despite the changed behaviour of the people now, it was still painful as it would have been, had we left earlier. The marks of the truck's

heavy tires on the road beneath it, seemed as faded as the unity and harmony we had once in the same place where we lived. As soon as the truck
crossed the Wagah Border, we entered a whole new country, Pakistan.

Even after so many months, the refugee camps were still running, and
we were taken to one in Lahore where we stayed for a day. People were
fed a bowl of boiled rice with beans. There were volunteers to help the
migrants. I remember them asking people where they wanted to go from
there. It was uncomfortable for people to answer that so early, as some
knew and some didn't, but no one knew if they would ever be able to find
a home anywhere anymore. Particularly a person who had to come to
Pakistan after living in India for almost a year even after the partition,
how could he answer that question? May be, they too knew it somewhere
in their hearts that people might never know the right answer to it anymore. We took a bus to Shakargarh from Lahore for our relatives lived
there, which cost us only ten to twelve annas. The people seemed the
same here, just like us yet so different. There was the same tension among
them, which was back home among us. We got to know about the rivalries as the consequences of partition and the same hate found its way in
the hearts of the people on this side of the border as well.

It was quite hard for us to make both ends meet after migration. I kept
on switching to different jobs, from general labour jobs to selling ice
cream on bicycle as well. We were not even given any claim of the land we
had before by the Authorities. In 1965, I got married. After struggling my
whole life, I finally get to relax at this age. Now, my children earn now and
take care of me. I was fortunate to go on the Hajj a few years back, which
was one of my most important wishes.

What about going back? I know my answer might be confusing to
some, given the circumstances my family had to face after the partition in
those ten months, yet here I am saying YES, I would go back if I ever had
a chance. What would I do? I would like to see my friends if anyone is still
alive. I would visit my house too. Who wouldn't wish to feel the soil of his
motherland? The Hindu and the Sikh pilgrims come to Pakistan every
year in thousands to visit their shrines. So, I believe the Muslims must
be allowed to visit there too so that they can also visit their holy places in
India. I would like to urge the government to take some steps in favour of
the refugees who wish to pay a visit back and re-live the memories they
once built there.

One could hear people saying that it was the Muslims who did it or the Hindus or Sikhs who took everything dear to us but were they really Hindus, Muslims, or Sikhs? Or rather, just human beings who got so much blinded by their pain, which resulted in bizarre thoughts leading them to believe that may be their pain would go away if they returned atrocities with atrocities! Revenge leads to nowhere but to a very un-peaceful and dark place where the guilt traps our soul and we make a hell for ourselves to dwell. We must remember only love can heal the pain, not causing more pain to others. This lesson of 'Tit for Tat' should be left for Allah to deal with, instead of taking it in our hands and ending up causing more damage to ourselves. The quest for love takes a person to every place where he thinks he can have it but where he forgets to look for it is, within himself.

I think if I die here today, I would have no regrets in my heart and I would be able to go peacefully.

27

Muslin Cloth

BASUDEV GANGOPADHYAY
DHAKA - BHOPAL

THE SPEAKING WINDOW

Standing on the left leg with the right foot crossed over the left, holding a flute in his right hand, as if balancing the whole universe while transcending his spiritual self with a peacock feather in his crown, adding colours to his persona and his beloved Radha standing beside him, Krishna seemed to relish all the sweet sound of ringing bells with the devotional songs sung for him by his devotees while accepting everyone who would come to him; such acceptance in humanity has been as rare as the sightings of a white rainbow. The priest in the Radha Madhav temple would apply tilak on the forehead of the worshipers and give them the Theertham (the holy water) with some prasad. And as a kid, the prasad was the sole reason for visiting the temple, which I believe Krishna didn't mind, either. Yet the ambience created with the sound of the conch shell, the chants of 'Hare Rama, Hare Krishna' and the Aarti (a Hindu worship ritual) would fill any soul with divinity and peace. This temple was nearby my village Khali, Bangladesh, so I used to visit it very often. The

The Speaking Window. Sandeep Dutt, Faisal Hayat, and Ritika, Oxford University Press.
© Oxford University Press India 2023. DOI: 10.1093/oso/9789391050733.003.0027

processions were organized at times with huge celebrations in the temple, which had a flair of their own.

Khali, the Arabic origin of the word, meaning eternal, adds a similar meaning to the kind of brotherhood which people shared there. Homes there were quite old with their ancestral roots as that of an old Banyan tree! I won't brag about the bond or the kind of food we used to share but what I would like to mention here is that people then were uneducated yet civil enough to accept the differences and make peace with them, unlike today where the differences are considered as a tool to either dominate or to demolish. I was the youngest of three brothers and a sister and without a doubt, the most loved one too. Being the youngest in the family has its own benefits, where everyone tries to dominate you, there everyone tries to protect too, cares a lot, and the love received is beyond what one can ever get. All the men in the house were Government employees. My father was an employee in court. One of the brothers was serving in Army and the other in the Railways. I, on the other hand, was a student and sometimes helped my mother with her household work. Our little family meant the world to my mother. She used to take care of the little things which were important to us. She was kind, empathetic, and very simple yet beautiful in her own way. I was a student at the Bengal Institution, Sadarghat in Dhaka. And friendship made my paradise even more beautiful. Asarudin Ahmed was the name behind that. Ahmed, the name of one of the prophets and Vasudev, one of the many names of Krishna, sound divine. Maybe not that divine, but our friendship was pious to us. He was my best friend, close to my family, my siblings liked him, my mother was fond of him, and he was one of the greatest human beings I have ever met. We used to play together, study together, and at times fought too but knew one or the other would always come back. The years passed, and we grew up, nothing changed but our age, and the rest got older but sweeter.

The news of my father's death in 1946 hit our family like a storm. Everyone was shattered. It is strange how a person just leaves one day, with a room full of memories for you to cry and smile about. In those tough times too, the people in our neighbourhood never made us feel alone and nor did Ahmed. He was there in my grief. I was studying in seventh standard then. It was the time to stay strong. Who could have mustered that much of strength but we all did somehow? My brothers took charge and became the pillars they were supposed to be and handled the situation. But, another news came in 1947, which broke not just one family but the whole country. It might sound a bit strange after all that has been heard, said, seen, and read about the partition but it changed nothing for us. People were the same, their relationships with each other were the same, and so was their attitude; nothing changed. What we found terrifying was the effect of it on the rest of the country. There were news about the genocide, people butchering other people, the Hindu–Muslim conflict, the train massacres, and much more but on our side, by God's grace, everything was not that insane! Since my brothers were serving the government in their respective fields, they were posted in different places in India. Hence, they had to leave. My brother, who was in Army, got posted in Pathankot and the one in the Railways was transferred to Madhuban, Bihar. As I was in my matriculation, we decided to stay for one more year for my studies to be completed. Thus, I was left with my mother and sister. But they didn't have to worry about us when they had to go, nor were we worried about living there in their absence. It was all due to the ambience, which remained peaceful, and didn't force the families like us to leave. Though we knew it was now East Pakistan, a different nation, with different leaders, but we still had the same people whom we had known for years.

Our migration journey started as soon as I passed my matriculation. So, from Dhaka, we went to Narayanganj by train and from there, we boarded a ship to Goalanda. Later we took a train again to Kolkata and reached Sealdah. People travelling in trains or ships were not having any fear on their faces. No threats or dangers were encountered on the way. Our journey from East Pakistan (current Bangladesh) to India was quite peaceful just like the days spent there.

Nevertheless, it was impossible for us to live with any of our brothers as both were working in far-flung places and we were new migrants, so it was decided to stay in West Bengal, with the people who shared our tongue, nature, culture, and tradition. It was easier that way. We settled down in Chandannagar, West Bengal. We got some money and property from the government, which aided us a lot. I resumed my education in the science stream and started my college life. I was determined to make my family proud and do something good in my life like my brothers, and I came across that opportunity one day. A newspaper published about a job opening in the Railways, in GIP (Great Indian Peninsula, prede-cessor of the Central Railway) in Bombay with an additional benefit of accommodation. So, without any delay, I went for that opportunity and was lucky enough to bag it too. From 11 November 1950 to 31 May 1988, thirty-seven years and seven months to be precise, I served in the Indian Railways.

It had been a great journey throughout. My job gave me a chance to explore the country. I got to travel a lot, saw stunning places, relished the beautiful sceneries of the nature and sometimes, great views in the sky. I finally got settled down in Bhopal, Madhya Pradesh where I got married on 4 December 1959 and fathered four beautiful children; three sons and a daughter who have now made me a proud grandpa! I am happy with all the joys and wonders, life has blessed me with. It's been really great so far and will be in the coming days too.

As far as the question arises of revisiting my birthplace, I did that once after the migration with my mother. The same people welcomed us with arms wide open, and a smile on their faces; nothing changed in their hearts or in their love for us. Like the Muslin cloth, which has been the speciality of Bengal forever, a ten-yard piece of cloth can fit into a small box; similarly, we all have been fitted into a similar box, packed in nicely with something beyond description and understanding, yet in existence. We never thought we ever had to leave our home, after all, who would have ever? And, why would anyone? When one's forefathers had been living in the same place for generations, the place becomes a heritage in itself, holding up the endless ties of generations that are gone and the gen-erations which are yet to come. But I can say one thing that we all were very fortunate that no one on the east side had to go through what West region had to suffer. We did have to migrate but didn't have to write our stories in blood.

With all the experience I have now, all I can suggest to the youth is that Politics is not something they need to get into. If they really want to serve the country, there are many other ways to bring the changes; but pol-itics. The politicians today only are concerned about meeting their own agenda, which can benefit them only. If change has to be brought, all one needs to keep a check on is one's own deeds, one's own thoughts, and one's own words. Just be a good human being; today's world lacks them.

28
Forgotten Bridge

CHAUDHARY SULTAN AHMED
KATHUA - MIRPUR

THE SPEAKING WINDOW

For four long devoted decades, serving in the public sector as a civil engineer, I have seen development at a pace barely anticipated by anyone ever before. Designing, building, and creating is all I have ever known, but no engineer neither in India nor Pakistan could come up with a design to map a bridge between these two nations. The nations which no longer know why but somehow know how they need to treat each other. I can only wish for a magic wand that I could use to make that rainbow bridge with all the goodness of the people who still miss each other on both sides, like I miss my home in Jammu.

An unmetalled road made its way from Jammu, in the district of Kathua, to our village; I cannot remember the name of it but it was populated by Muslims. Although our village was divided on the basis of casteism as the lower and upper-class Muslims lived on the different sides of the village, people cared for each other and were not interested in the communal hate which was consuming the rest of the country at the time

The Speaking Window. Sandeep Dutt, Faisal Hayat, and Ritika, Oxford University Press.
© Oxford University Press India 2023. DOI: 10.1093/oso/9789391050733.003.0028

of partition. I come from a politically sound family, my father Chaudhary Shahab-Ud-Din was a member of the Kashmir Assembly and had really intimate relations with Mushtaq Ahmed Gurmani who was a much-reputed politician of his time, which also means, I belonged to the upper-class section of the society. The neighbouring villages, which were at a distance of 2–3 km from our village, were dominated by a huge number of non-Muslims, but it was never viewed as a problem in our cordial relationships. In fact, my father had really close non-Muslim friends and so did my brother. We were three brothers and three sisters. I studied in the Government Primary school of Jasmirgarh, which was the tehsil for our village and then later in its secondary branch.

When the partition was announced, I can recollect that I was in 7th grade and thirteen years old. The ugly truth of partition, mounting hatred causing genocide and the pure blind riots, was not unknown to us. We got news of brutal killings from Lahore, Amritsar and the rest of the country. Extremists would gather at night in a big number, their voices could be heard at a distance raising unethical slogans and every night, one or the other villages close to ours, would become their target.

Our village was not an easy target for two reasons: first, it was on the main route from where people were migrating from Jhelum, Gujrat and Attock who used to go to Pathankot which made it crowded at the time and second, we had effective safeguard strategies which were protecting us from extremists, but we knew, those won't help in the longer run and attacks would follow sooner or later. One day we feared the attack, so we decided to migrate, joining the caravan, as that of the refugees who passed by our village. We took some amount of food, but not much luggage with us and buried the valuables in the house in a hope to get them back when everything would be back to normal. The border of Pakistan was only four miles away from our village but neither the path nor the villages on the borders were safe. The villages on the border were in a merciless condition. No one liked the idea of passing through them, for they were a treat to the blood-thirsty wolves who used to attack at night and leave the villages in flames. Therefore, to stay away from those villages and to reach Pakistan safely, we followed a route that was about 15–20 km long and it took us a whole night to cross it on foot.

By the first light of the following day, we found ourselves in a village, Chak Bela, which was on the border of Pakistan from where we left soon, being very much aware of the dangers we could get into if we stayed there any longer. Since we had a few relatives in Sagraan, we went there. One of the closest friends of my father, Ram Singh's house was in Sagraan, so we stayed in his house. Ram Singh and my father had a pre-arrangement in place in the situation if we were forced to migrate. It was decided that they would live in each other's house. We would live at his house in Pakistan and he could live at our house in India. Later on, he also migrated to India but didn't go to our house in Jammu and moved to somewhere else. He helped us a lot. Not only did he shelter us in our tough times but he remained a big support too.

The government gave us two hundred acres of agricultural land and some property in Daska, Sialkot. This newly formed nation had all sorts of challenges in the beginning, which ranged from handling the inflow of immigrants and establishing itself from the very base of a foundation. I didn't go to school in the first three to four months after the partition as there was no school for us to study at in Daska but later, I was sent to a school in the town, Sakrangian named Ghulaam Deen Islamiya High School. Afterwards, I continued my education at Murray College, Sialkot to get a degree in civil engineering. My elder brother who was working as a banker, suggested to my father to get me admitted in the respective field as one of our neighbours was in the same field and earned handsomely. Hence, I landed up in to the same course, which I went on to pass with flying colours. Even after the partition, my father didn't lose his connections with Mushtaq Ahmed Gurmani, Ram Singh, and Singh Dial. All of them, till the very end, were of the view that everything would be fine and believed Indo-Pak disputes were of temporary nature. They had a wish to go back to their respective homes, the wish they took to their graves along with them. My father passed away in 1953. Two years after his death, I got married and did my first paid job in 1956 in Muzaffarabad where I also got a house built in the year 1968. After serving for forty years as a public servant, I was released from my duties in 1994. I am a grandfather now and have six kids. One of my sons is Colonel in the Pak Army who also served as a Controller of Defense Accounts. I have seen this country in its ups and downs. After Jinnah and Liaquat Ali Khan, the country has not seen such devotion to the nation in any other leaders till now.

'If there is heaven on Earth, it is here'. This is what it is said about Kashmir and I miss my heaven. No matter how much I wish to see that paradise again, it isn't possible anymore. Peace is the only way, there is no alternative to it and should be promoted without a doubt.

Hindu-Muslim rivalry is nothing but a mere puppet show, where puppeteers aren't peace-lovers but are the ones who have a desire to fulfil their selfish ambitions, which are certainly not going to benefit anyone. Despite the tension which persisted during the partition, there were people who put humanity first and valued it higher than the chaos caused in the name of religion. Be it all the Hindu friends of my brother, who belonged to Dogras caste back home, or a Hindu-Dogra who became the best man at my father's wedding, or the Hindu fellow who had informed us that it was unsafe to travel to Pakistan from the closest route and advised us to a take the longer one instead which could take us there safely.

I hope that the future will find someone from both sides who would not only make the bridge a reality but also be able to bring the same trust and love to live and demonstrate to the world the true meaning of friendship and coexistence.

29

Folklore Monsters

RAJKUMARI TANEJA
JHANG - DAHOD

THE SPEAKING WINDOW

Love, the strongest emotion after hatred that either binds or breaks relationships. Love is selfless when it takes the form of empathy and love is
selfish when it takes the form of apathy. Love is also considered a 'rebel'
when referred to in romantic folklore. The book of time carries countless
such references in which the true romance has met a tragic end, but the
same stories are repeated over time with different names in different eras.
The state of Punjab has its own such legends; one of them is Heer-Ranjha.
The mesmerizing love notes of the flute of Ranjha, which made an un-
matched beauty, Heer lose her heart to them, led to a tragic end with the
deaths of two romantic lovers. As the story remains to live for eternity,
people still remember their love, and to celebrate and honour their love,
a fair used to be organized at their grave. The region had romantic songs
not only to sing but offered much more than that.

The five rivers, Beas, Chenab, Jhelum, Ravi, and Sutlej used to cultivate
the land of Punjab together to make its land fertile. The soil of Punjab

The Speaking Window. Sandeep Dutt, Faisal Hayat, and Ritika, Oxford University Press.
© Oxford University Press India 2023. DOI: 10.1093/oso/9789391050733.003.0029

bore fruits of compassion and love. This love had many faces; some loved their country so much that at the age of 23, they kissed the noose and left the fire of revolution burning in the hearts of people. Some loved their pride so much that it resulted in the demise of empires. The same love had many expressions like that of valour, fraternity, and romance. Such has been the history of Punjab. A place that has experienced all forms of love to the extent that has left a mark of its own in history.

Sometimes, it becomes so hard to believe how this much of love altogether fell short to save Punjab from the hatred which tore it apart. There is a reason which doesn't let people believe in the love which existed once, and again, for the same reason, there are people like me who still believe and long for the same love. My generation grew up experiencing that love and the later generations grew up experiencing the divide; which is why, I believe, they need to know what it was like, how it felt like, so that maybe, someday, they will rekindle it once again and learn to believe in the same dream, which are memories for us.

Astana was a small, calm, and really beautiful village near the river Chenab which had a beauty of its own. A small boat rowing in the full Moon, which filled it with countless silvery drops, presented a spellbounding view and when the Sun would set off, it seemed as if it was being engulfed in the same water. Names were not considered a mirror to reflect the religion of a person there. A small place with its little joy and enough peace reflected the same tranquillity in its people who owned it.

I was born in a family of a cloth merchant and raised among three siblings who were showered with affection from my grandmother and parents. My father used to work for five to six months a year, away from home in Kalyan, Maharashtra and would stay home the rest of the time, but his earnings were enough for the family to live off the whole year. My grandmother would help my mother sometimes and at other times, she would chant the name of God. Her stories would take us to the times of Kings and Queens, the supernatural world of magic, and the era of Gods. My mother would remain busy with her household chores, but she would make some time for us too. She would feed us with sumptuous dishes. She would take me in her lap, oil my hair, make braids, and dress me nicely. My father would play with us, scold us, but love us a lot too. I remember him taking us to a fair near Chenab River, which was organized every year in Jhang at the tomb of the greatest love icons of our history Heer-Ranjha.

I was studying in the second standard at that time. I had many friends and out of all, I miss Kisna the most. She was older than me. Whereas I studied only Hindi, she knew Gurmukhi too. We would play together, eat together, and study together. There was a garden of musk melon somewhere near where she suggested us to go and relish the sweet fruits, so we went there. Even she had no idea how far the boundaries of the garden spread. We kept walking deeper and further in it till we reached a dam from where the boundary of the village Berawali started. My maternal family used to live there then. We crossed that dam but there was a river on the way which we were unable to cross, so we decided to return. We had gone really far but there was no fear in us. We were laughing at our folly and returned after the sunset. We were walking in the dark fearlessly, laughing at our long careless walk and thinking how far we went. In those days, there were no street lights or electricity like today, yet the safety was not a concern for the people were so good at heart, unlike today where walking alone in light too is not safe anymore. May be there was light in that darkness then, which used to be a guide to us but there is darkness in the light now, which has led people astray.

The announcement of partition brought unpleasant news for families like ours. It shattered every family which was forced by the circumstances to leave their homes and set path to an unknown place if they desired to live. I remember some people came to our house and advised our family to leave as soon as possible. Some unknown danger was about to approach us and was getting nearer and nearer every passing moment. There were questions in every mind. 'Why should we go; leaving our homes, lands, and lives here?', 'We had everything here, everything which we could ever need. Then why couldn't we stay?' And most importantly, 'Where would we go?' The family did not give much time to entertain these thoughts and soon, I could see us all leaving. My mother was crying while packing all the stuff we could need, mostly some clothes and food. My grandmother, who had spent her whole life there, was looking at the walls as if her old eyes were trying to absorb every minute detail they could for the last time. My father was consoling and helping my mother.

Families like ours sensed the upcoming danger which was upon us already. We all rushed to the Gurudwara nearby to take shelter. There was a strange heaviness in the air. It was all very tense and scary. I never knew fear before but that day, I could feel it and sense it in everyone present there. To a nine-year-old kid, it was all very disturbing. I remember seeing a few women jumping into the wells. I can't forget that scenario. Those women were crying and shouting loudly. The splash of water could be heard and then the struggle between life and death as their bodies drowned within a few minutes. I could not understand then why we had to leave or why those women jumped into the well to kill themselves. It seemed like all the monsters from the stories I had ever heard, had come to life.

From the Gurudwara, we all went to the mosque and stayed there. Then we came to 'Jhang Maghiana' and then to 'Heer Mai' shrine and spent two nights there. People of that region helped us with food. After those two days, people finally had a sigh of relief on seeing the soldiers marching towards them since we had a sense of safety which did not last for long either. We were taken to the Jhang station under the protection of the army. A goods train arrived there which was supposed to carry coal rather was filled with humans. We all boarded the train. People were sitting even on the buckle joints of the train. The whole journey was dangerous. The route taken by the train was filled with terrifying scenes. All I remember is dead bodies on both sides of the track, cladded in blood, with a lot of scary scars on them. My mother covered my eyes. She asked us to look away, but the sight had already scarred our minds for life, leaving a lonely, scary feeling in us. It was hard to recognize which of those bodies were of Hindus and which of them were of Muslims but they lay rotting on the ground, questioning humanity and brotherhood, which seemed to be the things of the past now.

During the journey, we came across many problems; lack of water was one of them, which made it much more difficult. People were thirsty and were crying for a few drops of it. One of the stations had a pond nearby but its water was not clean, yet a person went there with his earthen pot to fetch some. The pond was filled with corpses, their blood and flesh were mixed in it, yet he filled his pot with the same water. No one agreed to have even a drop from it but whenever someone could not control one's quench for water any longer, they would take a few sips from his earthen pot. It is only the people who travelled on that train who knew how they had borne those death-like situations. Our siblings were clinging to our parents who were not wearing a strong face anymore. I had never seen them so scared and helpless before. When our train entered the borders of India, there was hope that we were not going to end up as one of the corpses we had seen on our way. Finally, the train halted at Delhi railway station and we all felt relieved.

The Government of India had made good arrangements in Delhi for the refugees. That August of 1947 had a merciless heat as if it was also burning in hate. The scorching Sun was testing the tolerance of the people and it was unbearable during that time. In the camps, we were served a glass of lassi to drink with food and clothes too. We stayed in the camp for a couple of days and then boarded a train to Jaipur. To make it convenient for the people to travel in those tough times, the journey through trains was made free by the authorities.

In Jaipur, the refugee camp was set up at its railway station itself. It was filled with so many people. There were volunteers who were helping them with different things. We were served food twice a day. And sometimes, wealthy people would come to distribute sweets and clothes to us. This is what we got when we came to Hindustan. People were sympathetic and were willing to help refugees. They were talking about their past life, their homes, and their land or the cattle they had there but they forgot to talk about the kind of ambience they had. It was as if they had simply forgotten that the love existed among them. It seemed they had accepted the hate which now ruled everything but after what they had endured, can you blame them?

After coming here, my father started working in various jobs and finally started a business in the clothing sector, which became our livelihood for the next seven years. After all those years, we shifted to Dahod, Gujarat. I studied till seventh standard in Jaipur but didn't resume my education as after shifting to Gujarat and got married. Over the time, we were able to overcome those harsh memories and some new, both bitter and sweet were formed but that's how life is. I have lived my whole life with satisfaction, but I still miss my home. As a kid, I never understood what was India or Pakistan; for me, my life and my world were confined to my village, which was my only known home and it was also taken away from me. My village was my only country and my home, which I had to leave.

After all this, I wish both the countries prosperity and hope they grow together. We must remember that it is the same people who live on this side and that side of the border. Before being a Hindu or a Muslim, we are humans and we must live like one. Any bloodshed on either side of the border only destroys a human life that must be valued, not annihilated. The corpses I saw on the way to India, whether of Hindus or Muslims, had shed the same blood. The real understanding of the religion follows the way of humanity, not violence. Killing people in the name of God to conceal our inner hatred for each other is no way to establish peace when we create a burning hell, here on earth.

30
Blood Betrayal

RAFIQUE AHMED
AJMER - LAHORE

THE SPEAKING WINDOW

The city where I was born has many stories of its own to tell. From the days when it was better known as Ajayameru; Ajmer has seen everything. Even through its downfall, it gracefully maintained its royalty and that of royal houses inhibited by it. It had been under the reign of Hindu and Muslim rulers who tried to rewrite their fate and that of the city. It has witnessed the rise and fall of many empires and houses but the city itself has withstood the tests of time and narrates the tales of its victories and defeats, which are written on the walls of its palaces and forts.

However, this is not the only part of the city I remember, there is one more integral part of it that has been an integral part of my life, too. Under the tranquillity and sanctity of Ajmer Sharif where millions of pilgrims visit the holy shrine of Khwaja Moinuddin Chisti to pay their homage every year in the annual fair held in the memory of the Saint. Every time it happened, the city too bathed in its serenity. People who desire for anything come and tie a Niya (thread) on the pole and wish for what they

The Speaking Window. Sandeep Dutt, Faisal Hayat, and Ritika, Oxford University Press.
© Oxford University Press India 2023. DOI: 10.1093/oso/9789391050733.003.0030

desire with all the faith in the heart and believe it will come true but what I have not seen is anyone tying a thread for the well-being of the city itself; may be, it could have prevented it from being torn into pieces.

My family resided near the main gate of Ajmer Sharif. I grew up with three brothers and two sisters, hearing the stories of Akbar, Prithvi Raj Chauhan, and their respective battles. My father used to sell milk and owned cattle too. My brothers used to help my father in taking care of the cattle. I learnt about Allah at the Madrassa with all the lessons of humanity which came along and played with my friends in the verandah of the mosque. I used to see people coming for Namaz at the Dargah. I saw sad faces, happy faces, some faces shining with hope, and some hopeless but they all used to come down there, sit together, eat together, and be together. Life was not as complicated as it is now, nor as fast-paced, which can leave one with no time to enjoy the little things in life. In the city, there was a school, but I never went there. The people never felt any discrimination for what they believed in or whom they worshipped. There was freedom to preach whomsoever one follows.

The partition happened officially in 1947 but it was seeded in the minds of the people and its sapling was watered with their blind faith much before that. The country had been divided later but the people had already started experiencing the changes in the behaviour of the others around. It was not that the differences among people never existed, they did but they never mattered but now the differences were used to create more divide, and all this was given a fillip politically now. The deep seeded feeling of being different from each other was weaponized into fear, so much so that it erupted like a volcano in 1947 which left everything around it in flames and ashes.

I was five years old at that time. The conditions were becoming critical and the safety of one's life had started becoming a matter of serious concern. The genocide was hitting higher numbers every day. When nothing seemed to get any better, we decided to leave. We were airlifted to Pakistan. That was the most unique thing about our journey, which made it the safest too. While flying, when I looked downwards, I could not see where the line was drawn so that I could understand what was different on the other side but to my amazement, everything seemed the same, except for a different intolerant perspective. I hardly remember where we boarded it, but I do remember the destination, Lahore. Another city with youth and beauty of its own and similar to Ajmer, it too had a royal heritage.

Nonetheless, the coming years had nothing but struggle waiting for us. We worked as labours for years till we were able to collect enough amount to buy some cattle in order to start a dairy business here. It took off and things were going smooth till that one big loss which we incurred and later could not recover from. My siblings left me and did not share my burden; they abandoned me instead and finally, I was left homeless to wander in the streets like a beggar. My loss was not financial only. Before that, I got married when I was 40. She passed away while childbirth and my child too could not survive long afterwards. I had also lost my parents too.

I tried finding work and ended up working as a garbage picker. So, this is what I do now all day just to earn enough to buy myself some food. It is not easy at all, but begging is something I would never do, and I pray to God, never to put me in such a situation. I am losing my strength every day, which puts me in a state of worry about how long I'd be able to work on my own.

After living and still stuck in the same miserable life, if I could change something, then it would be just one thing: time. I wish I had a winding key to it so that I could go back to my childhood. To the time when I was with my family, which was a loving and caring one, when my siblings loved me and genuinely cared about me, when I was back home, in India in the same mosque where I learnt all the lessons of humanity which other people forgot to learn and follow. To the time, when neither the country nor my family was divided.

31

Time Tailor

SURINDER SINGH
RAWALPINDI - PATIALA

THE SPEAKING WINDOW

The austerity and serenity of my village were spell-binding. The cool breeze carrying the bliss of rejuvenating petrichor rejoiced every soul. There used to be small hills around, with the trees which used to bear the sweet fruit called, Illachi Ber (the Indian Jujube) on one side of the hills and the vines of sweet melons on the other. I can still recall the sweetness of those fruits. I remember my grandmother reciting a shabad (a hymn), rhyming it with the sound of the spinning wheel, which she used to spin every day in the veranda of our house. *'Prem wali gali vichon koi koi langda, Taru Singh bhai hove, khopari luhayi hove, naam daan mangda. Baba Deep Singh Shaheed hove, sajji kali sees hove, khanda hove hath vich, naam daan mangda. Prem wali gali vichhon koi-koi langda ... '* Not to forget those Katlamme (Lahori snack) which Bashir and I used to savour every time there was a fair at Panja Sahib Gurudwara, whether on account of Baisakhi or Pooranmasi. Such were the joys of my village, Gheel where I was born in 1923.

The Speaking Window. Sandeep Dutt, Faisal Hayat, and Ritika, Oxford University Press.
© Oxford University Press India 2023. DOI: 10.1093/oso/9789391050733.003.0031

Where Gheel inculcated its ethnicity in me, there 'Pindi', which is a name given to Rawalpindi by its inhabitants, imparted me with the formal education; firstly, at Singh Sabha Primary school and Khalsa High School in Rawalpindi and then, at Khalsa College, Lahore. I was raised in a wealthy family. We had a big vineyard, a couple of grocery shops in Mohanpura and a Tonga, which was very dear to my father. It was so beautifully decorated that even the Britishers used to stare in awe and envy it when my father used to take us on the Tonga rides, on the Mall road.

I grew up in a cordial and warm Pindi, where the same enthusiasm could be seen for Eid and Diwali. I remember the grand scaled Dussehra festival organized at Pindi's Dussehra ground. The Lohri celebrations, was not just about the bonfire that provided warmth but the union of different communities, which was the harbinger of the togetherness. It was a well-known custom of visiting homes to collect sweets which not only by the children but also was loved by the teens too. It seems sorrowful to see how things had turned out after the partition where the same people became so detached from the sufferings and pains of the others.

It was early 1947 when the killings in the night had become quotidian; a call for help reached out to our family. Next to our street, there lived Sai Das, a very influential and wealthy man, who had three daughters. He owned many quarters in our street from which he earned a good amount of rent. The family had huge gardens and a big ancestral fortune. When the family feared the massacre that night then, one of the daughters sent a servant with a message for my mother, which was a help call. Our family suggested them to come to our house for spending the night, but they convinced us all to come and stay with them, saying they had sufficient space to accommodate the entire family, enough food supply to last for months, along with the ammunition which was much needed that time. So, we all decided to go there, leaving our house, which was just across the street but only to be lost in the dust of time. When the riots broke out and the drains were running blood, we could never get back home nor got a chance to see our house again. The attacks happened and we all got locked up in their place for days. Our Muslim neighbours were really nice and never ever thought of harming us. In fact, in those tough times, too, they helped us in all the ways they could.

But when we thought we wouldn't survive, there came help right out of the blue. Khan Abdul Gaffar Khan, more commonly known as the

Frontier Gandhi, had formed an army of his own at the time of need. He had sent a troop of his own to rescue us. We were safely taken to the railway workshop where we were sheltered in a rail coach and asked not to go outside till the army showed up. They took all our weapons but left us some food which was not enough. It was so painful to see the helplessness of the mothers who were forced to quench the thirst of their children with their urine. It was like living in a nightmare. The army came after almost five or six days and took us to Gurudwara Singh Sabha, Raja Bazar. There was a refugee camp where the ill-fated people like us were aided. Unarmed and terrified, we decided to make us some weapons so if the time comes, we would be able to protect ourselves. There were a few blacksmiths among us who made us the spears and then there were those who taught us to make bombs, which we used to scare off the attackers.

Not every door was shut. One day, the Maharaja of Patiala, Yadavindra Singh announced on the radio that the Royals were willing to help all those who sought shelter and he/she would be taken care of. This news brought us some relief and to verify the things, my elder brother and uncle decided to go to Patiala to see the arrangements all by themselves. The temple of God, which used to accommodate the faith and beliefs once, was now accommodating fear and sorrow. Gurudwara Fatehgarh Sahib and Gurudwara Dukh Niwaran Sahib, where the camps were set up, were too crowded already. There was this third camp to be set up soon, so they both came back and gathered all the family members and left for Patiala in March 1947. We left Pakistan via the Frontier Mail, which used to run from Peshawar to Kolkata. We took that train from Rawalpindi. We left all our wealth behind us and took along three pairs of clothes only, thinking when all of it would be over, we would come back, and everything would be normal soon but what we didn't realize was that every ascending mile was taking us away from home, our people and our land. On reaching Rajpura, a military truck took us to another refugee camp which was in the Dera Baba Jassa Singh. The tents were arranged in symmetry on each of the sides and the path was left in the middle. Castes didn't matter there anymore; what mattered was the fate of all those people who were now bound together with pain. It was their luck or misfortune that brought them together, but there they were, the survivors.

I would still consider us all lucky enough that we all arrived here in the early days of the partition that we didn't have to bear the pain of massacre, which has, without a doubt, left people with the scars of painful memories, but yes, we did see the trains carrying the dead running on both sides of the border.

The time there was not getting easier for anyone. On the very first night, an infant daughter of my elder sister died of a snake bite. And later, the crisis arose due to floods during the monsoon. In this ordeal, I had already lost three of my siblings, including two sisters and a brother. But, like every cloud has a silver lining, that time too had passed for good.

Time moved on and we all tried to build our lives from scratch. We started working in Patiala where I started selling milk on a bicycle and then, vegetables in front of the Lahori Gate of Patiala. I always wanted to wear a Churidar Pajama, so I went to a tailor to learn to make it but I liked the work so much that I ended up learning everything about tailoring. Then, someone helped me getting a shop in the main municipal market of Patiala where I started my tailoring business. It was the main road of Patiala, so many officers, ministers, and even the members of the Royal family got their clothes stitched by me. Now, as both my children are government officers so, last year, in 2016, I closed the shop, after running it until the age of 93. Now, I just rest at home, though I am absolutely fine, having all teeth, strong vision of eyes and still can run faster than you!. Life … it has given me many things to remember and not everything is bad, just like that incident which I still find amusing.

Walking down the road in the dusk, with great difficulty, almost about to cry and carrying a lamb on the shoulders, and a basket of six eggs with me, I saw a man coming on the bicycle, 'Bhai, zaraa aage tak chorhdo' (Please, drop me off to a fewer miles)—to which he agreed at first but on realizing the weight on the back of his carrier, which was not only mine but of the lamb too, he asked me to get off at once. And I had to plead him for dropping me off at least halfway through my original journey. This happened when I had roamed in many villages near Patiala, with the idea of buying eggs from villages and re-selling them in the city. The day was rough as I could just find a few eggs, so I bought a lamb for Diwali, thinking I had come so far so I must take something back but I didn't know it was habitual of walking in a herd. No matter how hard I dragged him, it just didn't move. So, I had to carry him on my shoulders and very soon, my feet gave up. I was far away from home. Trust me, though I am laughing right now while remembering that incident but when it was happening, I was just about to cry and curse the moment when I decided to buy it for a feast. Thankfully, the cyclist had pity on me and dropped me at Lahori Gate, Patiala and from there, I reached home.

Pindi was home to me. And unlike many people, I had been fortunate to get a chance to visit it not once but three to four times after the partition. In 1949, when I went there for the first time, it was to meet my best friend, Bashir, with my mother and wife on a tonga. When I arrived near his home, I saw some children playing there and asked them about his home despite knowing his address as he used to live next door. To my amazement, after knowing that we came from India to visit him and used to live here only, they took us to their home where they served us soft drink and fed us a variety of dishes. The warmth, they showed towards us, was so overwhelming that I could not control my tears. After that warm welcome, we went to my friend's home where we were welcomed with the same affection. I got so much love and respect that it cannot be expressed in words. People over there didn't change. The pain of separation was same on both sides.

Then in 1989, I went there again to visit the holy shrine Shri Panja Sahib, which was a ten-day tour, with a group of ninety people on account of Baisakhi. We also visited Maharaja Ranjit Singh's fort in Lahore along with, Nankana Sahib and Dehra Sahib. We also went to Nanda Mandi, which was famous for selling Japanese fabric called buski that I bought for Rs. 10. Since not many goods could be taken across the border, so we sewed it in the quilt to take it back home.

I have visited my home every time I visited Pakistan and still, I would like to go there again. It is so disappointing that the current generation would never know the bond that Bashir and I share. 'Hun lokan ch oh pyar nahi reha ... ' (That kind of love in people, now exists no more.) I wish people on both sides, could understand what they had lost and still have been losing. This hatred that is deeply seeded in us is not ours! Neither created nor chosen by us. A line stretched across the borders may have the power to separate nations and nationalities, but it is not powerful enough to separate the hearts.

32

Last Comfort

HAJI SABIR ALI
KARNAL - SILANWALI

THE SPEAKING WINDOW

The soothing sound of Azaan in all that tranquillity, around all the lush green trees, would even make a cool breeze slow down in a moment with the aura that it was blessed with at that time. All the residents of the village Kaithal, district Karnal would wake up to such mornings every day, and found it equally mesmerizing as any follower of Islam would, despite their religious beliefs. I used to see other children going to school in the morning with their bags carried on their backs, a smile on their faces after getting a lunchbox and a kiss from their mothers. They would see their mothers running behind them to make them drink a glass of milk. I never went to school, but I am sure the lessons taught to the toddlers didn't stress on identifying the letters of discrimination.

Our village had Muslims in majority, predominately hailing from Dogra and Rajpoot caste, with some houses of Hindus who used to visit the neighbouring village's temple for worship as the village had no Hindu temple of its own Nowadays, where some people get offended at

The Speaking Window. Sandeep Dutt, Faisal Hayat, and Ritika, Oxford University Press.
© Oxford University Press India 2023. DOI: 10.1093/oso/9789391050733.003.0032

the animal sacrifices made on Eid every year; in my era, that was never a case in our village ... ever. Neither the Hindus interfered in the rituals of Muslims nor did the Muslims question them for their beliefs. Children could be seen running in each others' houses where they were cared like their own as the love of a mother was not a slave of any differences back then.

Where today, Hindus and Muslims fight over sharing the waters of the same rivers; there our warm-hearted Hindu neighbours shared the land with us. Religion never became a problem neither for them nor for us. We used to cultivate crops together. Their family had two sons and a daughter. I remember their names too! Ratan, Mangal, and Sukhdevi, with whom, we used to play a lot. Their mother, Balari aunty, used to make sumptuous dishes for us in different seasons. She and my mother were like sisters to each other and used to exchange dishes, shared different recipes of various cuisines, along with their talks which seemed of never-ending nature! Both families owned a lot of cattle. I remember once asking my father about which ones were ours out of all the herd of cows, he smiled at me and he pointed his finger at the nearest ones first to say, 'These ones are ours'. Then he pointed far, saying, 'Can you see those ones? Those too belong to us!' And I smiled back.

I don't know how a flower that was nurtured by all became a liability to them that everybody thought it was not one's responsibility to care for it, so it started to wither. One day all the Muslim families of our neighbouring Hindu majority villages came to our 'Panches' seeking help as the extremists attacked the homes of the Muslim families there, threatened them, and killed some so they feared that their lives would end the same way. Since our village had Muslim-dominating populace, they felt safer here. The villagers welcomed them with open arms in the time of their dire need. They were sheltered and served food and it was made sure that they did not have to face any problems while staying with us, especially after what they went through. Even the Hindu families treated them as their own and helped them as much as they could. Soon, we came to know about the gravity of the matter and how real the partition was.

On the fifteenth day of the eighth calendar month of 1947, independence was announced at midnight with no shadow of doubt in it but then there was one more announcement made right before this one. A country was formed in the name of Islam so that no Muslim had to remain deprived of one's rights. Therefore, migration was a collective decision of ours. I am not sure of the exact date when we left. All I remember is, the Muslims of our village and those who came to ours seeking help agreed with us and decided to leave. All the Muslims in the village, in a moment, were migrants now. The people left almost everything behind. Farmers left their land on which they would work from dawn till dusk every day, tirelessly, along with their cattle that they raised, and took care of them like children. The adults left their homes, where they spent most of their life, seeing their kids growing up, and made it a 'home'. Children left their school, their friends, and even their smiles. People carried as much food as they could knowing they had a long way to go ahead.

Where Muslims were being slaughtered in other villages, there our Hindu neighbours were very much concerned about us. They were not happy to see us leaving and wanted us to stay back but we could not. I remember how Mangal's mother packed us a lot of food and gave my mother a warm hug with her eyes filled with tears. She took my face in her hands and kissed my forehead and asked me to be good always and take care of my mother. Their family took our luggage on their bullock cart to the railway station of Kaithal.

On arriving at the railway station, we got to know about a disturbing news. The previous train was attacked by the extremists, which carried only dead bodies after departing from the station. Some had a change of mind and decided to take the road instead but many like us, stayed there and boarded the train, thinking it might be the last chance we might have. Every passing station was bringing us a step closer to a new home and a step far from our own home but on every station, the train stopped for a few minutes, we prayed for it to leave safely. Fear could be sensed in everyone. The folds on the forehead, the desperation in the eyes, and murmuring lips, their thoughts needed no voice; they were apparent from their condition. An old lady with a rosary in her hand was constantly praying, another lady with a child wrapped in her arms and fear in her eyes was in panic, a man was consoling his family, and a child was lost in the thoughts of the game of death which he had never seen before. We were lucky that we were not attacked throughout our whole journey and we made it to Pakistan safely. We stepped out of the train and the board in front of us read, Muzaffargarh, the first city we arrived at, on reaching

Pakistan. Since there were no arrangements made for the refugees there, we moved to Silanwali.

'Why was the migration so tough?' Children ask sometimes seeming so confused, having this thought in mind that even now, people relocate in a hope of better life, but they forget that the decision to relocate is theirs now, not forced and certainly not written in a bloodbath. The real struggle began after the migration. The struggle with hunger, the struggle with people, the struggle with the life, and the struggle with people themselves. We neither got a shred of respect nor mercy from the people who were already living there. On taking even a single turnip from a field, people would mind and say, 'God knows from where this problem (referring to people) has fallen upon us'. Such was the bitterness in them for their own brothers! We neither had shelter or food, nor any hope of any sort of help. Even for claiming a land, we had to wait for two long years and we were finally given some land which was around seven acres, though it was very less than what we had back in India. After coming here, my parents wanted to impart some formal education to me, so they got me into a government primary school but in my seventh grade, they had to take me out of that school for not being able to afford my education any longer.

I even started working as a labourer, yet I could not sleep at nights, thinking about how I would feed my family the next day. What would happen to them if it never got any better? For a labourer in Pakistan, there weren't many facilities to aid their helplessness. I have gone through a lot of mental torture during those years, but I worked harder to give my family a better life, but all that hard work never paid off . . .

Now, I am a grandfather. I have three daughters and four sons. All my children are settled now. One of my sons has served in the Pak Army and is retired now. For a man like me who has worked as a labourer all his life, it was not easy to support my children. And in the times of today, where life has been so hard, earning enough even for a single person is as hard as climbing a mountain. My daughter decided to sell off her property and would live in a rental accommodation, only to support her child's education so that the younger generation doesn't have to live a life that we did. A parent does everything in one's power for the children to have a better life ahead. As my father did, I did, and now my children are doing too. But if I have any regrets, then it is all because I could not do enough for my own children so that their lives could have been better; or less tough maybe as that of now. This leaves me so sore that it doesn't let me be at peace.

Today if I close my eyes even for a moment to soothe my grieving thoughts, I find myself back in Kaithal where I was born. I picture myself being with the same people, playing with Ratan, Mangal, Sukhdevi, and their mother giving me a dish to take home to my mother and my mother ... I picture her fingers in my hair and my head in her lap, her smiling face as beautiful as the crescent Moon at Eid. I remember her reading Namaaz in the morning and evening and also, when she used to cook and would tell us the stories of her own childhood. Mother, the only comforting thought I can ever think of.

33

Memoir of Milkyway

DHAN KAUR
SIALKOT - TINSUKIA

THE SPEAKING WINDOW

From the historical Lahori gate to the majestic Gateway of India, I have seen it all. The glittering water of Dal Lake, which fascinates its visitors with its jaw-dropping serenity and scenic views, the soothing stillness, experienced in the Gurudwara Dera Sahib, Lahore and the freshness of Assamese breeze, I have felt the heart of the nation in its different rhythmic beats which extraordinarily synchronized with each other quite well. Yet this sync was distorted, among these united threads, which left them tangled forever.

I am a mother of nine—six sons and three daughters. Our family is referred to as the 'Milk King' in Tinsukia, Assam. Our dairy products are widely used in almost every nook and corner of the city. But the journey from Sialkot to Tinsukia wasn't a fairy tale. Our story was not ours to write. I could have never imagined, even in my wildest dreams to be born in an India, which was fighting for its freedom once and then to live in one, which forgot how it earned it.

The Speaking Window. Sandeep Dutt, Faisal Hayat, and Ritika, Oxford University Press.
© Oxford University Press India 2023. DOI: 10.1093/oso/9789391050733.003.0033

I was born in Muhadipur, Sialkot, in an upper-middle-class family where my father had a government job. He was a postman, so his job allowed him to be in contact with every kind of person. We had a huge family to take care of, as we were six brothers and two sisters. He used to adore me a lot. We often went on rides on his bicycle. The little treats on the way and the giggle and chatter, I remember how much he loved doing it. In those days, child marriage was a very common thing, more of a long-standing tradition abided by all. Our family was no different. So, I got married quite early. I was fourteen and a half when I took my marriage vows. My in-laws' family was an inhabitant of Lahore and they owned a shop at Lahori Gate but their ancestral home was in our neighbouring village, Kanpur. There was a custom associated with the child marriage called 'muklawa or gona ceremony', in which both families agreed to a period for which the bride could remain at her parents' home for a specific time period after marriage, which in my case was decided at one year. Even after that, mostly I used to live at my parents' home as I had a very understanding and caring mother-in-law who loved me like her own.

In 1947, situations were getting very critical in Lahore. Considering the seriousness of the situation, my in-laws sent me to my parents' house in Muhadipur. When the talks of partition started getting more serious, a meeting was called in Pindi Hiran Di, Sialkot by all the people nearby to discuss about the same. The things got out of control and in the heat of the moment, a person from our village got killed, which resulted in more raised swords and bloodshed. My brother got trapped in there. He was alone, surrounded by attackers with a least chance of survival. But he was well versed in the Sikh martial art form, Gatka, which saved his life. I was twenty years old when the partition was announced. Everybody around us was leaving their homes. This was when the fire of hatred blazed in Sialkot and our family decided to go and stay at my maternal grandmother's home, which was about two and a half miles away from our village. My father was told that relocating was not an option, he had to leave his life here and start travelling to India if he wanted to save his life, but he didn't want to till the day, he was attacked on his way back home, which made him change his mind. After staying there for a month, an official announcement was made in the village by the authorities to vacate it.

In that village, only four or five families left it immediately after the announcement, including ours. Both of my families decided to leave together. A very dear friend of my father was crying bitterly and wished if he could come with us. But a nation that was established on a religion didn't allow a Muslim to reside with a Hindu/Sikh anymore. After all, that is what was the idea behind the partition. Not a wise one, of course. A single announcement changed our land, homes, people, even our nationality, just in a fraction of second. What could a person possibly take with him then? Certainly not his house! A house takes years of struggle to build and then, turn into a home. It's not the lost land people were feeling bad for, it was the amount of memories that made it their home. And those homes were once again turned into a mere body of walls when their inhabitants were gone. We were only allowed to take our lives with us and that too, if we could.

We were around forty people in a caravan who started a long fifteen-day journey on foot to Jammu and that too without any military protection. We used to spend nights in the villages which came on the way. We were all in this together. Even those who were strangers to us treated us like family and provided us food at night wherever we stayed. We were served with tea and roti with salt. The people who travelled in groups, still managed to escape the death but the families who travelled alone, got slain. They were mostly robbed and then killed on their way. After reaching Jammu, we went to Pathankot and then to Batala where people asked us to occupy one of the homes in the nearby villages as the Muslim population which lived there had left. So, we chose to live in Gorewah, a village nearby, for it had a canal near it and the land was much fertile for farming. In all this brutality, hope for humanity was still left somewhere. People helped us in all ways they could. We were given clothes, quilts, food, and everything else we needed.

Due to so much of nuisance, it became very difficult for the authorities to maintain law and order. To add to the misery, crimes were prevailing. The villages used to get robbed at night and in the worst-case scenarios, even the lives were lost. A similar incident happened in our neighbouring village where a family was robbed, the helpless mother and daughter tried to stop the robbers but when they couldn't, they shouted and screamed as soon as the robbers fled. Our house was nearby and two of my elder brothers went there as soon as they could to help. One of my brothers got shot in his leg. And in fury, the other one ran behind them and got hold of one and wasn't letting him go. And in turn, he too got shot. On hearing the gunshots, many people gathered. They put him on a cot and tried to get him to the city, which had a hospital. He was severely injured, in severe pain, and every second was squeezing life out of him. On the way, there was a small stream where he requested some water and took his last breath there. He cheated death once, back in Muhadipur but this time, he got cheated by death. It was not easy on any of us. My father too, died shortly after we came here, and so did my mother-in-law who lived up to the age of a hundred years.

We had twenty-two acres of land in Pakistan and here we had gotten only two acres of it but we were fortunate to have a roof over our head. Some didn't get that too. We started doing farming and then my husband started selling milk on a bicycle. He used to collect milk from five villages and then sold it in surrounding areas. Later, he started selling milk in Gurdaspur where he had to travel 30 km of distance, only to reach there. He really worked hard a lot. After that, we moved to Tinsukia, Assam, and started the business of milk in which we got huge success there. All his struggles paid off. Now the people of Tinsukia, know our family as 'Doodh Waale Sardar ji'.

After all these years, even today, every day I miss my village. I can still picture all of it vividly. I dream about it every day. I see the streets of my village where my father used to take me with him, to deliver the mails. Our neighbours, the friends I had, the fort near Sialkot, and the Sikh historical museum—I miss everything.

All I can say to youngsters is that live happily! May you live long, prosperous, and meaningful life!

34
Demons of Banyan

MUHAMMAD DIN
AMRITSAR - LAHORE

THE SPEAKING WINDOW

Under the shade of a tree in a village of Amritsar, a man was standing with a mic in his hand and with an informative tone, conceiving deep grief in his voice, while addressing a huge crowd to which he broke this news which turned their world upside down and left them in disbelief. People simply refused to accept the decision. At least, this was that one thing that united them all.

My village, Mode in Amritsar, had both Muslims and non-Muslim inhabitants who lived there in harmony. They shared everything, whether it be each other's concerns, food, or chatters. The only thing they didn't share was water. There was a religious conflict related to this thus, it was not shared. Wells and ponds were divided but not the joys and griefs. So, in a way, they were all together, despite being divided.

Our family had cordial relations with Hindus and Sikhs as my mother grew up in a Sikh-majority region for which she had many Sikh friends and my father was a landlord, so he knew many people and was friends

The Speaking Window. Sandeep Dutt, Faisal Hayat, and Ritika, Oxford University Press.
© Oxford University Press India 2023. DOI: 10.1093/oso/9789391050733.003.0034

with many non-Muslims. And I was no exception as well; Joginder Singh was my childhood friend who used to visit my home often but I, on the other hand, visited him hardly twice but we never kept count of such things. To us, it was our friendship that mattered the most, so who visited whom and how many times, were not the things to be kept in a ledger. I had three brothers and a sister too. We used to play together, laugh together, eat together, used to tease each other, and plan mischiefs all day long. Elders might have had their conflicts with each other, but no family refrained their children from playing or talking with other kids. My father owned some cattle and used to cultivate corn on the land we had.

My education was limited to my family values and social norms imparted to me. No formal schooling was possible because the village did not have any educational institute. So most of the children of our village were like me, being educated by their parents, society, and most importantly, life. The nearest school was in Bachiwind, which was far from the village, as a result, people were also not much interested in their progeny's formal education.

The year 1947 brought historic changes, not only the regimes fell but also a nation. While the waves of revolution had engulfed the nation so much that just the thought of independence thrilled the people, at the same time, the tangled web of conspiracies was being woven, which found its origin from the very thought of freedom. Hundreds of years old Banyan tree with its long, strong roots, countless leaves, which homed various birds of different colours, species, and voices, was axed down by foreign hands and see the irony of it, its very own inhabitants raised the voice to make it happen in response to its life-long selfless services. I was thirteen at the time of the partition, young enough to understand the partition but certainly not as nearly prepared to cope up with the bloodshed and comprehend the need for it.

The news was confirmed soon through the official announcements made by the government. Government officials visited different places to announce the partition, explain how the migration was going to take place and how to avail the services provided by the authorities to help people migrate to Pakistan. A similar announcement was made in our village too. The Sikhs of our village were very supportive and empathetic towards us. They backed our decision of not leaving and swore to protect us if need be. But only if one could peek into the future may be through a crystal ball, millions of lives could have been saved. If there were people who stood by us, there were those too, who stood against us. The Muslim families of our region started receiving threats from the extremists who wanted all of us to leave but people decided to stick to their decision. The families locked themselves in their houses at night, the windows were shut, and the doors locked. They became prisoners in their very own homes.

Families were being slaughtered at nights, houses were set on fire, people were burnt alive, women were raped and butchered, and the young girls were abducted. The only crime of these people was their name, only Kahlons or Khannas were spared, not Khans. The religion which was the way of their life, not chosen but conferred upon them, became the very enemy of their lives. It seemed as if God had left the world to be on its own and, there was no one up in the skies hearing the prayers of those victims. Such disturbing news from nearby villages made everyone shiver in fear, yet no one thought of migrating as our village was still safe and no attack had happened till then.

These were not the only tales we heard. Our area had a demon of its own who wielded a sword, riding on a white horse, Makhan Singh was no prince charming but a villain, notorious for killing Muslims, especially the way he used to take lives; by beheading. He was once attacked by another thug, Gamaan Battar, but survived only to take the lives of other people. Death never scared Makhan Singh and may be that was the only reason that Gamaan Battar could not end the life of Makhan Singh after noticing a dead look in his eyes.

Neither the threats of extremists nor the disturbing news of massacre or the killings of Makhan Singh changed the decision of any family but we were left with no other choice but to migrate due to an incident that happened on the occasion of Eid. Everyone was trying to spare their mind from the tensed situation when out of nowhere, a bomb was dropped on the crowd. It was an improvised explosive device (IED) or roadside bomb, which is constructed or deployed in a non-military action. By God's grace or some unknown reason, it did not explode and no harm was done but soon, the extremists showed up. They were only successful in looting homes, but failed to execute their plan to spark a bloodbath. The Sikhs of our village fought them with all the strength and bravery. The day was saved but not for long for we all knew it was just a matter of time before things got even worse for us. It was by luck we survived that attack. We could have died if the bomb had detonated or our village's Sikhs were not there to protect us. We knew that the next time, no one would be spared. We left everything and decided to migrate. We took nothing but food. Noone from our village wanted us to leave but the sullen look on the faces of the people was telling everything that their words could not. The decision was taken, the farewells were bidden, and an unknown fate awaited us. My maternal uncle's wife and his son refused to leave when we left but eventually had to migrate later on, as the situations got more severe. During the whole journey, we travelled in fear of being attacked again but luckily, nothing happened. We stayed in village Jandiala Guru for a couple of days, and then spent approximately ten days in village Jhande. After reaching Tajpura in Pakistan, some people went to Amoki, near Sheikhupura but some like us, came to village Doori, near Lahore as we were allotted one acre of land there by the Pak Government. Since we were not able to afford the wheat seeds, we were not able to grow anything on that land for three consecutive years and were forced to survive by only consuming chickpeas.

The timeframe of the first five to seven years was not easy on the migrants. The bloodshed was not coming to an end in the beginning. It was all like living a nightmare over and over again every day, which we were not able to wake up from. It was like a deep sleep that wasn't coming to an end. Only this time, non-Muslims were being killed in the Muslim-majority areas. Demons like Makhan Singh chased us till here but this time, they had a new name and new victims. A subedar named Shah from Mendhar killed Hindus in Kamoke and another Muslim, Noora, gunned down many Hindu migrants on their way. And when the trains full of dead used to enter the boundary of Pakistan, this genocide was taken to a whole new level. Not many people had guns still there was such butchery but what if there were weapons like today? The intensity of red in the picture would have been even more and it is terrifying to imagine how it might have looked, then.

In our village Doori, Hindu migrants who were on their way to newly formed India, used to be attacked by the extremists. But one day when they were under attack, the in-charge of the nearby police station got there in time and fired a shot in the air to disperse the extremists and saved many lives. It is not easy to fight the people of the same community you belong to. The Sikhs of village Mode and the cop of Doori fought the people of their own religion to save the people whom they did not see as Muslims, Hindu, or Sikhs but as humans who had been suffering a terrible fate and that too, not chosen but forced on to them.

The memories of that time are not festive, yet the mind remembers every detail of the scenario it witnessed and the things it heard or read. Maybe, it is not the sorrow that is more painful but the time before, which was cheerful and peaceful, pinches the most as to why those cheers were trampled by the hatred to leave only hue and cry behind, I wish I knew. But the time keeps on spinning its wheel and as they say, if the happiness is not there to stay, so does the sorrow. We tried our hand at many jobs to earn our living and finally, around the year 1955, the same year I got married, I got a stable job in Water and Power Development Authority (WAPDA) and started at a salary of Rs. 67, which was increased to Rs. 72 soon after and in Ayub Khan's reign, by Rs. 20 again. I have three sons and three daughters who have made my life more beautiful and merrier, and my grandchildren love me with all their hearts. Oh, Life! It's full of surprises. It comes back to you when you least expect it to.

There is no doubt what I will say if I am asked whether I miss my home back in India. Ask any migrant, they all do. The people who came here from India and those who went there from Pakistan, they all share the same pain, experienced the same sort of joys, and miss their home with same intensity every day. Almost all of us would wish to go back to visit their homes for the last time, but some have financial issues, and some have health issues like me, which do not allow them to do so.

I am often asked how I deal with those painful memories when they start flashing in my head. Well, as I said may be it is not about the pain related to the incidents which happened, it was the love and affection attached to the place I was born and grew up in, the friends and the ambience there, and the people who shared Siwayyan at Eid and Kheer in Sawan.

The thing that agitates me the most is people pick Makhan Singh, Noora, and Shah to define each other's religion and as an excuse to fuel their preposterous hatred towards each other but fail to have a look at all those heroes who in the times of need walked an extra mile for people like me. When I look at the Sikhs, I see those who protected families like mine, irrespective of the danger that clouded upon their own lives and that of their families by doing so, yet they fought for us. I am sure the Hindus who migrated from Pakistan don't see Shah or Noora but the policeman in people of my religion who saved their families.

All I wish to say in the end is this, when people like us, who suffered all of what we had to and still don't foster hate or grudge in our hearts, no one else should either. The youth must understand this, it is not the religion that misguided people, nor any religion asked for it. It was people like Noora, Shah, or Makhan Singh who belong to no religion but exist in all of us that did the damage. So, it is up to us to get rid of them from within ourselves and value humanity above everything else.

35

The Airport Professor

The bursting bubbles of words in the stream of thought, emotions flowing through the ink; to the world, his world is confined to a single room in a suburb of Washington, DC in the United States, but to him, the world is what he is framing in those words. The expression of his pen is the mark of those innermost feelings that, pretty often, he doesn't share even with himself. Nonetheless, being a writer, he is blessed to live all the lives he wishes through his characters. Albeit never is the case when the words betray him; he is never short of them but there are a few things, not very often, but in some cases, whose realms remain just untouched.

Just like the river by which the notes of my flute were in a sync with its flow once, it opens the magical memory box with countless moments flashing out like rabbits jumping out of a magician's hat. And I wish to travel back in time to the decade of 1930s in Kot Sarang, Tehsil Talagang in the district of Chakwal (now in Pakistan) where then lived a mixed population of Hindus and Muslims with the exception of a single Sikh family,

The Speaking Window. Sandeep Dutt, Faisal Hayat, and Ritika, Oxford University Press.
© Oxford University Press India 2023. DOI: 10.1093/oso/9789391050733.003.0035

a timeline when, unlike today the spoken words and relations formed meant something. The friendliest time of that century, which meant everything to those who had seen it, lived and cherished it, and has been a fairy tale for those who have only heard about it. People were involved in different occupations there. In the heart of the village were residents, mostly Hindus, who plied various trades. Shopkeepers, money-lenders, and artisans like goldsmiths, tailors, or *hakims* were all Hindus and, on the outskirts, bordering open fields, was the Muslim population, mostly agriculturists along with some families whose menfolk were enlisted in the armed forces. Nonetheless, the seasons of festivities like Diwali and occasions of distress like Muharram were not exclusive to one community; but were shared by all. Maybe, it is the empathy of the people present then which confuses the youth of today who lack sympathy. Yet, the historical fact is that one may believe it or not, that time existed!

Counting my blessings, my family has been on the top of that list; loving parents and four adorable siblings. My father was a 'Pleader' (a term used for an advocate at that time) who had moved to Nowshera, a cantonment town in North West Frontier Province (now known as Khyber Pakhtunkhwa). The rest of the family including my widowed grandmother, my mother, and my siblings—three sisters and a brother—continued to live in the village till 1941 and then moved to Nowshera to join our father. However, we all used to visit our village house for spending the two months of summer vacation, to meet old childhood friends in both communities, and, of course, to get the freshness of its clear blue sky and cool summer breeze.

My schooling had been really superb … indeed, I have relished much at both the places. So many memories! Those even now, bring a smile on my face every time I recall them. The first school I went to was the village's Primary school for Boys. The only teacher was an old Muslim Rajput, named Munshi Rustom Ali Khan, a strict disciplinarian who taught Urdu and Arithmetic to us. I was rather a truant. Whenever I missed the school, which was done occasionally, I would go to the lake nearby and watch its water for hours. Sitting by the lake, I would play my flute, trying to coordinate its notes with the whistling winds, burbling water, and shrieking waterfowl. However, my casual approach to the school had a drastic change when the family moved to Nowshera. I was 10 and soon after moving there, I got enrolled in class 5 in an English-medium school.

The school had pretty good facilities for its pupils. It had regular drill periods, a sprawling hockey ground and volleyball courts. I became the captain of the school hockey team for being tall for my age and my track record on the field. I played volleyball too.

Nowshehra's Sadar Bazaar (the main market) was a busy place. The nearby Pathan villagers would come over to sell their field and garden produce there, and also to buy groceries. So it was a busy town. I would go to Sadar Bazaar every day for satisfying my quench for learning Urdu. There was a bookshop of one of our paternal family's relatives who would let me borrow, read and return Urdu magazines without soiling the pages. Because of the language barriers, the Pashto-speaking Pathans and Punjabi-speaking Hindus did not communicate much. Only a few people there knew Pashto, which I also thought of learning but ended up with learning only the cuss words. There were no conflicts with the local Pathans but no promises of long-lasting friendships as well. However, my interest in Urdu poetry helped me in making a few friends from Nowshera and Peshawar who would come over to recite their poems in the poetical symposiums. Yunis Saber, Arbab Yusuf Rija Chishti, Khatir Ghaznvi, and Fraz were such friends but with Fraz, my friendship lasted a lifetime ... indeed till his death when he was on a visit to Washington, DC here.

In the third week of August 1947, we emigrated. I wish if this part of the story could be reversed because the quicker it had happened, the tougher it was to sustain. The local authorities just moved the non-Muslims; no suggestions, no ultimatum given, no formality of asking one's wish, they just came and moved us, without letting us take anything but the dress that we wore. It was first to the nearby bus depot and then to the Chakwal's railway station from where we were made to board a train routed to Rawalpindi and then towards the Indian border, a train full of migrating refugees and, we were now one of them. Non-Muslims were being killed every day and thousands of women were going missing; trains were being looted and passengers being slaughtered as the unruly mob would just stand in front of the train and it stopped for the attackers to loot, abduct, and kill. We were aware of all this, yet the decision of migration should have been our own choice, not of the newly formed Government of Pakistan ... yet here we were, in a train, going to a place unknown to us and leaving everything known behind.

Despite every sort of fearful thought that had gone through our minds a thousand times, no nightmare painted in our minds came to life, fortunately. Thus, we reached India safe and sound. On arriving here, what we saw were the conical tents for *sharnarthis*, as we were called (the refugees). There were refugee camps on the outskirts of big cities where people had to sleep on the floor and had to line up once the volunteers brought food from Hindu/Sikh temples. This beggars' destiny for millions of the populace was not written by Gods but by man for his fellow men. There was such hopelessness and fear writ large on their faces. It was all very stressful seeing such long faces knowing about their hard journeys.

Starting afresh in India was certainly not a piece of cake. Our family, however, managed somehow and I could continue my education. We moved to Ludhiana where I got my college degree and then Masters in English from the Punjab University in Chandigarh with academic distinction. Later, I went for my Doctoral Degree in English Literature with the thesis titled 'Changing Concept of the Nature of Reality and Literary Techniques of Expression'. But I didn't stop there. Once I was in the United States, I went for another doctoral degree in Philosophy from the Trinity University, Texas. I got married in November 1957 and got blessed with three beautiful children; two sons and a daughter. Then I decided to share my knowledge with everyone and what better way could it be than teaching? I started teaching at the Punjab University Chandigarh where I was once a student. It was indeed a proud moment for me. Later, as a Visiting Professor, I undertook journeys far and wide in different universities in the country as also abroad, including the University of District of Columbia (UDC) in Washington, DC. I was a Visiting Professor at various universities that included South Eastern University in Washington, DC, University of British Columbia, Vancouver, Canada, and the British Open University in Milton Keynes, England. This earned me the nickname 'Airport Professor' a jocular but loving epithet. From 1992 to 1995, I was on a special assignment as a Professor of Education in the Department of Technical Education, Saudi Arabia. To cut a long story short, I have taught around the globe in each corner of which my students earned their graduate and post-graduate degrees. Thus I had the opportunity to visit different countries for seminars and conferences including Norway, Denmark, United Kingdom, Germany, and Turkey. Currently,

I am retired and live in Herndon, Virginia, a suburb of Washington, DC in the United States.

Apart from teaching, my passion for Urdu writing grew stronger over the years. In the early fifties, just in two years, I got my writing published in the form of collections of poetry, short stories, and novels. My first book of short stories was published in 1953, when I was 22 and still a student. In the world of Urdu writers and poets, spread all over the globe, my pen has earned its name and respect. Not only in Urdu, but my writings are also there in Hindi, Punjabi as well as in English. The books in English are all published in the United States and are available online. The Committee for 'Earth Preservation Day', sponsored by the UN, qualified my poem 'Thus Spake The Fish' for the award in an international competition. The Nehru Fellowship Award for my book, 'Promises to Keep', was given back in 1972. The prestigious Adaya Markaz Award (worth $5,000) and Shiromani Sahityakar Award by the Government of Punjab, India have been the honours I have been bestowed with. I have written, in all forty-seven books in Hindi, English, Urdu, and Punjabi. I have written my autobiography in Urdu under the title 'Katha Char Janmon Ki'. My Urdu books (twenty-seven in all) have been published simultaneously in Delhi and Karachi (Pakistan). However, in spite of all the success I earned, there have been a few disappointments along the way. In 1957, my Hindi novel, 'Chowk Ghanta Ghar', was banned in India due to its progressive (Communist) nature and the Government of Punjab ordered my arrest.

No matter how far we go, or how many milestones we touch in life, or the number of places we visit, nothing satisfies the soul, but home. I got a chance of visiting my ancestral village thrice; in 1991, 1999, and 2011. Accompanied by my literary friends in a caravan of cars from Rawalpindi, I could pay my first visit. I met a few old folks who remembered my family, but none could remember a child of 10 seeing the same face after these many decades, except for one old friend who was blind and didn't need his eyes to recognize me. He just touched my face and kissed my forehead and that was it. The place had grown older and so did its people who lived there but the memories were still fresh in their hearts. I saw the school I went to. This Primary School for Boys was upgraded to the middle school and a new primary-level girls' school too got built. I noticed that the Jogi *dargah* had been destroyed. Also, my house had its woodwork and brickwork looted, with only one room left intact at the back. This is now a home to a husband and wife, a Kashmiri refugee family. Time is indeed a leveller, a destroyer but never a preserver.

And now, back to the present. If I am asked, what is my message to the young blood? Hard work, hard work, and MORE hard work is the single answer to this question. There is no shortcut to success in life nor any elevator to skip the stairs, so don't look for shorter ways but for better ones that not only benefit you but everyone around too.

And about the partition, what I believe and understand is that its foundation had been laid by the British rulers from the day they had to fight the very first rebellion against them in 1857. And for a ruler, a shaking throne will make the crown fall, so a simple trick of divide and conquer helped stabilizing their ground. Keeping Hindus and Muslims apart was their policy so that the strength of a unified populace with a common cause be destroyed. The current state of affairs between India and Pakistan is the penultimate result of that policy. At 87 years of age, I can give only one message, Keep your home safe. Treat all as Indians whether they are Hindus or Sikhs or Muslims.

36

Abandoned Virtue

FATIMAH NOREEN
DELHI - RAWALPINDI
THE SPEAKING WINDOW

Having the virtue of parents in life is the greatest blessing one can ever wish for. Not only the parents shower their progeny with all the love, affection, and blessings they have but also, they help them to become a better person in life. Where the strength of a father ensures a sense of protection, the shade of motherhood helps in providing a healthy environment to nurture them. The days of endless work change into the countless years of sacrifices and back-breaking efforts they make to see their kid become successful. But after that, when the same child raises the finger at the same parents whose fingers he held when he learned to walk, when the same child refuses to extend a hand to support their old bodies to help them walk, when the same child becomes selfish enough to forget the selfless services of his parents, then what should a parent do? Blame him, him/herself, or the fate? It was not the first time as I had to go through the pain of losing home twice in my life.

The Speaking Window. Sandeep Dutt, Faisal Hayat, and Ritika, Oxford University Press.
© Oxford University Press India 2023. DOI: 10.1093/oso/9789391050733.003.0036

Sialkot was my first home where I was born in 1938 and spent the first five years of my life. Our family, which included my parents and my five siblings—five sisters and a brother—was rich in terms of love. We all were caring towards each other and helped each other in any way we could. My mother who was a homemaker used to spend her whole day in her household chores, taking care of us and of my father. Her Dupatta, which she used to sometimes cover me with while making me sleep, always made me feel the warmth of her love and care for all of us. My father was no less caring, either. He was a very diligent man who worked as a messenger in a government organization. However, his salary was little but not his heart. It was difficult for our family to make both ends meet with the little earnings we had, but our parents never made us feel the burden of the financial crunch they had. It was the little joys we had that mattered, like the sweets which my father used to bring for us while coming back from his work or the delicious food which my mother used to cook for us. The little doll of clay we sisters used to play with or the walks when I would see the world sitting on my father's shoulders are experiences that are still close to my heart.

When I was five years old, we moved to Delhi because the government official my father used to work with, got transferred there. In those times, the city was way different. It was one of the most beautiful places I had ever seen. It was big, clean, peaceful, and liberal in thoughts. Whereas in Sialkot, the majority of the population was of Islamic followers, but here it was completely different as it welcomed all kinds of faiths without offending anyone, making them all fall in love with itself. And, its historic essence with its majestic heritage made it even more unique and attractive. My father, who wished to impart education to his children, made all the possible efforts and ensured they bore fruits. I was sent to school at the age of six. The school resembled the heart of the city. Never before, I had ever interacted with someone who was a Hindu, a Sikh, or a Christian. The best thing I observed from my interactions with them was that they all looked like me. Only the practices of worshipping were different, but they were taught the same as what Islam did, love for humanity and peace. I was happy there, having so many friends and to them, the communal difference didn't matter. This was Delhi. Refreshing, accepting, soothing, and simply beautiful. My school life was going great. I was one of the bright students in my class who were in the good books of their teachers.

The charm of Delhi got eclipsed like the Moon, which lost its silvery shine in the darkness of hatred. The partition of 1947, which happened during the holy month of Ramadan, brought with itself the unholy scenarios which cast a long-lasting shadow on the oneness of the people. Like everyone else, my mother was also been saving money for two months now, just for the shopping at Eid but what she didn't know was that her savings were about to be spent on a shroud and the ever-deepening loss that no one would get over. It was the third week of Ramadan, which is called Ashura, I remember how the extremists started attacking streets, only to threaten the Muslims to leave the city. The banging on doors, beating the innocent, threatening them with their sharp knives and swords, leaving them wounded; all just to make a statement; if we did not leave, it would not end well for people like us. They warned the houses of their own community that if they tried to help any Muslim family, then they might suffer the same fate as them. The big heart of Delhi was stabbed and being cut into pieces and everyone was trying to stake a claim on those pieces. Such an outburst, that too in such a short time, was beyond acceptance. People, who were nice towards each other, were still the same but the fire of extremism was burning every form of unity to ashes. Even if someone wanted to help the other, the fear of losing one's own family would become so suppressing that surrendering to the threats for the sake of one's own well-being was the only remaining option for them.

The same night, the Imam of our mosque got murdered and the rage which took the city by storm was unbelievable. The Delhi I stepped in was big, clean, and beautiful, but now was left unclean and ugly. Neither the historic heritage nor the communal harmony of centuries could then curb the violence which was spreading like a wildfire with every passing moment. More and more people were being killed, relationships distorted, families scattered, and the spirit of the city butchered. My family knew that one more day spent there could make us join those people whose limbs were scattered in the street. Thus, on the twenty-fourth day of Ramadan, we started our journey of migration, a journey to Pakistan.

For the way, we didn't pack a lot of things, since we knew it was going to be a really long journey which was not going to be so simple or safe. So, only the necessary things, along with the food, were bundled together. We were not alone in that; hundreds of Muslim families were migrating with us. We started off on foot first, making our way through the narrow maze of the street leading to the Red Fort. Considering it a safe place, many people started gathering there and stayed there for some time, but it was a folly. Hundreds of people who were already threatened with attacks were now gathered in a single place, which was more like an invitation for a cat to hunt and it did. The extremists attacked the Red Fort. There was only mayhem. People were running here and there in panic and only falling in the way of the extremists who were standing there as their reapers. Dead bodies were falling everywhere, children were crying, women were being stripped off their dignity and murdered, families were lost, and men were being butchered, everything was happening simultaneously and in all this, I lost my brother too. That was the point when it felt like the world had just stopped moving as I saw him lying there ... still, as if he was in a very deep sleep. I can't forget the cries of my mother and my father who didn't know how to wake him up from his sleep. Somehow, the fellow families helped us getting out of there and we were saved. People around us were very sympathetic towards our loss and were very encouraging. They helped our family a lot during that time and motivated us to carry on the journey.

This incident caught the eye of the government and the rescue trucks were sent to get the people out of there. We were taken to Amritsar where we spent the next couple of days in a refugee camp. For those two days, my mother who had lost her only son was in deep grief, and my father was trying to strengthen her will with all the courage he could muster at that point. After two days of struggle, we reached Lahore, Pakistan where we thought of starting a new life with a new hope, but that hope was not strong enough to hold things together. We were given a small house near the railway colony, Lahore. However, we got shifted to Jhang merely four months later. Getting an education became a distant dream due to the poor financial conditions but things started falling into their place after some time when my father got a government job in the Union Council because he knew some office work.

Life took another turn when I got married in 1960, to a man who worked as a labourer at my father's office and after a few years of marriage, we got shifted to Rawalpindi. Our family got big with six children, and we

were happy. We did every possible effort as parents to get them the education that we both were deprived of so that our children did not have to go
for labour jobs. And finally, our children stood on their feet; that was indeed a proud moment for both of us that after years of hardships, we were
able to make our children capable enough that now they could do something for themselves in their lives. But this happiness did not even long,
they left us. At this age, when now we needed them to be our support, to
help us walk through the streets, we took them as a kid, when it was their
turn to take care of their aging parents whose hands are now losing their
grip, they left us.

I wonder how their kids would treat them in future, if they had treated
their parents with such disrespect! My husband met with an accident a
couple of years back because of which he has some neurological issues
now, so I stay with him all the time, help him with his daily chores, take
care of him with all the efforts I can with my declining health and aging
body. I help him selling clothes in the streets too. *'Beta uparwaaley se ek
hi dua hai ki marney se pehlay kisi ka mohtaj na karey'* (I pray to Lord, not
to make me dependent up on anyone, before I die.) This is how I lost my
home twice. Neither the madness we suffered in Delhi, which forced us to
leave our home nor the selfishness of children, which made us homeless,
I can never understand it.

37

Strong as Steel

ISHWAR DAS
GOJRA - LUDHIANA
THE SPEAKING WINDOW

'A friend in need, is a friend indeed'.

#friendshipquotes #friends #friendship #friendshipgoals; such never-ending captions or posts fill endless pages of countless social networking sites. It shows how much the youth seems fascinated towards the relationships formed based on friendship which is loyal, determined, and honest. However, the obsession of display takes them far from the reality and maybe, that is why the love and affection of friendship portrayed on screen, the tales of which are written in books and the legends narrated by their older folks, fascinate them. Because, what they see through all these mediums is the friendship of Hindus and Muslims but what people like me see is, love which knows no colour, caste, religion, or nationality.

In my entire life, I have never known or understood people by their religion but as a human being which is why, Nissar Ahmed, a Muslim, had been my best friend. Mohammad Shafi, another Muslim, was again a close friend and Amar Singh, a Sikh, was one of those friends that everyone

The Speaking Window. Sandeep Dutt, Faisal Hayat, and Ritika, Oxford University Press.
© Oxford University Press India 2023. DOI: 10.1093/oso/9789391050733.003.0037

needs and should have. Though Nissar had been my best friend but he became more like a brother after an incident that happened at my home.

Although there was no apparent discrimination that existed yet some orthodox minds, forced by their ideology, were able to draw lines among humans whom they used to consider different from them. One of such people who were radical in their approach was, my mother.

However, she loved and respected everyone and as a mother, she has been great but sometimes, the same motherhood makes mothers selfish too. She is not able to feel the love and affection for others' children as she is able to feel it for hers. When Nissar used to visit home, he used to touch her feet, seeking her blessings. On the first three visits of Nissar, my mother served him water in the glassware glass, so each time she would break it, every time he left. Now here, a Muslim child, was following a Hindu culture of touching feet, out of respect but there, a Hindu lady who could only see the boy's religion but not his heart. But when he visited home for the fourth time, she served water to him in a steel glass that time. It was surprising but later when he left that day, she started crying, saying that she felt shameful for her cold behaviour towards a boy who always had considered her like his mother. And at that moment, she changed, and her heart melted for him. Since then, he has become a son to her and a brother to me.

I came across a similar situation in my life one more time but this time, after many years of partition, when my other best friend, Mohammad Shafi, was on a visit to India on the occasion of Rakhi. He saw the wife of my younger brother tying Rakhi on the wrists of her brothers. Since he didn't know much about the custom, so he inquired about it from me. I explained him, how a brother promises to protect his sister from every bad thing that falls in her way, and the thread of Rakhi is what symbolizes this promise. He asked me to request my sister-in-law to tie him a Rakhi too, which she gladly accepted. Shafi noted that date and started sending gifts to her on the very same date every year, for the next five to six years. There was one time when he couldn't do it, so he sent her a money order of ₹100 with the help of a friend living in Qadian, Gurdaspur. ₹100 was a big sum at those times, so this money order came into the notice of the authorities and got everyone stuck in a huge misunderstanding. An enquiry was made by the state as well as the central police on me for 1 to 1.5 years. Eventually, I was found innocent. I remember how an officer, dressed in civil, came to interrogate me. I got so annoyed at his questions, for they were quite weird, that I asked him to explain why he wanted to know what he wanted to know. In response, he started laughing and said jokingly, 'What kind of friendship you have there! You're giving us a headache unnecessarily'. After that, I barred Mohammad Shafi from sending any further gifts.

Surprisingly, all these long-lasting friendships originated in Gojra in district Lyallpur, now better known as Faisalabad where I was born in a Hindu joint family which was into the crop brokerage business. I was the second eldest among the eight siblings. There, differences were not defined as discrimination but were dealt with in understanding. Gojra had no big glorious history like many other cities of Punjab. It was more of a forest called Nilibagh, cleared for agricultural purposes. The Britishers sold the land at a negligible price of ₹16 per acre to the people. The first inhabitants of it were farmers who needed land to grow crops. They set up their shops to sell their crops too, so the village started to develop gradually. Thus, the forest was cut down to shape cities like Gojra and Lyallpur out of it. Gojra, which was more of a big village to people, was very much developed for a village; it had wide-concrete roads, grain markets, et cetera.

Unlike the current times, money was important back then too but wasn't the life itself! People didn't run after it, leaving and hurting everything and everyone on their way towards it. They were happy even when they didn't have much of it. The economic gap between the rich and the poor was not becoming a deep ridge every five years as now. Even they owned at least a buffalo or a cow, so their homes never ran out of milk and milk products. Consequently, they didn't have to worry about what to feed their children.

As far as the subject matter of religion is concerned, there was harmony in the surroundings. There was no temple during that time, but the Hindu worshippers never felt the need for one too. The Hindus of Gojra would visit a Gurudwara which, along with the Guru Granth Sahib, had the pictures of Lord Rama and Lord Krishna also. At the time of Kirtan, if the harmonium was played by a Sikh, a Hindu would be playing the Dholki; such was the understanding between people of different faiths. Intercaste marriages were not a surprising incident back then. In fact, my grandmother was from a Sikh family. The only difference between the two was the practice of growing a beard, while the Sikhs kept it, it was absent in Hindus. However, despite being a Hindu, my grandfather had a long beard which he had kept by choice. He had a look like that of Rabindranath Tagore. He didn't know Upanishads of Hindus, but one could hear the chants of Gurbani from him.

In our village, the Muslims were mostly labourers whereas Hindus and Sikhs were either into farming or business. There was no bigotry existing between Hindus/Sikhs and Muslims. The only scuffles seen among them were during the Kabaddi matches organized at the fest of Baisakhi at the riverside between the Hindus/Sikhs and the Muslims. Thus, there was a sense of competitive tension in the air but none of it was a negative vibe.

My life in Gojra had been no less than a dream; it's been extraordinary. It was young, wild, and beautiful in its own sense. From the beginning, I had been a bright student who bagged the first position throughout my schooling days. I studied till matriculation in Gojra and went to Lyallpur to pursue my college education as there was no college back home. I remember at our college, we were around thirty students who were nationalists and anti-imperialists, not only in our thoughts but in our ways of life, too. The national flag of any country is important to itself as it reflects the pride and prestige of a nation but when a nation is ruling the other, the individuality of the nation being ruled gets crushed under its suppressor, which hoists its own flag as a mark of its dominance over the enslaved. Back in date, Union Jack was given the honour of a national flag for the British ruled our nation and any disrespect shown towards it was considered a matter of treason which was a punishable offense. Despite knowing all this, a sixteen-year-old boy did something which shocked everybody who got to know about it.

I was in 10th standard and it was the prayer time in school. I went to the terrace and burned the Union Jack hoisted there, the flag of the British Government. The news soon reached the police station. I was only sixteen when I got arrested and was put behind the bars. The revolution of earning complete sovereignty had already begun and more and more people were joining the fight for freedom every day. So, when this news got out in public, people came forward in support. I got bailed out because of my family's influence and the public pressure which was being built and could have made the matter even more sensitive. A case was filed against me, so the people approached the Sub Divisional Magistrate who was the judge at that time. I was a kid, so he sent me to prison for only a day and as a punishment, I was declared ineligible for any government job, which anyway, I never wished to have.

In 1943, our family was struck with a huge crisis. My father passed away. I was in the second year of my college and now had a big family to look after. At that very moment, I grew up and shared the responsibility with my elder sibling and got into the family business. I left my education in the middle to work for three to four years and later got married and had a son in Gojra.

Even after leaving college, my will to learn more never died. I missed the books, the lessons, the teachings, and the learning. There was a Municipal Committee Library nearby, but it was rarely open. When I shared my concern about it with my friends, we came up with an amazing idea. We all decided to build a library in Gojra. All of us had a certain number of books at our houses, so we collected all those books and took a rented room for two rupees per month. It was decided that we all would spend at least one hour there every day. Then as we managed to save a certain amount, we started buying books. By the time of the partition, the library had over 9,000 books and it was still there when I went back to Gojra after the partition. Once again, my friends didn't let me down.

I was twenty-three years old at the time of the partition. Things were bearable, if not fine, in August but became critical in September, which made us take the toughest decision of migration. One of our broker's sons was at the rank of Captain in the army and in those tough times, the people in the military were provided with a truck so that they could take their own relatives out of the country. We requested him to take us with them, but he had his own relatives to take with him. Being a benevolent man that he was, he said he could not take all of us, but he agreed to take the ladies of our house and the children with him. Thus, my sisters, my wife, and my son, all the female family members, were able to come to India with them in early September. Fortunately, they took some gold jewellery with them, which became instrumental to our survival, once we were in India.

The circumstances there were not getting any better, so when it became impossible for us to stay any further, we moved to the military camp set up in the grain market for the refugees. The boundary of the grain market was already secured with walls and was under the watch of the police. Our shop was in the same market and our house was adjoining the market, but it was no longer safe to get out of the camp so we could never see our house again. My ninety-year-old grandfather was suffering from Alzheimer's. He once went outside the camp to defecate, and forgot to return and never came back. We looked for him everywhere we could but never found him. A Muslim informed us later that an old man resembling my grandfather was hued with swords by a group of extremists but we could never be sure of what happened to him; such helplessness was not easy to deal with.

My friends stood by me through every thick and thin. The partition, which broke many friendships of many people, on the contrary, deepened ours. I had a friend, comrade Wazir Chand, who had served jail time with Mridula Sarabhai who was a progeny of Ahmedabad's industrialists' family and an independence activist. She had good relations with Pandit Nehru, too. She was called by Wazir Chand, who told her that the city was in danger and it needed to be saved. It was after that call only, military trucks arrived to rescue Wazir Chand but he was such a good person that he refused to go with them until the whole city was evacuated and stayed back until everyone was transported. People were sent in trucks to a camp in Lyallpur. Not only did he was the last person to leave the city, but he also sold all the belongings of his near and dear ones for whatsoever price he could manage to get in Pakistan. He sent that money in drafts to the respective people here in India. It was for him that day, not only us but also the people of the city were able to breathe again and so many families had something in their hands to feed their members. An unknown hero, such a man!

Nissar, in those days, was posted as a bank manager in Agra but after the partition, he was asked to take up the position in Lyallpur. He refused to take that position because he wanted to know about my whereabouts. He didn't take that position until he found me. Since we were brought to a refugee camp built in Khalsa College, Lyallpur, he was able to find me there. He enquired about my health and family, if they got out safely and then took charge in Lyallpur. But soon, Muslims were barred from visiting the camp for the fear of extremists' attacks, so we could not see each other anymore. After seven to eight days, a few military trucks of the Baloch Army were passing through the city. One of our relatives requested one of the officials to take us to Lahore, for which they demanded

₹1,000. A very big amount in those days, and that too in such a crisis! Our relatives were somehow able to arrange that, and they took ten to twelve of us. However, we were afraid of getting killed by them on the way but were dropped safely in Lahore where we stayed for four to five days in a military camp at DAV college. The government had arranged freight trains in which people were being carried like livestock.

The journey was not easy for anybody. The tears in the eyes of people had dried enough to not appear anymore. Especially after witnessing what they did, one could only feel one thing: nothing. There were a husband and wife on the train. The wife felt thirsty, so her husband went down to take water from the hand pump for her when the train stopped at a station. By the time he came back, the train had started moving at a fast pace, so he ran trying to get on it. His foot slipped, and he fell down and was cut into pieces. His wife who was traumatized and blaming herself for his death, was crying bitterly. People were trying to console her and told her that he was gone and wouldn't come back. Everyone there had lost someone, and they were tired of crying by then. They did feel her pain and understood that well, but their empathy had now been consumed by the hollow inside them.

We reached Amritsar while the ladies of our family who came before us were in Nakoder. We had a relative in Amritsar who lived near the Golden Temple. We searched for his home and reached there. The rest of the family also sought the same relative out and thus, we got reunited. Everyone but my grandfather reached India safely.

After coming to India, for a few days, we stayed at our relative's house. After some days, we met a known face who was the chairman of Amritsar grain market and had been one of our clients whose lands were being taken care of by us in Gojra. He had a very big Haveli with over twenty rooms in it. He asked us to stay there in his guest rooms. It is still there in Amritsar and has been turned into a school. We were thirteen to fourteen people who stayed there for two to three months. For a month or so, we were provided food by them but later, we asked them that we would make our own food as it didn't feel right to trouble them anymore; they had done more than enough already. We didn't have any money, so we used to sell my wife's jewellery to buy food. She had around 1.5 kg of gold, which was very much at that time also. After this, we tried searching for jobs. One of our relatives suggested us to come to Ludhiana as he could help us settle down there. He was a Lawyer in Pakistan earlier but now was a Settlement Officer in India. He was helping refugees in settling down. By then, we had found a room at ₹25 per month in Ahmedgarh with the help of a relative who was working as a postmaster there. We decided to stay in Ahmedgarh because it being a small village near Ludhiana, would be cheaper than the city.

So, we started our journey to Ludhiana but when we reached its station, the Settlement Officer came to meet us. He suggested us to stay in the Ludhiana city itself, else we might not be able to know about any government announcements, if we lived in a village, like Ahmedgarh. We told him about our financial problem, so he offered us to stay with him. For being a Settlement Officer, he had been given a big house with seven bedrooms. There were four vacant rooms in his house which he gave to us. The people who were crop brokers back in Pakistan, were given a single ration depot to run. My uncle and his family were given a ration depot and I was given a tin shed.

The shed was full of scarp and bum shells. I used to cut the bum shells to make scrap out of them, using a hammer. Since I hadn't experienced such work in the past, I had blisters on my hands. My mother saw them one night and asked me what kind of work I had been doing. I told her everything and knew she wouldn't do it after that, so I left the place and that work as well. Then I asked someone what I could do to earn some money. Someone suggested that there was a market for floor mats in Nakodar and if I sold them in Ludhiana, I would get fifty paisa or a rupee for every mat. I used to pick twenty mats on my shoulder and sell them, but I couldn't do that also because I didn't have the habit of doing such physical work as we were quite well-off in Pakistan. So, soon I quit that work too.

My uncle, who had got a depot here and was running it just fine, asked me to take care of his business for he was in his old age then and couldn't work anymore. The price of sugar was six annas then, but it was sold at much higher rates on the black market, which was against my work ethic. So I asked our clients who were mostly from UP, to buy sugar from us at six annas and sell it at ₹2 in the market, which was beneficial for them too. This earned us much name for the only depot there which didn't sell anything in black. I was able to save ₹200 from the depot out of which I would give ₹100 to my uncle. Our family was big—we were twelve members.

We used to buy one kilogram of milk every day and made tea with it. We would have a cup of tea and a single chapati as our breakfast daily, but this meal turned lavish soon. And let me tell you how.

One day I was coming back to my house for lunch when I came to know that a factory was being auctioned on the Shahpur road, Ludhiana. People were standing there as spectators. To control the crowd, only those who were participants in the bid were allowed to stay and the rest were asked to leave. The base price was ₹165 per month and I thought the price would go upto 300–350, so I said ₹170 just to stay there but no bid was raised after that, and it was sold to me! I was forced to pay ₹340 as rent for two months, which was the ration money I had in my pocket. I went back home crying and told my uncle about what had happened. He asked me to forget about the past and worry about the ₹170, which we were supposed to pay from the third month. We asked people at our depot for suggestions they had, to start any work in that factory. An old person who owned eight mills suggested us to put a unit of four machines worth ₹1,500. He helped us set up by ordering these machines on his own. As we were allowed to run the factory only during the night time, so I worked there at nights and at the depot in the daytime. I started earning 1–2 paise per meter till I came up with a brilliant idea.

There was an actress named Suraiya. She had worn a striped dress in a movie which I copied the pattern of and made striped clothes. People loved Suraiya and they instantly fell in love with that cloth too. From 1 to 2 paise per meter, I started earning 4–6 paise. Then I bought another four machines with that money. Eight machines operated for six to eight months and I became financially sound. Things went on and we established ourselves as one of the leading business houses in the textile business. We also ventured into Cycle manufacturing which was another success story.

After six to seven years of partition, I went back to Pakistan as I was missing our lands, our home, our village, and my friends too. Our agricultural land was at a distance of one mile from the town. On reaching our Haveli, I found that Christians had been living in the village now, who were working as laborers. I saw one of them working on the lands we owned once. It was dusk, and nightfall was around the corner. When he saw me standing there in nostalgia, he figured out who I was. He ran back to the village and soon the word of the 'Owner's return' got spread. In no time, people carrying sticks in their hands appeared before us, so I started running with my friend with whom I went there. People were chasing us and we were chasing our lives in the dark. At one point, both of us were panting and stopped to catch a breath but by then, the crowd had caught up with us, which was breathing heavily too. 'Shah ji, Shah ji! We have come to meet you', they exclaimed. It was hilarious that all this time, we mistook them for having an intention of ratting us out of the area or may be killing us, in the worst-case scenario. The confusion happened because it was common for the farmers to carry sticks in their hands during those days. We laughed heartily and talked to them. They agreed to let us go if we would visit them the next morning, which we did. The next day I went to the village and believe me the whole village had spread mats on the ground and was waiting for me. Then we shared stories of both the nations for about an hour or two. Coincidently, many people from Ludhiana had migrated there. The people of the village welcomed and treated me very well. The warmth in their hearts is indescribable.

Time had only brought us closer. Neither I nor my friends had forgotten each other. In the 1960s, I revisited there with my wife for a cricket match in Lahore. We were provided passes that allowed us to stay only in Lahore. The match was just an excuse to visit Gojra but we weren't allowed to go there. So my friend Shafi arranged for a car for us with a Pathan chauffeur who took us to Sangla first where my wife belonged to. It was between Lahore and Gojra. She saw her house and factory there and probably felt the same as I felt on my first visit. Then we went to Gojra and stayed at Nissar's house who had shifted there from Lyallpur.

We roamed around the city the whole day and by the evening, we had to go back to Lahore. When we were taking his leave, he asked his sons to accompany us to ensure we reach Lahore without any hurdles. Though we had Shafi's chauffeur with us but Nissar insisted us to take his boys along. The travel distance between Lahore and Gojra was of four hours and I didn't want his children to travel so far for such a long time with us, so I suggested them to roam around the city for four hours and after that go back home and tell their father that they had dropped us at Lahore. They went back home in two or three hours and Nissar grew suspicious. They tried to convince him, but he got so anxious that they had to take him to the hospital!

We had been the same. Our concern for each other, our love for each other, nothing changed when the borders did. Neither before nor later. Our bond only grew stronger. So, my message to the youth is very much clear; stay together. Be smart enough to ignore the communal differences and be kind enough to accept the same by heart. If the amount of money being spent by both the nations on the artillery is spent on solving the socio-economic issues of the both, then instead of rising tensions, they might be able to foster love.

38

Corrupted Hearts

DEEN MUHAMMAD
RAJPURA - SARGODHA

THE SPEAKING WINDOW

'Two thousand Rupees and the land will be yours!'

It was the bribe demanded by the Patwari (the land officer) at that time when we were supposed to be allotted a piece of land after the partition as promised by the Pak Government. It sounds hilarious and insane at the same time considering if we had that much amount of money back then, we wouldn't be surviving at the mercy of others. This makes me question the morality of people who make money out of the misery of others. And then people say it was religious hatred which makes it even more hilarious. Religion, at times, is just a tool that is misused to blind the vision of believers, that is why I am so thankful to my father who taught me true lessons of Quran, which have in turn led to the foundation of my values, and I grew up in an ambience which put humanity before anything else.

My father was a cleric in the mosque of my village, Manakpura Khera, Rajpura, which falls under the territory of Patiala. In those days, there was no fixed income for those who were in the services of Islam and followers

The Speaking Window. Sandeep Dutt, Faisal Hayat, and Ritika, Oxford University Press.
© Oxford University Press India 2023. DOI: 10.1093/oso/9789391050733.003.0038

would contribute as per the weight of their pockets. Since the age of 5, I started learning the Holy Quran, under the teachings and mentorship of my father who was a simple man with an austere lifestyle. My father who was already married twice, could not be bestowed with any progeny, so he married the third time and finally got blessed with four children—three sons and a daughter—no doubt being the youngest of us, my sister was adored by all. The village was filled with tranquillity and harmonious bond among its inhabitants who were both, Sikhs and Muslims. There were two Gurudwaras and a mosque. I used to spend most of my time with my best friends, Dharam Singh and Pritam Singh and we would play all day long! No one ever stopped us or refrained us from staying together. Our friendship sustained because we kept religion out of the talks. I can still recall the celebrations and joys they felt, even more than me when I got married at the age of 16 to my cousin.

The change in behaviour and attitude of people became much apparent even before the news of the partition was confirmed. All of a sudden, religion started to matter over everything else and disturbing news from all over the country started pouring in, in the form of headlines in newspapers. I was nineteen years old and still quite young to understand that sudden change of heart which was of discomforting nature but the thought of migrating never crossed my mind until it actually happened. My wife's parents lived in the village near to ours and she was going to visit them, but she could never make it ... She was attacked by the extremists on the way who chased her like mad dogs hunting for their prey. When she found no way to escape and knew what would happen to her if she got caught so, she jumped into the canal and got drowned. My family knew nothing about it till our neighbours came and informed about the incident. And to me, any incident like this is the true face of partition.

We were still in Manakpur when the extremists from the other villages started invading our homes. There were many families who wanted to migrate with us. So, before things could go worse, we left. From Patiala, we went to Ambala first, where we stayed in a Government Refugee Camp for five days, but the brutality was yet to be witnessed. At the midnight hour, our camp was attacked. There was a hue and cry everywhere. The extremists were slaughtering everyone. Their swords were sparkling with blood on them. No one was spared, not even the infants! Women were running to save their dignity and children were crying by the side of their dead parents. All of us tried to run to save our lives and we managed to do it somehow but my brother Asghar got stuck in the camp during the course of massacre. By the time, we gained our consciousness back out of that incident, we realized that we had lost him. We tried to find him, but we could not. A day later, we found his lifeless body, all wrapped in blood and wounds. It was no less than another shock for us. We knew it was almost impossible to leave Ambala in all of that bloodshed. We knew the risks and were aware of the circumstances too but anyway, we decided to leave Ambala as soon as we got our first chance in order to avoid any more fatal contingencies resulting from these massacres. After crossing almost ten to twelve cities, our train arrived at Lahore, which had chaos of its own.

The border ... only the partition was certain but the border wasn't! No one was certain about which part of the country would be carved into Pakistan and which would remain with India. At least the common folks were unaware of it. We were sheltered in Lahore at a refugee camp known as Walton camp for two months where we were given food only once in a day. Every day, we would watch an escalating number of migrants, seeking shelter with an expression like that of a lost wanderer on their faces. No one had any hope of lightening the burden that they carried in their bundle of grieves. Finally, we decided to move to Sargodha. We were supposed to be allotted a plot by the Pak Government to settle down but the Higher Authoritative Officers in-charge that time, didn't let it go through. They repeatedly harassed people and took bribes and those who could not fill their greedy bellies, had to suffer like us. The Patwari there, who was supposed to assign us a plot, asked us for bribe, and that too, of Rs. 2,000. If we had a sum of Rs. 2,000 at that point time, we would not have been living our lives in such misery, of course!

We earned our livelihood by selling wood in the city, which we used to cut from the forest. And later we did labour jobs. I used to pick heavy things on my head to move them from one place to another on foot. I was already Hafiz-e-Quran (Hafiz-e-Quran is the title given to honour those who have known Quran by heart, remember the verses very well, and can narrate them beautifully) when we moved to Pakistan, so later on, I got a position of Imam in the village's mosque.

In 1957, I got remarried and had four children—two sons and two daughters. But the time tested me once again, and for some reason,

I remained deprived of the love of my daughters who passed away at an early age of their lives. I don't even know if anyone of Dharam or Pritam, is still alive but if I ever could, I would surely go back to see them. We do have a few relatives back there even now but it has been a long time. Generations have passed since we last saw each other. The faces we used to recognize exist no more. If I could roll back time to the period when there was no hate among people, I could have taken this generation to witness the true meaning of friendship, love, empathy, and compassion.

39

Recipe to Revive

SHAKUNTALA MALHOTRA
LYALLPUR - HOUSTON
THE SPEAKING WINDOW

'Posted to….' There was stress in my husband's voice, I could sense some pain but couldn't understand why until he added:

'Lahore.'

'Lahore?' I repeated. Images of the city of my birth and the events from a stressful time went through my mind as if they had all happened yesterday as he continued:

'Yes, my first posting is at Lahore', he replied in firm confirmation; disappointment reflected in his words had melted any delight of expectation.

'No! We can't go there! How can we go there? No, we won't! We can't!' I exclaimed, tears welling in my eyes.

'Lahore', the word that sounded haunting to me, was the city of my birth but the name brought back memories of the horrific events of 1947, which reminded me of the horrible nightmare we had gone through and barely survived.

The Speaking Window. Sandeep Dutt, Faisal Hayat, and Ritika, Oxford University Press.
© Oxford University Press India 2023. DOI: 10.1093/oso/9789391050733.003.0039

I was born in the dazzling city of Lahore, the capital of an undivided Punjab, when it was part of pre-partitioned India, but I left it as an infant. We moved and settled in Lyallpur, about two hours to the southwest, after my father, Sunder Lal Talwar, became the postmaster there. So the memories I have of my childhood are mostly of Lyallpur, which is where my *nanaji* (maternal grandfather) Mastan Chand Mehra had a respected position as the Municipal Committee Secretary.

Even today, I remember every detail of Lyallpur, like the Bell Tower with the clock, which we would run to the rooftop to see and tell the time and the bazaar around it, and those memories still bring a smile to my face. Such a happy time it was! My schooling was done in Lyallpur and our rented house outside the city wasn't far from the railway station. Across our back boundary was a church and the padre would speak to us in heavily English-accented short sentences in broken Punjabi. Adjoining our quarter was a Muslim family and we would exchange food or roti across the common wall or send each other bowls of freshly made dishes in a bowl through a small opening we had created by pushing a loose brick out. Later, my nanaji moved to another house that he had built and gave us his old house to move into. It had a walled-in courtyard with one end with a lean-to roof where we could tie a cow overnight. I was happy with my extended family who lived close to each other.

My husband's family was from Jhang, a small town where retired people lived and others came to enjoy the countryside, about two hours away from Lyallpur, and they were known to my elders as my father's family was also from the same town. Our families all owned ancestral farmland there and at each harvest, we would receive jute bags full of grain and other foods from the tenant farmers who would tend the crops. If a young man from the family didn't show much aptitude for studies or wasn't too bright, he would be sent to oversee the family lands.

It was 1940 and I was 12 and in the seventh grade at the time when my family started looking around for a suitable match for me. The elders discussed among themselves and announced that we were to be engaged. His name was Jagdish Chander Malhotra and was considered a good match and from a known family in Jhang. He was twenty years old and had already been working as a stenographer (since he was very good in shorthand) for two years in Lahore to support his large extended family. It was very customary for young men to leave their homes after they passed matriculation and go away for work, leaving their families and wives behind.

So it was in 1942—five years before the partition—that my eldest brother Raj who had found a job in the Ministry of Education and relocated to Delhi with my mother and two younger brothers, while my nanaji and his family and my father stayed behind in Lyallpur in his government quarters. There was no hint or fear of a partition at that time, but moving to a government job in the capital was a much sought-after opportunity.

At the same time, my husband-to-be landed a job with the Viceroy's office in Shimla and moved his parents and six siblings there with him. But three years later, he resettled them in Lyallpur again while he himself stayed on in Shimla. Around that time, in 1945, when I was 18, we were married in Lyallpur. By now, my husband's work required him to be in Delhi, so we then moved there to a two-room rented house on Original Road in Dev Nagar. His younger brother Sham and sister Savitri accompanied us.

Eighteen months later, we learnt of the impending partition and started to move our families from both sides to Delhi. We were all ignorant to think that after the partition, we would be able to go back to our ancestral homes. My nanaji even said, 'Governments might change but the public cannot change' and years later, when he would think about it, he'd swear it was the cunning of the British that broke up the country. He refused to move and stayed with his own extended family in Lyallpur. When the agitation in the city got louder and the chaos of mobs in the streets became scary, my father moved in with my nanaji. A few days later, mobs set his quarter on fire.

So naïve we were that, in March 1947, while there was unrest all around in the Punjab, the rest of my husband's family came over to visit us in Delhi during the school holidays of the younger children, believing they could go back in a few weeks. But when we heard the drumbeat of terrible events of massacres, lootings, and homes set on fire in the country, they all decided to stay with us in Delhi where it was much safer. Soon there were thirty people living with us in a two-room flat. To make ends meet, all the women would pitch in to make meals and do household chores and as I knew sewing well, I made clothes for everyone who needed them. We had left all our possessions and farmlands behind and long after the partition, we found out that we could file a claim for compensation from the Indian government. It was nearly nine years later when we received a small amount of money for all the land we had lost.

We heard about the impending date of independence from the radio and newspapers and, at the urging of his family who had left everything behind, my husband decided to venture back to Lyallpur to retrieve their belongings and took me along. We expected to return within a few days, just a week before Independence Day and it never occurred to us or the rest of the family that it was a bad idea. We boarded at night from Old Delhi Railway Station, which was heavily crowded; we found seats going to Lahore. Though the train was heavily packed with Muslims going towards the west, we got through the entire journey uneventfully, arriving in Lahore at dawn. The station was deserted save for a few Pathans roaming around, and we changed trains for Lyallpur.

When we arrived at Lyallpur train station, it was still calm and we took a tanga to get to my nanaji's house. When we knocked on his door, he was hugely upset, scolding us, 'Why did you come here for these belongings? You have brought this young girl (I was only 19) here?! They are kidnapping girls and women and assaulting them and there is danger everywhere. Saving your life is the most precious thing right now!' He hurriedly pushed me inside the house and told my husband to immediately take care of whatever belongings we came for in his family's house, which was on the other side of town and leave back for Delhi.

And he was right. Many Hindu and Sikh houses had been abandoned and were being looted or taken over. We heard about people being murdered every day and women being kidnapped and killed after they were treated even less than an object. Women were learning how to fight with swords to defend themselves and generally, there was a sense of fear and desperation. Even getting out of our own house was not safe anymore, but once I carefully sneaked through the streets with my cousin Mohan to check on how my husband was faring, packing everything into bundles and bags, which took four days.

We left our house in Lyallpur a few days before Independence Day with the few belongings we had come for, leaving everything behind: the house, the rest of our belongings, and never imagined that we would never see them again. We booked the larger items to arrive by train back to Delhi, hoping they would turn up, which they did many months later. We only took the valuable items with us in a small steel trunk.

Lyallpur Railway station was packed and we waited on the platform with our belongings but for three days, no train arrived, so we were forced to stay at the railway station with hundreds of other people, witnessing every good and bad thing happening around us. Each minute, we were scared by hearing about atrocities, looting, and women being kidnapped and we hoped that nothing bad would happen to us. Every kind of a bad thought would cross my mind and every day, I would be grateful to God for keeping us safe. Then finally, a train arrived but it was completely jam-packed. In those days, the train's windows didn't have bars like today. My husband barely squeezed on board. When my cousin Mohan saw there was no way of getting into the train, he lifted me up and threw me inside the bogie through the window.

But all of my nanaji's family members were still left behind and waited on a military truck to take the old, women and children to cross till Firozpur where they ended up in refugee camps. My nanaji wanted to stay in the house even though it was not safe anymore as marauding mobs had taken to the streets and were laying claims to property. He stubbornly refused to get on the truck, so my father picked him up and forced him on. The able-bodied men had to walk on foot till they found any form of transport across the border.

Our return train did not stop though it travelled slowly through Lahore railway station, which was turned into a slaughterhouse. Thieves, thugs, and murderers were roaming, looking for a chance to take advantage. The situation for Hindus, Sikhs, and Jains was not favourable and the lives of their men were in danger. Many were killed, their women and daughters were abducted and assaulted and children were either left to cry over their dead families or were cut down like vegetables, just like their parents.

During the entire train ride back, everyone was crushed together. We were terrified by the stories we heard from the crowd and every second regretted why we took the decision to come back; at least we would have been safe back in Delhi.

In our two-bedroom flat in Delhi, we had more than thirty people who came there in crisis looking for shelter. Many areas of the city had fallen into lawlessness and many young men were fighting to guard Hindu and Sikh colonies against Muslims. Even so, we all sought some form of work to make ends meet. 'No one would call you "Refugees". You're not a refugee! You'll live with us', declared my husband who asked every relative who reached the newly independent India to stay with us. Many other people were indeed refugees, forced to take shelter in a tent or by the roadside, to remain dependent on others for food, and drown in the grief of losing their homes. So, we sheltered around thirty to thirty-five people in our little flat and needless to say, it was not easy. We were sleeping on the floor, hardly able to manage the food and every day brought a new challenge. After somehow managing in the rainy season, nature tested us in the cold. Soon winter arrived and we had no proper clothes or even blankets to protect ourselves from the chilly winds.

It was a time of total chaos; people were crossing the new border to reach Amritsar, Firozpur, and other border cities and finding their relatives was really difficult. In all that chaos, many of our relatives went missing whom we were trying to get as much information as possible and we're making efforts to find them. Two of our uncles, Ram and Inder, remained missing for almost half a year. Another uncle, Lal Chand Mehra, arrived in Delhi and was able to place an announcement on the radio that he was in Delhi searching for his family and told the place he was staying. My father heard the announcement by chance and was able to locate him.

Another uncle, Bahadur Chand Talwar, who had joined the Azad Hind Army, was captured in Burma and held prisoner for five years. When he was released, he sent a telegram to his younger brother (my father) as he knew he was the postmaster in Lyallpur. He was sent by ship from Burma and arrived in Bombay where my father went there to meet him. One of our family friend's sons who was just a young boy of 10 at the time, survived by hiding behind a door while the rest of his family in Jhang was slaughtered. And my father-in-law died in a refugee camp in Kurukshetra.

With the future, in the British Government, looking bleak as my husband worked in the UK High Commission so immediately after the partition, he resigned to try his hand in business but when it didn't run per his expectation, he decided to go back to government service. In 1954, he joined the newly formed Indian Ministry of Information and Broadcasting and took on his first overseas assignment in Indo-China for three years. There he took the Foreign Service Exam and joined the Ministry of External Affairs.

On his return, my husband learnt that his first posting would be in Lahore. Though I was happy at the prospect of a better life in the Foreign Service and having a chance to go out of Delhi, I was saddened that we would have to go back to a part of the world where we had seen so much misery. Knowing what we had seen and gone through, I didn't want to go down memory lane to relive that horror. I remember, we both cried a lot and decided we would not go there. At his request, his place of posting was changed to London and we with our two sons left in July 1958 and stayed there for four years.

The next posting was to the Indian High Commission in Karachi for three years and once again, we were disheartened. I expressed my desire to see my birthplace, but we were not permitted to leave the city. Moreover, time had changed and had made Lahore an alienated place. It was too familiar to be unknown, yet unknown enough to be known by anymore. Afterwards, we lived in Tehran, Iran for the next four years and then were also posted for four years, to Switzerland, which, quite rightly said, if there is paradise on Earth, it is here. Our youngest son Jawahar was now of college age, so in 1969, we arranged for him to study in Houston, Texas, United States where my brother Shyam Talwar lived and could help with any hurdles that he could not handle.

From Switzerland, we went back to India where my elder son, Jayant got married. Then we were posted to Romania for another four years and survived the 1977 earthquake in Bucharest, which took more than 1,500 lives and we lived in our broken flat for several weeks. Then in 1978, my husband retired from the Foreign Service and we returned back to India. But even after his retirement, he visited Kabul, Afghanistan for some government conferences and meetings very often. At that time, Kabul was really a beautiful and peaceful city, unlike the Kabul of today.

My husband died quite suddenly in 2003, passing on quietly like a saint. After his death, I moved to Houston in 2004 to live with my son who has been publishing the local community paper, Indo American News, for the past thirty-seven years. Here in Houston, I write Punjabi vegetarian recipes, which are published every week in the paper and because of this, even at the age of 90, I have become quite well-known in our community. People encourage me and thank me for the recipes, which makes me very happy and confident. I have always been a very devout Hindu and often participate in religious functions.

As time goes on, I remember the Lyallpur of my childhood, and how much sacrifice and hard work we had to do as a family in order to persevere and survive the partition and put ourselves on our feet again though we had lost everything we had. But I believe that you cannot be inflexible in life and must avoid wasting energy on anger and hatred. Many opportunities will come your way and you must be willing to see if they are best for you. Have faith in the Almighty for guidance, trust your intuition, and keep your social ties and family obligations.

40

Dying Reflections

JAAFAR ALI
KARNAL - GUJAR KHAN

THE SPEAKING WINDOW

A mirror reflects everything one is, one has, one used to have, and wishes to. It doesn't lie or demand anything, but it does reflect everything in the present and reminds how the past was. Every time I look into the mirror, I see a reflection of me that has everything today. The wrinkled skin tells how many lives I have lived in this lifetime. The eyes may have grown weak in vision but can see minute details of everything. I see a Patwari, who has served in many places, earned enough for the family, and lived a good life. Everyone sees this side of me—healthy, wealthy, and contented—but if you look at the same reflection closely, you would see a seven-year-old kid who was scared, helpless, and traumatized, who didn't know how to soothe his worrying parents and was terrified of himself. That boy had almost forgotten to smile but he was normal like the other kids before the partition. He used to play, laugh, be into mischiefs, and wander in the streets in summer. It was all before 1947, a year that took smiles off millions of faces.

The Speaking Window. Sandeep Dutt, Faisal Hayat, and Ritika, Oxford University Press.
© Oxford University Press India 2023. DOI: 10.1093/oso/9789391050733.003.0040

I can still imagine the streets, the house, the doors, and the cattle of that time, right in front of my eyes. I remember visiting the fairs of Kaliyar Sharif. It was all very much exciting; however, my ancestral roots led me back to Nawagaon, in district Karnal, the birthplace of the first Prime Minister of Pakistan, Liaquat Ali Khan. The village had ethnicity in it. A river flowed down by it, making it even more beautiful in terms of natural beauty and people living there made it a home; full of warm-fuzzy-feeling with clear blue sky over our heads which never showed discrimination towards anyone nor did we all. Women used to go together, chatting all the way, to the market and buy things not only for their homes but for each other too. I remember little girls playing with their dolls and boys with their marbles in the street. If anyone got thirsty, the doors of every house welcomed them. A pat on the back with a sweet smile on the face, this was the way people used to greet each other. Most of the people were into agriculture so was our family who owned almost sixty to seventy acres of land, which made us financially sound enough to live a lavish life. I have lived a childhood with unforgettable memories of friendship, brotherhood, and family. There is a reason why old folks like me think that the time in the past was much better than the present we have today. People were more tolerant towards each other before, and they were kind, respectful, and accepting. Religion was neither a business nor political tool but every time it has, it has shaken the world.

When the disturbances began, we used to hear the news of attacks in different villages and fear we were next. Situations were so tensed that when we were informed, there might be an attack on our place, we all left our homes and remained out all day till we got a confirmation back it was safe to return. Many times, attackers attacked and many times, they didn't. Even when we were misinformed, we all would run every single time, as no one could take any chance of risking one's life, if it were true. It was the month of Ramadan when in the name of religion, we left everything, our home, our friends, and our lands. Before departing, our father took all the jewellery and buried it in the ground in a hope to return back home after some days, and we started our journey by joining a caravan that was moving to Pakistan. Migrants kept on joining the caravan and it kept growing. We were four families on a *Kirachi* (an ox-cart) and carried wheat and millstone along, thinking we would buy something if needed on the way but we didn't, due to the low quality of things.

'Don't be afraid, our destination is near! Don't be afraid, our destination is near! Don't be afraid, our destination is near!', these were the words heard by 1.5 lakh of people including us every single day just to keep us motivated so that we could keep walking, a walk which lasted for continuous sixty long days but despite being a part of this big caravan didn't prevent the attackers from making several attempts on attacking us. Attacks were happening more on the people travelling at the end of the caravan or on the small groups, which used to get at a little far from the rest of us, as they made an easy target. We would only get news of being attacked. Some would say, today four people died, or six got missing, and figures used to get changed every day but not the situation. So many times, there were false alerts made about extremists' attack and we would all get together but then nothing would happen, and we would continue our journey.

It was not easy for us to carry on this long journey which we never thought to be as stretched out as it came to be. For two months, we were stuck there, spent countless sleepless nights fearing an attack, lived in unimaginable conditions with the scarcity of food and water and most of all, and we started doubting if we would ever reach there alive. Of 1.5 lakh people, there were those who were old, sick, disabled, and got injured in attacks. There were days when we used to think that we might never make it but then our leaders used to encourage us to take a few more steps and we'd be closer to Pakistan. And with every step we took, we would think, we were about to reach, even though we were a lot more farther than we thought. Just like a lost traveller in a desert who looks for an oasis, we felt the same; long lost.

We didn't only watch other people losing their family members, but we did one of ours too. My grandmother got sick and passed away. It was a really tough call to make on what to do next. Neither we could halt our journey nor we could carry her along, so the family decided to bury her there only. I remember when she was wrapped in a shroud and we bowed down and bade her goodbye. And from there, we continued our journey only to face the biggest hurdle in our journey—Ludhiana; where our own stories were falling in the shadow of death which could have ended everything there before we could begin something new. Since it was a Sikh-dominant region, who were not pleased at all with the slain trains coming back to India, so we feared to become victims of their wrath. But troops which were with us from the beginning of the journey restrategized their security protocols and made sure no danger would come in our way and we could be able to make it to our destination safely.

After a long tiring and terrifying journey, without losing any more people, we reached Lahore, Pakistan. People were bowing down in honour and some were expressing their gratitude to the Almighty for their safe arrival. Families were crying in joy and hugging each other. There was finally a sense of joy felt in a long time, which delighted every single soul. People made camps where they thought they could. Everyone was trying to find a place for himself to fit in and we were no different. We had no resources, no possessions, and no money. We all knew now there was no going back since we all had just lost everything. Even after making several efforts when my father could not see any solution to sort out our financial crunch, he realized he had buried the jewellery in the house back in India. So, after three months of partition, he went back, risking his life as the bloodbath spree was not coming to a halt. However, to his surprise, when he reached our house, he found it still abandoned; nobody had come to live in it; at least not yet. He dug out the bundle he had buried in the house and came back with it as soon as he could. This helped us a lot in those times when we didn't have to be at the mercy of the people or the government but they both did help us too.

We stayed in Chak, near Hafizabad for two years where I saw burnt houses of Hindus and Sikhs. In Chak, we were given fifty-four acres of land to cultivate crops and make our living. After that, we moved to village Kantrili, for my maternal Uncle was living there. We were given land there too, so we shifted. There was a government school in Kantrili that was owned by Hindus before the partition, but not anymore. It was in that school, I completed my education till matriculation, after which I got a government job and served in the position of a Patwari. I got married in 1962 and have ten children by the grace of God with countless grandchildren!

What I believe is that the life before partition was better because of the people who were understanding, caring, and empathetic towards each other but after that, if we say it is not the same or good anymore, it is again because of the people. But everyone had suffered so much at each other's hands that all they can remember now is the pain. But not all hope is lost. There are our relatives from the maternal family in India today who have visited us twice. They haven't changed a bit nor we have, I believe or maybe, it is just the age that did.

The circumstances which arose in partition, no doubt, were really unfortunate and I firmly believe it was the Rulers of that time who plotted this all. There were manoeuvres that they planned and executed to benefit themselves and harm people. It was not easy to annihilate centuries-long relationships of various families but the fear of being different from each other rusted their bond, which was no longer impenetrable. I have seen the partition, remained witness to the wars of 1965 and 1971. I have seen patriotism in people during those times and have also seen it being changed when it becomes only a matter of themselves. I have been to Mecca and Medina, which is a religious duty of every Muslim to fulfil. But after seeing everything, when I am asked if I would ever go back? If I had a chance, I would say YES, I would. After all, I belong to that country and it belongs to me. It is my motherland and which child doesn't want to be reunited with his mother once again? You, tell me, wouldn't you want to?

41

The Light Preserver

PREM SINGH BAJAJ
SARGODHA - LUDHIANA

THE SPEAKING WINDOW

Time: After the announcement of partition

The refugee camp of Shahbad, Markanda was already filled with the woes, cries, and sorrow of people when all of a sudden silence engulfed it, after the stamping feet of the soldiers marched into the camp and brought something, for which, no one was ready. All eyes suddenly filled with a strange emptiness. In that chilling silence, the sight of a cold corpse was the last thing anyone wanted to see. A chill ran through my spine when I realized that that lifeless face seemed very much familiar. It was the corpse of Mehtab Singh, the English teacher at my school. A face full of life once was now lying lifeless in front of me. The flashes of his memories filled my mind. His talks, scolding, laughter, and motivation, existed no more. The feeling of being lost, the feeling of losing someone, the feeling of nothingness. He was killed in Sargodha, while trying to reach the railway station. It was so un-believable back then to imagine the same place which happened to be

The Speaking Window. Sandeep Dutt, Faisal Hayat, and Ritika, Oxford University Press.
© Oxford University Press India 2023. DOI: 10.1093/oso/9789391050733.003.0041

my birthplace, preached harmony and brotherhood once, was now draining blood everywhere.

Born in a village, Baaran, Tehsil Shahpur, District Sargodha, I never knew what was religious hatred despite having different communities living in the same place in which only one-third population of Hindus and Sikhs and the rest were Muslims still, I don't remember anyone having conflicts with the other, just because one was a preacher of 'Allah', who is 'Ishwar/Rabb', to the other. I remember, my school, Khalsa High School was situated in the neighbouring village, Farooqa. It was started by a re-nowned Raagi (a Sikh devotional singer) Gyani Heera Singh. Children from all walks of life used to come to learn there. We were never taught how saffron or green was more than just colours. But since when and how they have been thought to signify religions, is something that amazes me. My matriculation examination had just gotten over when the news of partition broke out. Its result was out after my family migrated to India, which back then, used to be declared by the Punjab University, Lahore.

Imagine you have a house, and one day somebody comes and claims it, forces you to leave, and takes everything away from you. Those walls having your memories hung on them, the garden of your house where you used to play in the Sun and the veranda, where you had spent your childhood, were all gone. Even the petrichor which used to mesmerize you in monsoon, no longer belonged to you. And, the tragedy is, you are not asked to choose it; rather forced to leave it. And, you can't do much about it.

15 August 1947 was a black-letter day for everyone which not only brought the news of freedom but also, 'the cost', which we never thought of paying. An era of centuries of slavery had come to an end but the sound of all the trumpets and victory drums-beats seemed to have a deaf-ening effect over the supposed new masters of it... The sighs and mourns seemed to be lost in the whistling winds of victory. The massacre was a heart-crunching reality on both sides of the border, which lasted for days and left the present generation wounded and the generations to come scarred. Waking up to the smell of burnt houses, rotten flesh, and sight of blood all around was something much more than just fear. Like everyone, we were frightened for our life. At that moment when we all knew that we had to leave now.

To take the people, stuck in the madness, out, a special train arrived, escorted by the Sikh regiment, from the Silanwali station, which was luckily boarded by everyone who was present there. It ran non-stop until it reached Shahbad Markanda, Kurukshetra, where a refugee camp was set up. Here, we stayed at a mosque. My brother was desperately looking for a job in order to earn bread and butter for us and then one day, somebody helped my brother to get a job at Patiala Municipal Committee and my family got shifted to Patiala. There, we got a shelter too, as after some time, we were allotted a refugee house there only.

It was a tough beginning for every one of us who were forced to leave our ancestors' footprints and our motherland behind. Not everyone was as fortunate as I was. I got to continue my education. I did my Gyani at first and then F.A. English. I then did B.A. with English, along with a job as an Account Clerk in Mohindra College, Patiala. Though I wished to pursue M.A. in Economics but my teacher suggested me otherwise and I did my masters in Punjabi, which I did while working in the same college. The Principal of the college, Mr. A.R. Khanna, who was quite pleased with my work, called me in his office one day. I still can recall that while having tea, he said to me, 'Son, if you'll see any vacant post of lecturer anywhere then let me know I will help you to get that job because you deserve it.' And with his assistance, I got a job at the Satnam Dharam College, Hoshiarpur where I worked for four years. By that time, my whole family got shifted to Ludhiana and I started looking for a job nearby. In 1959, a new college opened in Jagraon, by the name of Lala Lajpat Rai Memorial College (now known by the name of Lala Lajpat Rai Memorial D.A.V. College) where I got myself posted as a Lecturer; I stayed there for thirty-one years, from 1959 to 1990. At first, I worked as a lecturer, then as a vice principal, and finally as a principal, the position I served for thirteen years. After retirement, I started a library at Punjabi Bhawan, Ludhiana, with the help of my seniors. I began it with 700 books and today, there are more than 70,000 books. Here, I have been teaching Urdu to people for twenty-two years, which I fell in love with, back in Pakistan. This library has the treasure of approximately 3,000 Urdu books. It's all because I want to save the culture for the upcoming generation.

People say that once time passes, it never comes back. I believe, you get to relive and rewrite your story once again in your lifetime. The time, itself gives you time to take back some of what you have lost completely.

In the 1980s, I got a chance to visit Lahore, with a few friends, to watch a Cricket match. Back then, people were easily allowed to visit Pakistan. There, we got so much love and affection of the people that cannot be expressed in words. I always longed for visiting Sargodha; but not alone. Neither I ever got the company of anyone to visit it nor could I muster a little courage to visit there all by myself.

After years of experience, and in the life-long process of gaining and losing, I have realized that it is very easy for us to think that 'we suffered more and they suffered less.' All I want to say is that the culture of 'our' people is one. We are just victims of extremism, which has always been a bane. If these two countries, forget their woes with each other, let go off their grudges and live like good neighbours then, many of the problems would get resolved automatically, which they are facing now. We need tolerance for each other. And I hope that they realize this someday.

42
Colour of Blood

ASHFAQ AHMED KHAN
DELHI - KARACHI

THE SPEAKING WINDOW

A rainbow has seven different colours, spread at different levels of a spectrum, but the thing that makes it so extraordinary and awestruck, is how gracefully those colours come together without overlapping but amalgamating into each other to form a huge band across the sky which makes it look so dreamy. Now, if the colours instead of getting along, ask, 'Why your spectrum is better, brighter, and wider than mine?' or 'Why red is on the top and violet at the bottom?' Trust me, we would have never been able to relish such a beautiful natural phenomenon. The pre-partition era was just like that rainbow, to which the world bowed down until its colours chose religion over collectiveness and decided to form a rainbow individually where every colour perished except for all the red that was left.

I never understood how people now say that the differences and conflicts were there already, even before the partition. They reason it with the fact that the chain of murders which started, went on to such a large scale, but it was not the case. Or, was it just half of a complete story? Very

The Speaking Window. Sandeep Dutt, Faisal Hayat, and Ritika, Oxford University Press.
© Oxford University Press India 2023. DOI: 10.1093/oso/9789391050733.003.0042

few people know or talk about the conspiracies, incited by the controversies, which were again a result of the misrepresentation of the facts to give birth to the conflicts that happened. Hindus and Muslims were never the Hindus and the Muslims which they are presented like; as if they are the North Pole and the South Pole, meant to repel each other. At least they were not like this in the place where I come from.

I was born in Rohtak but we used to live in Delhi where the majority was Hindus. Religion was just a way of life before. People would celebrate and cry together. At a funeral, the tears and the sense of loss did not come to a person, after inquiring about one's religion; it was the same for everyone. And on joyful occasions like wedding ceremonies, they used to get together to share the responsibilities of the bride's/groom's family. People were more into making things easier for each other rather difficult. The modern schooling lacks the lessons of empathy, sympathy, ethics, and morals in it but these were the teachings that were much more important to the people back then, which is why they used to send their wards to temples, or madrassas for getting the education and learn the values of life. The formal education was not much preferred by them but yes, the religious education was given more emphasis.

However, the region had Sikh residents too, but they were in minority and they were not as close to us as the Hindus were. People would gather at each other's place and have conversations the whole day. The men could be seen sitting on a cot outside their houses, under a tree, smoking Hookah. They would sit together, puff the pipe and pass it on to the next person sitting beside them. No wonder considering the current scenario, imagining Hindus and Muslims sharing the same pipe to smoke seems a little overrated thing but that is the whole point; it was a normal thing back then. Not only did they share the pipe, but their problems too with a whole bunch of chatters and laughter.

I was born into the family of Yousafzais (the ethnic Afghans and Pathans). The street in which we used to live was named after my father, Faiz Muhammad who was a cop and died when I was one year old. I could not get a chance to know him, but I did have a chance to know my brother, more in a father's role than that of an elder brother. After the death of my father, he took the responsibilities of our family that included me and my two sisters, who also saw him more like a father figure. He got a job in Police Department. He did a lot for all of us and never let any of us feel alone. He practically raised us all. Apart from him, I did have a lot of friends who were Muslims and Hindus as well. I can recall Lala Vaid Nath with whom I used to stroll in the streets and play all day long. He was like a brother to me and I was to him.

Before the partition was announced officially, the affections once held in the eyes of the people turned into a gaze of detest. The sweet talks, 'How is everyone home?', 'It's been a long time, when are you coming home?', 'Mother has made you Kheer today!' shockingly turned into: 'Go where you belong!', 'This is our place not yours!', 'You should go where you belong to!' 'This is not your home', 'Go back to your land!' But where were we supposed to go, leaving our own home? I was born and brought up there. My ancestors had been buried there. My father died serving the people of that place. If that was not home, I don't know what it was then.

The government had started setting up camps in the nearby villages for the migrants. Soon the people were brought in, loaded in trucks, on foot, and from all the directions and were sent to the railway stations. This was when we came to know about the partition. And then the killings began. Sikhs, Hindus, and Muslims were blaming each other for it but what they forgot to see was the loss that spared no one. The people tried to hide behind the locked doors of their houses which were burnt down to the ground. They tried to run but were chased and butchered. The few, who tried to fight back, were brutally murdered to set an example.

I had never expected that the same could happen to us. I used to work in a mill which was located in Abdullahpur. On my way back, I was stopped by a group of extremists, along with the other people who were Hindus. I knew if they came to know that I was a Muslim, my life would not have been spared, so I thought of disguising myself as a Hindu. I re-membered a Bhajan which I had heard in my childhood as I was friends with Hindus. So, I decided to recite it so that they would think of me as a Hindu. As they were talking and enquiring the others, I started reciting, 'Meine Ram naam dhan paya, Na mein Ganga gayi nahane, na mein Brahm rajaya, Ram naam dhan ghatat ghate nahin, mere dum dum Ram samaya, meine Ram naam dhan paya . . . ' These words saved my life that day and I was able to escape my death. Strangely, in this part of the na-tion, Ram saved a follower of Rahim, but somewhere else, the followers of Ram were struggling with the followers of Rahim. I wish, both groups instead of just following their idols, if had understood the meaning and importance of their teachings, then maybe nothing of such perilous nature ever would have happened.

As soon as I got home, I told my brother all about it and he decided that we would migrate. We carried only food with us and left everything else behind. We decided to leave via train, so we went to Delhi railway station. In those days, the trains were not safe at all and were the easiest and perfect target for a genocide that had already happened so many times in an endless loop. As soon as we boarded the train, we noticed the seats and the walls that had blood stains on them. It was a terrifying scenario. We hesitated a little and for a moment, we had to rethink our decision of leaving via train, but we had no other option but to take that risk. The more time we lost, the lower became the chances of our survival. So, we decided to stick to the plan. Before the train left, the army came and we took a sigh of relief. They travelled with us to ensure our safe journey. Most of the passengers were Rohtakis (from Rohtak). In spite of having the Army protection, people were still worried if the extremists could become successful in stopping the train on its way or if the driver stopped it, then what would happen to us all? It was a journey of two days and one night with a persistent sense of worry. It was like we were keeping track of every second but no such thing happened. All the way, I had the flashbacks of our home, our street where all the homes were of Pathans. And, how I used to play with my friends there, where now there was nothing but empty houses.

We finally reached Pakistan, safe and sound. We stayed in Multan for a few days, but we were not welcome there and people were so insensitive towards us that we were denied any kind of help but they did shelter us temporarily. Then we went to our relatives in Karachi. We received Rs. 12,000 and a few properties in Pakistan by the authorities, which helped us getting settled down a lot. I started my own business here and with time, our family got settled. I got married and now have two sons and two daughters. My eldest son was a Sergeant in Pak Airforce and passed away serving the nation. And now, I have no wishlist and I am happy with what I had and have today.

In my perspective, I hold the Britishers responsible for the whole mass murder. They should have and could have done something to prevent it, but they chose to become mere spectators. And it was the folly of the people who not even for once, thought that the blood was scattered on both sides and it was not something they chose or needed to do. A political decision, taken without the consent of the people, claiming it was for their betterment which I see none of till date after all these years since the bloodshed that happened.

Ask a mother who lost his son, a father in front of whom his daughter was taken, a brother who could not save his family and a five-year-old child who lost both of his parents; they would define what betterment really is and if it really has been such a blessing. It is easy to write and document about the number of people who lost their lives or those who witnessed it but the families who suffered it all, are the only ones who know what they had lived through and lost. The barbarity we had to witness cannot be described in any words. The limbs of a body were scattered everywhere; a hand was lying somewhere in the corpses with the glass of bangles stuck in its flesh. There was a head with its eyes wide open which were filled with the horrors of its final moments and they were looking at me as if penetrating my soul. I could barely look at it. Many bodies were beheaded and wells and rivers were filled with corpses of the dead. There was no water to drink, and in the trains, the nails were hammered on the seats so that people could not sit. Ah! It was all so much disturbing. Some memories, no matter how much we try to erase, keep coming back, and these are some of those.

After the partition, people from Rohtak contacted us and informed us about the possessions which we had left entrusting them, thinking when the things would cool off, we could go to take them back. But the situations were not favourable, so we didn't go back and asked them to keep them for themselves. This way, at least we knew they were with our own people who had been a part of our family. My father was a benevolent man too. He once donated a major part of our land for a graveyard to be built years before he died.

For me, India and Pakistan are the two sides of the same coin. We share the same culture, land, people, and water too. If I ever could, I would definitely visit my home once. I have lived a blissful life in both the countries. I have lived my whole life minding my own business, with dignity, honour, and without any worry.

43

Passed Era

LEELAVANTI GAMBHIR
SIALKOT - SURAT

THE SPEAKING WINDOW

In the refugee camp of Amritsar, some were mourning over their dead and some were reunited with their loved ones but there were those like me who didn't know whether to wait or learn to live with this deep gloomy emptiness inside of me. I was waiting for my husband whom I had not seen since I had started my journey to India. The pain after the first labour, the sense of loss of leaving her home behind and fearing for her child's and her own survival, there was a wife having her son in her arms, waiting for her husband to return to her, remembering all the vows they both made to each other and countless memories of their time together which came back haunting her now. I spent those days in these thoughts with eyes constantly searching him and fighting the darkest fears which petrified me every second on hearing the tales of this bloodied timeline, to which the generations were going to question in the future.

'Partition' may not be happening for the first time in the human history but at this extreme and grand level, it was. Millions of homeless people

The Speaking Window. Sandeep Dutt, Faisal Hayat, and Ritika, Oxford University Press.
© Oxford University Press India 2023. DOI: 10.1093/oso/9789391050733.003.0043

travelled in the hope of a better future, leaving their homes to seek a new one, which many could never see. The leaders had spoken, the fate of the nation was signed, and the partition was real. The people who shared same heritage, fought for the same freedom, were now fighting each other. It rewrote the past, which people knew differently till then.

Sialkot, the place where I was born, brought up, and studied up to fifth grade, knew quite a different era. It was the time of authority in life. Ethics and morals were highly valued and there was an ease in the understanding and acceptance of the differences which did exist then but never conflicted with the beliefs of others. The Arya Samaj School where I received my formal education had pupils from all backgrounds.

Daska was about twenty-five kilometres away from Sialkot, where I moved at the age of fifteen, after getting married. The farms of cauliflower, potato, and other vegetables, we owned used to have this fresh fragrance all around. We had a well-established shoe business there and life was good. It was our ancestral home; our forefathers and their forefathers had lived there all their life and had never even been out of the state. With the rising voices of freedom, there was a strengthening demand for partition too, which caused violence in many areas. The police told us to migrate but like others, we would just close our shop and lock our house from inside for some days and then go back to living a normal life. We thought it was temporary and everything would be fine soon. After all, how could anyone go leaving everything behind? Our generations had lived there, how could we …?

In August 1947, the government orders came in asking people to migrate and with that, a new struggle began … a struggle to be alive. If war knows no mercy, the communal hatred is even blinder. It didn't matter if it were the same children who used to play in their streets, or the same women who would have welcomed their guests with sweet delicacies or the expected mothers like me, for whose wellbeing they might have prayed at some point of time. The hate-mongers knew none of them when it came to the merciless slaughter. I was twenty-one years old and wasn't only worried for myself alone but also for the child who was about to open its eyes to this cruelty. I was nine months pregnant and had come to my mother's place for delivery when we had to leave immediately.

There was no time to inform anyone. My husband, who was in Daska at that time, was not informed that we were leaving. I didn't get a chance to visit him, considering the severity of the circumstances, which were just getting worse and precarious with every passing hour. We didn't even get a chance to take our belongings and had to shift to a refugee camp, at once. This is the last thing that a mother could ever want for her child; to come into this world in such chaos. And the time came, I got into my labour. I remember the ladies gathering around me to help me in giving birth to my child while their sarees were hung around me to ensure privacy.

Those four days in the camp with a newborn were extraordinary for there were no joys of celebrating a new life but a constant fear to save it. From there, we were asked to board the train which was leaving for Amritsar. Our journey to the 'New India' began. It was by the virtue of the Gods that we reached India safely, without any slaughter or bloodshed and under the military protection. On the way, the train was stopped on a bridge where we all were instructed to walk in the caravan to Amritsar. There were people who told horrifying stories. Some said they had to drink their own urine because no water was available. The people who migrated in the train which came next to ours were not as fortunate as us. Even the infants were not spared. Few of my distant relatives also suffered the same fate. And my husband … till then, I had no clue of my husband and his safety. I didn't even know whether he made it alive or not. I didn't know if he would ever be able to see his son's face or not.

After walking for four long days, struggling with thirst and starvation, we reached Amritsar. My family and I were sheltered at a relative's place there. And then, about fifteen days later, my husband made his way to India and we finally met.

Seven years! It took us seven long years to rebuild a house of our own, combined with ceaseless efforts of re-establishing our shoe business and finally, after a long struggle, we tasted success. At present, my children and grandchildren are well settled in different parts of the country. My husband had visited Pakistan once, but I didn't.

They say, painful experiences make one colder, less empathic, or more insensitive. I don't agree. It is said, 'Don't let someone dim your light, simply because it's shining in their eyes'. This is what I have learnt from what experience I have in life. I believe there's goodness in people, which is why one must not hold grudges. Ek daur tha, jo beet gya (It was an era, which has passed).

The rule of karma says you reap what you sow, so my message to the young generation, which owns the power to change the world, is to give love, and you will get the same in return. You cannot fight hate with hate, just like the darkness cannot be driven out with more darkness. Only love and light can illuminate your path. So, just love each other and live your life to its fullest.

44

Horror of Horrors

SYED ABDUL WAHEED
AMBALA - RAWALPINDI
THE SPEAKING WINDOW

A child, when born, brings nothing but its joyful presence along with it; without a name, religion, culture, community, and everything else that distinguishes and establishes similarity within a particular group with beliefs which has its own unique teachings and preaching practices. If thought about it deeper, people use fashion and symbolism to identify themselves within a social structure. A Shikha and a Janeu mean the child belongs to a Hindu Brahmin family, a Taqiyah on his head will introduce him to Sunnites, a cross on his neck means he should be given lessons of Catholicism and with the shabad in Gurudwara, in the naming ceremony, he will feel the holiness of Guru Granth Sahib for the first time while getting the first letter of his name from the holy book. Strange but true, the world is so lost in seeing and understanding religion and God cladded in the rituals and traditions, unique to every belief system that the real essence of his existence is lost somewhere in the process.

The Speaking Window. Sandeep Dutt, Faisal Hayat, and Ritika, Oxford University Press.
© Oxford University Press India 2023. DOI: 10.1093/oso/9789391050733.003.0044

Dressed in a white saree with blue piping but swathed in fear, not knowing what would happen next, with a little faith in heart, my sisters stepped out of the house with my father who was wearing a Rampuri cap to conceal their Islamic identity with a Hindu attire, hoping to deceive the eyes which would look upon them with detest and wrath which fails to understand even God's will. We left for the railway station to catch a train to Saharanpur at 5 pm, which we did on time. I was twelve years old at that time and was trying to understand what exactly was going on. Only a few moments ago, my father had come home with the lines of worry on his forehead and the pitch of his voice ringing with fear, which was something I had never seen before. As soon as he got into the house, he told us to get dressed like Hindus as we were about to leave. No one questioned him, and we simply did what he asked us to do. The place I lived for twelve years of my life was not mine, anymore. Peeping out of the moving train's window, I could see my home getting farther and farther at the pace of the moving train. The trees, the grass, the lights, and the houses outside seemed blurred with the fast-moving train, which eventually disappeared at the nightfall. And then, all I could recall were the memories I loved and cherished in the past.

Ambala, my hometown, the simpler, the beautiful, and the calmer it had been, so had been its people. A Hindu majority region, having Muslims and Sikhs in minority but still, there was a lot of affection among them. The city was a major cantonment. So, the sight of heavy tanks and big-armed forces with decorated officers and infantry marching around was a common scenario. The British and Indian soldiers could be seen exercising together. Thus, the presence of military made the city safer for the general population. There were schools, colleges, district court; everything a big city has, Ambala had it all. Ambala Cantt and Ambala city were at a distance of 6–6^1/2 km from each other.

People—working for the government had good contacts and, so did my father. He was known to many and knew many more influential people. His job paid him well too, ₹130 to ₹150 monthly. We were living in Ambala Cantt for my father was a railway employee; he was a guard. Though Cantt had the biggest station with Government quarters, but we preferred living in a nearby rented accommodation in a house of a Hindu family who was nice to us. Our family was big—we were six sisters and three brothers. Our father was a family man. He loved spending time with us at home. He used to plan vacations, organize celebrations on various occasions, and would talk to us about our day too. I remember spending every summer at Ambala in our main house where all my siblings used to play hide and seek a lot. We would run in the whole house and plan mischiefs there. There was one more place where we used to go. It had coldness in its atmosphere, beautiful snowfall view, and was famous for its beautiful dawns and dusks and had the world-famous toy train, which had its own joy to travel in, Shimla. I also remember an elite Hindu friend of my father, Raghu Nath Rao who was as aristocratic as his family name. His life was lavish, and he made it larger. He was good with Britishers also, as he was an A-grade driver. But during the partition, his attitude got changed. Their friendship turned into communal enmity, which was for no apparent reason.

I was in grade 7 studying in CB School near Ambala Cantt. At the age of 12, when I heard about the partition, I didn't know that decision would have such consequences. It was my father who returned with a scary news. He got to know that the extremists would attack us the next morning, so we all had to leave by night. This is when we all dressed like Hindus and dodged many extremists, but we knew somewhere that we needed something to stick together. My father was aware of all the tactics which the extremists used to create hurdles in the ways of Muslims. In those days, the people working with extremists used to board the train as a normal passenger and would pull the chain where the attack was supposed to take place and sometimes, there would be trees placed on the railway tracks because of which the train had to be stopped. So before boarding the train, he went to the driver, Nathu Ram and asked for his help and said, 'We have known each other for a long duration of time. This might be our only chance to escape and probably we might never see each other again. So, don't betray me' and requested the same to Muslim firemen to be on alert. Consequently, the train only stopped at a few important stations and the firemen didn't disappoint him. They kept the fire on thorough out the journey and we reached Saharanpur at 9 pm.

After reaching Saharanpur, we went to the house of one of my father's friends in Muhalla Sherazan where we spent a couple of days and planned our further journey. My father wished to migrate by sea from Mumbai to Karachi. However, the sudden financial crunch didn't allow him to do so. Therefore, travelling by train was the next fastest option left but with a degree of greater risk of life given the fact that train massacres were happening every day during that time. However, all of us stuck to that decision.

To ensure our safe arrival in Pakistan, my father requested a Colonel of the Baloch Regiment to let us board the special train which carried the soldiers of the Baloch Regiment, to which he agreed. The Beas station was defaced to an unrecognizable form. There was a hue and cry everywhere. We got to know that the extremists had attacked a train that arrived before ours and no one survived. People were crying over the dead bodies of their relatives, and crows and vultures feasting on the corpses. My paternal uncle's son, Abdul Shakoor was a sub-inspector who was also migrating like others from Ambala to Pakistan but unluckily, he and his family fell victim to that attack. He had his daughter Noor Jahan and his mute son, Qamar with him. When the extremists attacked, the boy ran and hid in a pool of dead bodies while the girl was standing behind her father who was fighting the attackers but lost his life when one of them cut his belly open with a sword. He fell unconscious in the pool of his own blood. His wound was so deep that his guts fell out. His sixteen-year-old daughter, scared to death, lying beside his lifeless body, tried to cry for help when she herself fainted, witnessing the horrors unfolding in front of her. Since she was smeared in her father's blood, she was left unharmed as thought to be dead. His brother, who was mute, neither could even cry out loud to express his pain on seeing his father being butchered in front of him nor could he hold his sister to take her away from all of that. He was forced to run and hide and see his family being annihilated in front of his very eyes but he could not even utter a word. Nevertheless, the siblings made it to Pakistan later.

On 9 September, we arrived at Atari railway station, which was our last station in India. The loud shout for 'Long live Pakistan' could be heard loud and clear and with this, we bade goodbye to our home, our old life, and old motherland. At Malakwal station, two friends of my father received us who had already migrated there a year ago. In the beginning, people started occupying the empty houses left by Hindu/Sikh families who migrated on the other side, so when we arrived there, we went to a house which was a three-storey building, with a really beautiful garden which had a captivating sight. It belonged to Dr Ram Laal Bali, a renowned person of his area who probably had left his house deserted because of partition. There was a Persian Wheel (a water-lifting mechanism from open wells) in the garden itself. My father was determined to live there after seeing the house but as soon as we explored the place, something made him change his decision instantly. The house was really beautiful from outside, had a beautiful architectural design inside and old artefacts in it. As we started ascending on to the stairs, we noticed blood on the steps, a lot of blood. Chills ran down our spines. The stairs led us to a huge room which was painted with the blood of a body that hung upside down in the middle of the room, with its head missing. And that was it. My father immediately left with us and decided not to reside in that house.

This is not the only house that was wailing all the atrocities its dwellers went through. The whole city was screaming in pain. Eighty percent of the Hindu houses were burnt in rage. The house we visited was in a lane called *Bank wali gali* (Bank's lane) as it had a bank nearby, which was left in shambles. The place reeked of death and the haunting pictures painted in every corner of it were retelling the story of its recent events. The scattered papers, torn registers, looted lockers, and blood on various spots were not signs of mercy. We were not able to bear the sight of this and it gives me goosebumps even today when I think about those who had to go through all this. Nonetheless, some people were trying to help people like us too. There was a person named Ghulam Ali Bajwa who helped a lot. He gave us food to eat and helped us in finding a place to get shelter.

As things started to cool off and people started to go back to their normal life, my parents decided to get me admitted to a school. My school here was M.B. School which had some of the great teachers who loved their students and helped them get over the brutality of partition but for our family, things never got normal. In 1950, my younger brother fell into a well and passed away and I never saw my father smiling ever again after that. And soon, he followed him to the grave too. We were asked to evict the house and there was again a big crisis. However, as it is said, if one door closes, the other one gets opened. My sister Suraiyya got a job and she took all the responsibility of us. And finally, I was able to complete my graduation from the Government Degree College, Sargodha. From 1957 to 1995, I served in railways. My children are also serving the nation now as they are in armed forces. I am a grandfather now and living my life in peace.

For the youth to understand what their ancestors went through, I penned down my whole story in my autobiography, کہمندانم—Ke Man Danam, which means I only know myself. I have no desire to go back as we have no relatives there anymore. I believe that human desires know no limit or end to it, but on counting the blessings which I am bestowed with, I think I am content with what I have.

45

War of Blinds

AMARJIT SINGH
KOT RADHA KISHAN - DELHI

THE SPEAKING WINDOW

9 March 1947

An unusual sound of drumbeats entered the Khukhrain villages; not of the celebrations but it was a sound of the footstep of death, stepping slowly inside those villages, however, this time not silently but with a charade.

'Convert yourself into Islam or leave the village, if you wish to live!'—a voice ringing with extremism said.

Fear struck everyone. There were those who left silently, and those who could see the blood splatter on the walls of others and could not bear witness to the same fate for their family, so they cut their hair and accepted Islam. Then there were those, who could not decide whom they should betray. Their Gods, or themselves? Thus, they consumed poison with their families, leading to a mass suicide. But then came those for whom the Khukhrain clan have been known for so long!

The Speaking Window. Sandeep Dutt, Faisal Hayat, and Ritika, Oxford University Press.
© Oxford University Press India 2023. DOI: 10.1093/oso/9789391050733.003.0045

The clan has marked its claws deep into the history to the origin of the civilizations of Taxila and Mohen Jo Daro. Residing near Jhelum, our ancestors had been the target of the attackers coming from Khyber including the attacks led by Ahmad Shah Abdali and Nadir Shah Abdali. I belong to the very place, where the historic defeat of Alexzander the great had been witnessed by time. The clan moved to the river Soan later and we had served in the army of the Maharaja Ranjit Singh. Originally, farmers and warriors, the Khukhrains had been known for their courage! Even the text from the ancient Hindu scripture, Mahabharata has a reference to the Khukhrain clan. When, at the time of the war of Kurukshetra, Duryodhana went to Lord Krishna one evening and requested him to spend the night in his camps, two Khukhrain Kings—Anand and Bhaseen, were also present there who were fighting from the Pandavas side. To his reply, Lord said, 'I will prefer to live with the kingdoms of Anand's and Bhaseen's rather than yours, Duryodhana'. Such has been the loyalty and faith in Khukhrains and that day, we needed to exhibit the same.

With the announcement of life threats, the genocide began with a drum roll as if they were on a hunt and enjoyed every kill. People were being killed, even children were not spared, the women were being dragged by hair and their pleadings were having no impact on the perpetrators of hate. It was rather giving them a feeling of joy. The houses were set on fire with the people inside them, burnt alive. With this gruesome act, it was Allah and his teaching which were being disregarded.

My maternal family who was living in Dheri, which was one of those villages that were attacked, took the third way; of fighting back. The family got divided into two groups and was trying to reach out to the nearby Gurudwara when one of the groups got misled by a Muslim neighbour who misinformed my maternal uncle by telling him, 'Shah ji, a group of extremists are coming from that side, hide yourself in our haveli (mansion)'. And so, they did and got trapped. When they entered into the haveli, they sealed the door with the wheat bags present inside and everyone went on to the roof. As soon as they reached there, what they saw was terrifying. A huge mob had surrounded the haveli. There was no way they could go out and the mob could come in any second! Their naked shiny swords swinging in the air were getting restless to taste blood. Again, the same scenario transpired but only this time, there was nowhere to run.

'Convert yourself into Islam or leave the village, if you wish to live!', they declared!

The people there were terrified and whispering about what they should do when all of a sudden, one of the extremists threw a brick towards my maternal aunt who was holding her one-year-old son. The brick hit her, the child fell down from her arms; her tears and screams filled the sky. A helpless mother cried to my maternal uncle, 'Let's accept their conditions to escape from here and save our lives. We'll go straight to Amritsar, and take Amrit and return to Sikhi'. But her husband got enraged, took out his sword, beheaded her, and yelled 'It is time to die!' He, then, opened the gates to fight, and yelled, 'It is the time to die!!!!'

The gates were opened and a blood-thirsty mob entered that mansion, leaving the dead bodies in their way. There was only a handful of people, in hundreds maybe, who were nothing in front of the thousands standing there to kill them. In no time, almost everyone died; only a few women and sixteen children were left. When they were too about to face death, a Muslim woman named Allah Ditti came there and pleaded for their life in front of those extremists who were blinded by hatred. She said, 'Tuhanu Allah da vasta, ehna baccheeyan nu na maro! (For the sake of God, have mercy on these kids)!' She saved them including the one-year-old kid who fell off the roof. The corpses were displayed like exhibits to make a statement. Most of them were either burnt or dumped into the river. However, interestingly, my maternal aunt was buried by them.

The other group of my family was saved by their Muslim friend, Deraab. When the extremists started searching the houses of the Muslims whom they doubted were helping the non-Muslims, they knocked at his door too. He was hiding my grandfather but when he was asked to swear in the name of the Holy Quran as no true Muslim would take a false oath, he took the oath and said that no one was there in his house. Technically, he was not lying. He was hiding my family in a separate building; not in his house, so the oath he took was not really false.

In the night, my grandfather and the rest of the family decided to move towards the Chakri village, which had a big Gurudwara and I knew many other families were trying to reach there as well. They walked all night to reach there and found that around 265 people from a nearby village had taken shelter in that Gurudwara, which was still under construction. They knew they were not safe, so they started taking measures to safeguard themselves. By dawn, the extremist arrived there and sieged the Gurudwara. As the Gurudwara was still under construction, there was a lot of marble lying on the floor, which on the instructions of my grandfather, was used to seal the gate. Everyone went on the roof. In the name of ammunition, there were only a few guns, with limited bullets but a lot of courage. They started firing and killed five extremists. The extremists retaliated too but, on this side, no one got injured. Now that the extremists knew that the people were armed, they stopped firing. The SHO of the area came there and requested us not to take law in our own hands and appealed people to come out as the police would save them. My grandfather replied, 'We don't believe you! Everyone is backstabbing!' Then, the area counsellor Hayat Khan arrived and said, '*Khatriyon kyon marde o?*' (Why do you want to die?), and continued, 'We'll save you, just come out'.

The people started thinking over their 'too-good-to-be-true' offer but few of them believed it. My grandmother stood up and requested my grandfather to kill her as she didn't want to get abducted or be killed by the extremists. Seeing no other choice and considering the fight seemed certain, he respected her wish and she was martyred. Then he addressed the people saying, '*Guru Gobind Singh de puttran de khoon naal likhya Sikhi da itihaas, Shahidiyan da itihaas, kale pochhe maar ke na marna... Zindagiyan te kayi wari mildiyan ne... Guru shabad vich maran da eh subhaag hai... hune shaheed ho skde han... apna farz ada karo*' (The history of Sikhism, which is written with the life sacrifices of the sons of Guru Gobind Singh Ji, ought not to be blotted like this. We will get many lives but to be martyred like this, is an honour. We must do our duty.) Hearing this, my newlywed maternal aunt stood up and offered her life to be sacrificed and was martyred, and so was the kid of one of my relatives whom she was holding. Here, my younger maternal uncle who was at the age of 11 then, got up and said, 'Guru Gobind Singh Ji was nine years old when he took the charge. We are also his sons. Give us the swords we too will fight till death'. My grandfather asked people to leave if anyone wished to and if they chose to stay, a fight for their honour awaited them.

Thirty to thirty-five people including the pregnant females and Malik Singh who was one of our relatives, went outside. He was the last one to leave and had a sword hidden in his umbrella, in case the situation needed it. Since he left at last, he was at a considerable distance from the rest of the group. Upon going further out of the Gurudwara, he saw the women getting slaughtered by the extremists. It was then he realized that my grandfather Gurmukh Singh was right; it was time to make sacrifice. So, he returned back to Gurudwara and informed that the extremists had killed all those people who went out.

For the next two hours, the extremists tried to get inside the Gurudwara, which was still full of people who were praying now. The chants of Japji Sahib were getting louder and louder and so were the threats and voices of extremists. However, the prayers were answered. A truck full of the Sikh Regiment came in time and rescued all the people. The extremists fled the place. Sixteen of my maternal family members sacrificed their lives for their religion and their dignity. Some people, including my grandfather and two maternal uncles, were safely escorted to a refugee camp made in the Panja Sahib, Rawalpindi. And some days later, they were moved to the Dukh Niwaran Gurudwara, Patiala where the Maharaja of Patiala Yadavindra Singh had made arrangements to aid the refugees.

An attempt was made to assassinate the Maharaja of Patiala for his sympathetic attitude towards the refugees. This sparked violence and a large number of Muslims were killed despite the fact that Muslims were in majority there. While studying in Patiala, I heard that the Nullah of Patiala was filled with the corpses.

This did force me to wonder how all of this got this far! People whether in Pindi, Lahore, or Patiala were never like this. I have lived in all these places because twenty families on my paternal side belonged to Chakri village, and twenty-five of my maternal family's relatives were from Dheri village. Both villages were in Rawalpindi. I remember visiting both very often while visiting Panja Sahib Gurudwara, which was near to them. All these areas were Muslim majority but the dominating number of one community had never been a threat to the other. We were farmers and landlords and were also into finance. In our fields, we had a majority of Muslim workers but all were honest and hard working. Never even once, the faith and love needed any explanation for approval.

I was born in Kot Radha Kishan near Kasur. My father was a government employee in railways and in 1945 went to Second World War as well because the railways was under British Army and my father was assisting them in Assam. Thus, my own family, which included three siblings, my parents, my grandfather, one brother, and one sister of my father were living in Kot Radha Kishan. Though we are six siblings in total, three of us were born in new India.

Kot Radha Kishan being a Sikh-dominating region, remained safe throughout this massacre. Besides, people were sure that Kasur would become a part of India, so nothing was much disturbed there. However, this misconception which we thought of as a fact was cleared soon when Kasur was announced to fall under the boundary of Pakistan.

From March 1947, we had been hearing about the bloodshed. Our own relatives also lost their lives in that but we didn't leave till 11 August until we were sure Kasur was not a part of India anymore, after hearing the confirmation by the Authorities in a radio broadcast. To avoid the deadly situations faced by my maternal family in March, my family decided to migrate.

My father had bought a Tonga for Rs. 500 and all the children were seated in it with the goods which we could carry. On the way, a river was to be crossed, which proved to be a bugbear. The Tonga got stuck in the river and was soon turned upside down. All the jewellery and valuable items got lost in the rapid pace of the river. But we all survived somehow. Now the only money we were left with was Rs. 50, which my grandfather kept in his shoe. The second half of the journey was covered on foot. We joined a caravan. It was raining at the night when people were staying in a temporary camp but God sent help for us. A friend of my father, Prem Singh, a military official came in his jeep, looking for my father. Since it was dark at night and so many people were there in the camp, so he was shouting his name, 'Sardar Navneet Singh!' to find him. As soon as my father heard his name in the voice of an old friend, he knew who it was. Both, so happy to see each other, couldn't contain their emotions, but the criticality of the situations did not let them spend a single moment when dangers loomed around. We were then taken to Patiala in a military truck immediately. If it weren't for him, who knows what would have unfolded? Our rest of the relatives from the village were already living there, after surviving the killings of March 1947.

We spent some days in the refugee camp. Since my father was a government employee before, he was appointed as a food supply inspector in Sonipat and we moved there. I studied for two years and then moved to Patiala where the education level was better. I studied till eighth standard.

Having a knack for sports, I participated in many sports events which took place in the National Stadium of Patiala. By that time, my interest in the religious teachings also got much deeper, so I opted to study the Guru Granth Sahib.

In ninth standard, the family moved to Delhi as my father started a Motor Parts Business near Kashmiri Gate. I used to study the Guru Granth Sahib in-depth at home for I sought knowledge and peace which I believe, it did impart to me. After completing my eleventh standard, I completely left my studies and joined my father's business.

I started working at the age of 16 and till the age of 32, I used to work for eighteen to twenty hours a day. I have seen the 1947 partition, wars of 1965 and 1971, the emergency of 1975, and 1984 Sikh genocide, which broke my heart. I felt so helpless during the 1984 riots that I could not focus on my business anymore and wanted to do something for the people. Therefore, I went into public services and worked for Sikh widows for four years after the riots. Then in 1988, I came back to the normal way of life, but gradually, I let go off my position in business, and started giving public speeches and communicating with people. I do Satsang, I teach people through Guru Granth Sahib, and I teach Bhagavad Gita as well. Apart from the many states of India, I've been to Maryland, Virginia, Washington, Singapore, and Bangkok as well.

The 1947 partition was the biggest swap of population and a huge genocide in the history of time. It has definitely left the nations and their people wounded. But if the wounds are not treated properly, they turn into sores which, if left untreated, can infect the whole body. Even after such tragic events, in all the stories I narrated, there were those who became hopeful in those dark times. The boy who fell off the roof of that haveli, is Dilwant Singh who is right now in the United States. The eleven-year-old boy who told his father that he would fight, is right now in Guwahati, Assam. Malik Singh who came back to the Gurudwara and told my grandfather that he was right, he met me many years later after the partition. They all are in touch with me and still sometimes, discuss about the partition but not to remember the hate, but the love which people had and the sacrifices they made. The difficulties we went through to get here, to start a new life, and to remain rooted with our ancestry.

By now, I believe that you must have taken sides already. Haven't you? Must be feeling hurt and betrayed? Must be feeling angry? A lot of anger on that Muslim neighbour who got his own people trapped in the haveli and on that SHO and counsellor too, who were trying to convince people to come out of that Gurudwara. So, what about Deraab who took an oath of the Holy Quran to save the innocents? Didn't you understand yet? He was a Muslim too! But, he didn't help in killing people but saved them, risking his own life. Then Allah Ditti who saved the lives of those sixteen children! What about that? It was not the religion but the people who hid their evil behind the mask of religion. If there were those Muslims who killed all these people, then there were those who were saved who knew the love of God lies in humanity, not brutality; and religion doesn't define it.

Neither now nor then, were people wise enough to see that religion had been and has been used merely as a tool to gain the support of its followers. It is used to benefit one's own selfish motives, which were and will always remain a part of the power game for its preachers. But why do you care? When we all love to give a verdict over the name of a person than their deeds! It might be a Radcliff Line that divided the nation, but it was us who darkened it enough to remain intact till the present time. This Hindu–Muslim line inside and outside us, is created by us.

So, a Muslim who lied to kill people and was blindfolded in hatred, or a Muslim who lied to save people in the name of humanity on which Islam is also based, who between these two incidents, is a true Islamic follower, is for you to decide. Or maybe if you are able to see beyond the religious boundaries, then you might one day be able to erase that line. Like I said, it is for you to decide.

46

Beyond Barbed Wire

MANDOWARI KARMANI
MITHI

THE SPEAKING WINDOW

Not all stories of the partition are written in blood, narrating the saga of stabbed brotherhood. There were some which did not let the star of hope get lost in the dark nights. In fact, they became the pole star for those who thought they might forget the way to home forever. Help comes to those who really seek it and may be that is what happened when I was looking for the same. When the whole nation was getting divided and people were forced to leave their ancestral homes in order to save their lives and that of their families' we, on the other hand, didn't have to. I am Mandowari Karmani, a Hindu residing in Sindh, Pakistan and I did not have to migrate.

I was born in a small town, Chelhar, in the district of Tharparkar in Sindh. It was a small desert area with a population that was the majority of Hindus. People living there were quite peace loving and believed in living a simple life, so it was never the case that anyone would have had any conflict with the other. The sand of the desert, with camel hoofs' prints

The Speaking Window. Sandeep Dutt, Faisal Hayat, and Ritika, Oxford University Press.
© Oxford University Press India 2023. DOI: 10.1093/oso/9789391050733.003.0046

on it, nomadic songs in its air on the tunes of Algoza and Chang, and the temple Murlidhar in the heart of the town where the chimes of bells and sound of Aarti would create a very positive aura all around. And may be, it is the same aura that protected us here when it was needed.

In spite of all the scarcity of resources, the town had a school. Many families sent their wards there including mine. I studied till fourth standard. There was no such thing as communal differences among us. People would stand by each other in their good and bad times. There had been moments in my life when we also feared for our lives. The most terrifying time I witnessed was the Second World War. It was a very fearful experience to see the skies echo with the thundering sounds of the fighter jets, so we would remain inside our homes, fearing the loss of our lives.

About 30 km to the North, another town named Mithi was located, which is now the capital of the district Tharparkar in Sindh. I got married in this town. Even Mithi was no different than Chelhar. It had the same peace in its surroundings and the same kind of people. Like Chelhar, it was also a Hindu-majority region. Everything was going well and nothing much changed even after the partition. I was around twenty-two years old when the partition happened. Because of the lack of resources, the communication facilities were not much available and due to that, we got to know about the partition two days later from the time it was announced. That too, from a person from a nearby village, who came to deliver the news to our town. It was shocking for us to know that now there were two nations, India and Pakistan, and people had begun migrating from one to another because we were told India was for Hindus and Pakistan was for Muslims.

Mithi was in Sindh, which became a part of Pakistan. It was scaring us all that what would happen to us. Would we too have to leave our lands, our homes, and our lives here like the millions of people who had to do the same? Was it not our country anymore? Were we now aliens to the very soil we belonged to? So many questions were popping in the mind, but we had no answers to them. When everyone stood worried about it, there came the answer, walking towards us, all in flesh and bones. The Muslims of our region visited us requesting to stay. They assured us nothing would happen, and we need not think of migrating to an alienated place where we would have to re-sketch our lives from the beginning, which would not have been like eating a cake.

Where, in rest of the country, the states were engulfed in the communal violence, Muslims, Sikhs, and Hindus could only see the blood in each other's hands and were getting infuriated in response to the communal killings in their communities and killing people to avenge the deaths of their own but there, somehow, peace still prevailed in Sindh. The desert area of Sindh might be cold in winters, but its people were still warm. They didn't forget their years old relationships and while they may be less educated but did know the lessons of humanity, which they also upheld when the circumstances asked for them. As a result, the Hindus of Sindh have always been so grateful to the Muslims here for being so empathetic towards them.

However, the Hindu migration still happened and surprisingly not in 1947 but in 1965 for various personal reasons. Though, our community tried to convince them to stay but all attempts to reason with them failed as everybody had their own reasons to leave. When one has made up one's mind to leave, it is hard to mould it with reasoning. On the other hand, if one really wants to stay, the significance of a single reason can weigh more than hundreds of reasons to leave. Watching them leave their lands, their work, and their lives here, including us, was difficult and somewhat painful too. If we wanted, we could have left with them but unlike them, we had our reasons to stay. The ambience in which we were living was still peaceful, the people were good to each other, even the Muslims living in nearby villages were still friends with us, our work was here, our roots were here, we had a good life here, so how could we pack our stuff one day and leave forever? Who can leave one's home just like that? We decided to stay till anyone forces us to leave, which by God's grace, till now, has never happened. This is the main reason why our region is known for brotherhood even today, the very same brotherhood that we have kept intact; always.

However, like those families who had their own reasons to leave, many of our relatives had too. My relatives from my paternal and maternal family, left after 1990. Three of my daughters have migrated to India; two of them in the 1990s and the third one in 2010, and many other close relatives have also left Sindh. I have not seen my daughters for the last thirty years now due to the border and visa issues and only two months ago, I was informed that my grandson had passed away in an accident. I couldn't even go to see him for the last time. It was such a big loss to my daughter, to our family, and to me!; who neither could hold him when he was young nor could go and see him when he was taken away from all of us forever.

For thirty years! I have only cried in silence every time I felt like hugging them, when I wanted to be with them in their sorrows, or when I needed them as my friend. I missed playing with my grandchildren, I missed the feeling of joy a grandmother feels as she holds her grandchildren, I had to miss the experience of sharing stories with them, and I had to miss keeping my hand on their heads to bless them! I had to miss thirty years of their life in which there were times of joys and distress only because of some barbed wires between us. This is when the borders become stronger, higher, and dominating over the love of parents who can do nothing but to surrender and wait, wait for this higher form of power to understand that the love for one's country must not be weighed along with the different faiths people hold. I wouldn't have to miss all those precious and important moments of my children's lives as their mother if there was no stress, if the relationship between both the nations was not this strained. And like me, so many mothers have only felt helpless and lost a share of their motherhood.

In my life, I have seen the partition, the wars, and heard the horror stories of the barbaric murder of humanity. What I have felt is that Hindu–Muslim was not even a thing before the partition but since then, it has been more than just communal differences. I am not much educated. I do not possess a degree, nor have I seen much life; I don't even have much knowledge of today's world but what I can tell you is what I know and that is, 'peace is the only way'. No one wins the wars but the loss it brings along is neither bearable, nor it is something that anyone would like to leave as their legacy for the future generations to inherit because they will question, and they certainly will!

And, no progress made in the past or the inventions have done till now will appear to fit as an answer because none of them will ever be able to fill the deep ridge carved in hatred that only ramshackle their future.

47

An Independent Imam

MAULANA HABIB UR REHMAN SANI LUDHIANVI
LUDHIANA
THE SPEAKING WINDOW

Shah Shuja Ul Mulk, also known as Shah Shuja Durrani, the fifth ruler of Durrani Empire (also referred to as Afghan Empire) was overthrown by his successor Mahmud Shah Durrani in June 1809, and was exiled with his brother Zaman Shah Durrani to Punjab. During this time, after staying in Attock and Kashmir, in 1813, he reached the then capital of Sikh Empire Lahore, and stayed with Maharaja Ranjit Singh. Shah Durrani might have lost his throne but what he still had was almost as precious as the throne itself, the Koh-i-noor.

The diamond has had a history of its own. It was said to be cursed and responsible for changing the fates of rulers who possessed it, often leaving a trail of blood behind wherever it went. When Shah Shuja Durrani met Maharaja Ranjit Singh, he gave the Koh-i-Noor to him with a hope to get his assistance in regaining the throne of Afghan empire at the time of need. By 1818, both Durrani brothers set their foot in Ludhiana city with the help of their old ally East India Company which gave them the status

The Speaking Window. Sandeep Dutt, Faisal Hayat, and Ritika, Oxford University Press.
© Oxford University Press India 2023. DOI: 10.1093/oso/9789391050733.003.0047

of the *Royal Guests*. They even started their own court in the palace they were staying at.

The road of politics and betrayal, which they took to satisfy their high ambitions, came to a crossroad with spirituality. Balliawal was a village on the outskirts of the city, situated on the bank of the river Sutlej. A very well-known Islamic scholar by the name of Maulana Abdul Shah Qadri, the great-grandfather of my grandfather and the sixth predecessor of our family, lived there. His aura and fame came to the notice of Durrani brothers, who went to seek his blessings. The way to his village was very hard to cover, so both the brothers requested him to come and live in the city, to make it easier for his followers to visit him. The request was accepted and consequently, he started living in the city and also got a mosque built in the Mochpura Bazaar.

He was staying at the mosque when one day, Zaman Shah visited him with a proposal of accepting the position of Shahi Imam (the Royal Imam) to provide his valuable advice and wise guidance to the Durrani brothers. However, this time the acceptance came with a condition. 'I will accept your proposal only if continuously for forty days, five times a day you will come to the mosque barefoot, for the Namaz prayer'. Maulana Abdul Shah Qadri declared. Zaman Shah gracefully accepted his condition, and for forty consecutive days, he visited the mosque bare-footed, five times a day for the Namaz prayer. It was after this event the designation of Shahi Imam was conferred to Maulana Abdul Shah Qadri and from then on, this designation has stayed with our family. After almost three and a half decades, in 1839, the throne of Afghan Empire was once again seized by Shah Durrani with the help of Maharaja Ranjit Singh and the Brits. He went back to rule his empire, but Zaman Shah stayed. He spent the rest of his life in Ludhiana and passed away in 1844.

It was the time when the Britishers had already been working on the 'Divide-and-Rule' policy. Religious scholars were offered government positions so that Britishers could make them their mouthpieces to steer people into a particular direction. The same proposal came across the Shahi Imam too. In 1832, Sir Kultan Bahadur, then deputy commissioner of Ludhiana, came to him to convey the message of Governor, offering him the position of an Islamic Scholar under the British Government, which to everyone's surprise, he refused to take. 'If I'll become an employee of Britishers then my upcoming generations will feel ashamed on me', were his words that made him less of a scholar and more of an anti-imperialist in the view of East India Company.

The spark of revolt had just been born, which was soon going to turn into a fire. By 1857, people were already preparing for a big rebellion and their leader, the last Mughal Emperor, Bahadur Shah Zafar, wrote letters to many influential people, including Shahi Imam, requesting their support to rebel against the Britishers. So, on 9 June 1857, an announcement was made by him in response to the request, 'Time has come to fight for independence!' Following this quote, the supporters of Maulana, attacked the fort of Ludhiana city to drive away the Britishers and hoisted his flag. The news of the attack spread like wildfire and resulted in more people coming in to support the cause over the next one week. Religion didn't come in the way of faith people had in the cause of independence; his supporters were both Muslims and non-Muslims who marched under his leadership to Delhi via Patiala, along with his sons.

Anticipating the slip of the power through their soft hands, the government plotted its next move very carefully and effectively. Islamic scholars, who were hired as the mouthpieces of the British Government, pulled a few strings of religious beliefs and served them a lie, which stated, 'It is not the duty of Muslim to declare the war against British, in the name of the Independence'. In response, Maulana, by getting the support of various other Islamic scholars, issued the first Fatwa (a ruling on a point of Islamic law given by a recognized authority) against Britishers, in which he declared that it was necessary for every Muslim to fight for the independence.

The revolt went down with serious casualties including the wife of Maulana, who is now resting in peace in the Fatehpuri Mosque, opposite the Lal Quila. The death warrants were issued in the name of all the rebellions. The Great Revolt of 1857 turned into a great defeat in no time. Maulana went underground for two years in Shutrana, Patiala which turned out to be the last two years of life.

A decade later, the British Government in India made an announcement related to the revolt of 1857. It was informed through the announcement that the supporters of 1857's revolt who were in hiding had been pardoned and therefore, free to return back to their homes. It was, in fact, a trap set up by Britishers for getting their hands on those whom they were unable to find, including the sons of Maulana who returned home only to be imprisoned. The three sons of Maulana Abdul Shah Qadri were arrested but after some time, acquitted of all the charges on account of the status they held in the society. However, their repercussions came in a different way, as their home and the mosque were both demolished on the order of the Deputy Commissioner. The land where the mosque and home of Maulana were made, was sold and bought by a Kashmiri woman, Zanto who gave back the possession of their land out of respect just for Rs. 1 so that they could build the mosque and their home once again.

Around thirty years after the first war of independence, the efforts to attain freedom started picking pace yet again. Revolutionaries realized that the mere use of swords was not enough to attain independence. The Indian National Congress was already formed, which started voicing the collective opinion of the nation. On one particular occasion, Abbas Tyabji, the pioneer member of the Indian National Congress visited Ludhiana from Bombay and met Maulana Shah Muhammad Ludhianvi, son of Maulana Abdul Shah Qadri who was then holding the position of his father. Tyabji asked him, 'Isn't it possible if all the Muslims could join hands with freedom fighters coming from every faith, to fight together against Britishers for Independence?' Years ago, his father had received a similar request from the last Mughal emperor seeking support for freedom and the same was asked of him. Patriotism was in his blood, so following the footsteps of his father, he did something his father did in his time. Another *Fatwa* was issued, which urged the Muslims to join the Indian National Congress and fight for their motherland. These two Fatwas played a great role in the Freedom Movement. The latter one was reprinted and released by Jawahar Lal Nehru and Mahatma Gandhi in the 1936 session of Congress.

Time went on, generation of our lineage kept changing but the family's stance against Britishers remained the same. Then in 1892, a great freedom fighter named Maulana Habib Ur Rehman Ludhianvi, whom I have been named after, was born in Ludhiana. He was my grandfather and grandson of Maulana Shah Muhammad Ludhianvi. He grew up listening to the stories of his great-grandfather and those of loyalty to the soil which he inherited from his forefathers.

In his time, the revolution had begun. He started participating in independence movements from his childhood. One night, some friends of Maulana Zakria Ludhianvi, the father of Maulana Habib Ur Rehman

Ludhianvi, visited their home, only to tell him about his son and his fearlessness. They were worried that he had started walking in the footsteps of his great-grandfather and would get arrested, which nobody wanted. It doesn't matter how strong fathers are, but they always worry about the well-being of their children. In order to restrict the participation of his son in independence movements, he took his son to Darul Uloom Deoband (Islamic school in Deoband, India where the Deobandi Islamic movement began) overnight by train, where they were greeted wholeheartedly as the school held great respect for Maulana Abdul Shah Qadri.

Call it fate, or anything else, but Maulana Habib Ur Rehman had reached a place that was already working for the independence of India. In five to six years of his education, his intentions to struggle for a free India only grew stronger. He was twenty-seven years old when Jallianwala Bagh Massacre (also known as Amritsar Massacre) happened, which disturbed him a lot, so he organized a protest against it.

With the help of his friends, the arrangements were made, posters were pasted across the city, and announcements were made on the important spots. People were informed in one way or the other. The name of the Maulana was new to the city, but his roots were not. Some knew it and others were about to know. The stage was set in the Committee Garden where Maulana Habib Ur Rehman addressed the people, delivering a fierce speech against the British rule, which forced the Captain of the Police department to hold an emergency meeting that night. Jail became his second home. Being a freedom fighter, he was into many freedom struggle movements which threatened the government and moved the masses. Many times, he was offered his freedom in return for an apology from him, which he never accepted. Why would anyone apologize for voicing their opinion to safeguard the honour of their country? They knew it yet they tried to manipulate him because they were aware that if he bent his knees, a large number of his followers would too.

An incident in the court of law stands witness to the kind of person Maulana Habib Ur Rehman was.

'Maulana if you ask for an apology then I can free you right now'— these were the words of the judge, Justice Vidya Sagar, who was about to sentence him.

'It is my responsibility to oppose the British Rule and if in your view, it is a crime then I accept it'—Maulana replied.

'Maulana then I am compelled to punish you'—replied the judge.

'Today in this court, I understood the difference between a slave and an independent man'—said the freedom fighter who knew that he had sealed his fate with his own hands.

This was his first sentence. In the second one, along with the jail time, he was also fined heftily with a ridiculous amount of Rs. 2,000, which of course, he refused to pay. According to the law of that time, in case the fine was not deposited, the person failing to pay it was liable to serve an additional jail time but to trouble his family, a British officer decided to collect his fine by auctioning his household things.

All of his household things were brought to Clock Tower in Ludhiana for auction. Everything was sold and while Britishers rejoiced their little win, they didn't realize that possessions can be bought but not one's loyalty. The people of the city loved Maulana Habib Ur Rehman. The affection, the love, and the kind of respect he had earned, the authorities could not auction that. People had bought all his things only to return them to his family. By the end of the day, every single thing got back to its original place, where it belonged.

Just to give him hard times, he was constantly transferred from one prison to another. There was hardly any prison left where he was not kept. During his first sentence, he had to go through many torments. In summers, he had to bear the heat waves in Multan Jail and in winters, the cold-harsh weather of Shimla. However, all these atrocities could not affect his will to fight for the independence.

Maulana Habib was one of the founders of Majlis-e-Ahrar-e-Islam, founded on 29 December 1929, an anti-imperialist nationalist Muslim movement. He travelled to various parts of India to have Muslims join it. In 1930, an Indian flag (used by the revolutionaries at that time) was hoisted by him on the top of the Royal Mosque of Ludhiana in the presence of 300 British soldiers.

The British Government extended their policy of divide and rule a step further by installing two different earthen pots at the railway stations and other places, with a mark of Hindu and Muslim on them to distinguish between the two. The idea was to have these communities drink from different pots and create a subconscious rift between the two. To reunite the people, Maulana gave a speech in the city and while addressing the people, he said, 'If we want to make our country independent then we have to break these pots'. And his volunteers broke those pots at various places, which got him arrested again.

If he had foes in the form of authorities, he had friends too who were no less than a revolution in themselves. Whenever the elder brother of Bhagat Singh, Kultar Singh, and his sister visited Ludhiana, they would stay at his place as he had good relations with Bhagat Singh and his family. He had an inclination towards the ideology of Subhash Chander Bose as regard to the methods which should be used to gain independence, so he shared good relations with him, too. When Bose went to Japan through Afghanistan, he sent his son to accompany him till Peshawar.

Talking of good relations, Lala Lajpat Rai served two years of jail time with him in the same barrack in the jail of Dharamshala. Once Governor of Punjab was scheduled to visit Ludhiana and a welcome ceremony was being held in his honour in which Governor was supposed to chair the Municipal Corporation. After getting this news, Maulana said, 'We won't let him chair the corporation. Lala Lajpat Rai ji will chair it'. Lala Ji was in Jagraon at that time and a message was sent to him to inform him about it, to which Lala Ji agreed.

On the scheduled day, Lala Ji and all other freedom fighters from nearby places reached the spot before Governor. Maulana offered the re-served seat of Governor to Lala Ji and asked the corporation to start the proceedings. The Police captain became furious and ordered Lathi charge on them. The sons of Maulana shielded Lala Ji to protect him. He had great relations with Mahatma Gandhi as well. Both served jail time to-gether. He had cordial personal relations with Master Tara Singh too.

When the theory of two nations popped up, he was against it. When Muhammad Ali Jinnah visited our home in 1936, he suggested him to support the idea of a single nation.

Not just Maulana Habib but his family was also equally participating in the freedom struggle. In 1941, when he was sentenced to another jail term, a hefty fine was levied on him. The British officers came to our house and took every valuable thing they could to make up for the fine. They even took the earrings of the wife and daughters of Maulana and de-molished the walls of his home while leaving. Maulana's wife lived in that house by placing sacks in the place of walls for two years. When someone asked her to send a letter to his husband informing about the situation, as he could send some help, she replied 'He is not alone in this fight'.

In 1945, Shimla Conference (also known as Wavell Conference, named after Lord Wavell) was about to be conducted in which all the big leaders were going to partake in, to discuss the independence. Maulana was imprisoned in Multan at the same time, for the last five years, still serving his sentence.

A few days before the Conference, Maulana Zakariya Ludhianvi, the father of Maulana Habib, sent a letter to Maulana Abul Kalam Azad in Shimla through his grandson in which he wrote about the imprisonment of Maulana Habib. He questioned him about his son's freedom when all other political leaders were freed and also inquired about his absence from the Wavell Conference. After receiving the letter, Maulana Abul Kalam Azad informed the authorities that he would not attend the conference until and unless Maulana Habib was freed. Following the defiance of Maulana Abul Kalam Azad, Maulana Habib was immediately brought to Shimla and thus, he attended the conference with all other leaders.

In the year 1947, Maulana Habib Ur Rehman Ludhianvi and his family who were fighting against British Raj alongside other freedom fighters, felt they had lost the battle even after the Britishers had left the country. They did leave but also left the country divided into two parts. Mass migration started with chaos, bloodshed, and violence which went on for four to five months.

All our relatives, including the brothers and uncles of Maulana Habib, left the city for Pakistan except his immediate family because he wasn't willing to leave his city at any cost. He was not ready to accept partition or migration after fighting for India's freedom for all these years. Many relatives were killed, as well. Things were turning ugly day by day. The city started to fill with new people who were migrating from Pakistan's side. Those people had lost many things including lives of their dear ones and they were not liking our presence in the city, they wanted vengeance for their sufferings that they had to go through at the hands of the people of our religion. They held us responsible for everything and wished the same fate for us.

Jawahar Lal Nehru, who had visited our home in 1936 and then again in 1946, despite being busy with the administrative responsibilities, had not forgotten his old friend and had strictly ordered the authorities to protect us. Later in October of 1947, the Deputy Commissioner of the city came to our house with the suggestion of migration, for he knew things were about to get uglier and in such a scenario, he might not be able to get hold of the situation and protect us.

Then at the end of October, on the continuous requests of the Deputy Commissioner, Maulana decided to leave the city and wished to move to Delhi. A special train was arranged for it, but we couldn't board it as there were some inputs about a planned attack on him, then he tried to leave the city by road, but it couldn't happen as well. After two failed attempts of leaving the city, Deputy Commissioner suggested that a train was leaving for Lahore, which was not to stop anywhere before reaching there, so he should at least leave his children in Lahore for the sake of their safety and then, return back. Considering all the failed attempts to leave the city and running out of options, he agreed to it.

He reached Lahore with family, but extremism and violence were following him there as well. Extremists of Pakistan wanted him dead as well because he and his party had always been against the partition. In Lahore, he was staying at the house of Maulana Ahmed Ali Lahori, a renowned personality of Lahore. When the Nawab of Bahawalpur came to know about Maulana's safety being at stake, he took matters into his own hands, being his close friend, he sent a fleet of cars to take him out of Lahore to Bahawalpur, along with his family. There he allotted many acres of land to Maulana. After around fifteen days of staying in Bahawalpur, one night, the wife of Maulana and my grandmother Shafaq Beghum asked him to move back to Lahore. When asked for the reason, she said, 'Ludhiana is nearer to Lahore than Bahawalpur', and they moved back to Lahore. They stayed in Lahore for some time and then moved back to Delhi.

While in Lahore, a chartered plane was arranged by Jawahar Lal Nehru to escort Maulana and his family to Delhi. Delhi was also burning in riots at that time. Maulana decided to travel all around the country to request people to stop this bloodshed. My grandmother got so much depressed that her health kept declining after the partition. She kept on asking people how did they have the heart of taking innocent lives. After a stay of a few months in Delhi, the whole family came back to their home, in Ludhiana. He was welcomed by the Deputy Commissioner of the Police and other officials upon his arrival in Ludhiana.

When they came back to their home and knocked on the door, they saw that there were refugees living in it. They insisted us to come inside but my grandmother started crying and refused to enter her house, saying 'You too are displaced just like us, you too have lost your home . . .'

And with that, the family returned to Delhi. She hardly survived a few more months after that and breathed her last there.

After staying for another two years in Delhi, the whole family moved back to their home, Ludhiana. Though there was an order given to the authorities to get the possession of mosques and homes of Maulana back to him, but he refused to take their possession until the migrant refugees were given some other places to live, which eventually authorities did, and he shifted back to his home. He knew the pain of the people and was empathetic towards them. He could not take a sigh of relief sitting in his house while seeing the people without roofs on their heads outside. It was his empathy and compassion which made him people's favourite.

He served a combined jail time of fourteen years and seven months in prison for the sole purpose of attaining independence for his nation. After all those years of struggle, he had a new aim to achieve; Peace. The dream of independence had cost the country its peace and harmony. People got divided sooner than the time they took to come together. After independence, he undertook different activities for harmony. He helped in the renovation of mosques. He was the founding member of Punjab Wakf Board. He also founded and became the chairman of Phir Basao Committee, which surveyed, found, and helped children and females abducted or displaced in the partition, for which he visited many places in India and Pakistan. Borders could not stop him from helping people and he never hesitated to extend his hand for help.

In 1953, when India wanted to start the oil trade with Saudi Arabia, Maulana Habib was sent as the leader of a goodwill mission where he met the Saudi King. He passed away in 1956 but his legacy has lived on through us.

This is the story of my inheritance, my honour, and me. Today, when I see people surrounded in chaos, losing hope and peace, I wonder if this is what my grandfather and his grandfather had dreamt of. Of course not.

At last, I, Maulana Habib Ur Rehman Sani Ludhianvi, Shahi Imam Punjab, descendent of Maulana Abdul Shah Qadri and grandson of Maulana Habib Ur Rehman Ludhianvi, would like to advise the Punjabis on either side of the border that you are the people who can do anything, you are the warriors from thousands of years, and you should remain united. You should promote love and harmony among all religious communities. Begin from home, start loving your family, and start giving utmost respect to them.